VILLAGE EDUCATION IN NINETEENTH-CENTURY OXFORDSHIRE

GW00642862

The Oxfordshire Record Society

VILLAGE EDUCATION IN NINETEENTH-CENTURY OXFORDSHIRE

THE WHITCHURCH SCHOOL LOG BOOK (1868–93) AND OTHER DOCUMENTS

Edited by Pamela Horn

VOLUME LI

Issued for the years 1975 and 1976

1979

ISBN 0 902509 13 6

Printed in England by
W. S. MANEY AND SON LIMITED
HUDSON ROAD LEEDS

TABLE OF CONTENTS

LIST OF TABLES

LIST OF PLATES

FOREWORD

I believe that no School Log Book has hitherto been published in full, though Mr Ronald Blythe in *Akenfield* (1969) printed extracts from a Suffolk village school log book for the years 1875–1941. Dr Horn explains on p. liii why the log book for Whitchurch was selected for publication by this Society.

I am grateful to Dr Gillian Sutherland of Newnham College, Cambridge, for encouragement and help at an early stage of this project; to our printers, W. S. Maney & Son Ltd (and especially Mr Derek Brown) for invaluable help with the difficult problems presented by a new type of text and by the need to achieve both clarity and economy in printing it; and to Miss Shirley Barnes and Mr Malcolm Graham for preparing the lists printed in the Appendix.

CHRIST CHURCH, OXFORD   J. F. A. MASON
March 1978   *Hon. Editor, O.R.S.*

PREFACE

I should like to express my gratitude to all who have assisted with the preparation of this volume. In particular, my thanks are due to the Social Science Research Council for financial help in carrying out the project, and to Miss Shirley Barnes and the staff at Oxfordshire Record Office for much efficient assistance. I am also indebted to Mr John Garne, M.C., Chief Education Officer for Oxfordshire, the Revd T. B. Pelham, rector of Whitchurch, and the National Society for permission to quote from documents in their possession. The Bodleian Library, Oxford, Christ Church Library, Oxford, the Oxfordshire County Museum at Woodstock, Berkshire Record Office, Culham College Library, Oxford, Borough Road College, Isleworth, and the Public Record Office have likewise given invaluable help. Finally, I am grateful to Dr Mason, the Society's general editor, for assistance in the preparation of this volume and to my husband for aid in checking the texts of the documents reproduced.

March 1978   PAMELA HORN

LIST OF ABBREVIATIONS

Berks.	Berkshire
Bodl.	Bodleian Library
Kelly's Dir.	*Kelly's Directory*
MS. Oxf. Dioc.	Oxford Diocesan Papers
O.C.M.	Oxfordshire County Museum
O.R.O.	Oxfordshire County Record Office
O.R.S.	Oxfordshire Record Society
Oxon.	Oxfordshire
P.P.	Parliamentary Papers
P.R.O.	Public Record Office
Soc.	Society
V.C.H.	*Victoria County History*

All letters and punctuation which are superscript in MS have been printed on the same line as the main text.

New Year's Day in the years covered by the Whitchurch log book fell as follows:

MONDAY	1872	1877	1883	
TUESDAY	1878	1884	1889	
WEDNESDAY	1873	1879	1890	
THURSDAY	1874	1880	1885	1891
FRIDAY	1869	1875	1886	1892
SATURDAY	1870	1876	1881	1887
SUNDAY	1871	1882	1888	1893

INTRODUCTION

OXFORDSHIRE VILLAGE SCHOOLS IN THE NINETEENTH CENTURY

'We break off a fragment from the education we suppose necessary for our own children — its mechanical and technical part — and give it to the poor man's child in charity. The inveterate prejudice that education in any higher sense is a privilege annexed to a definite social position, and graduated by it, associates itself with all our educational efforts'. Comment by the Revd Henry Moseley (1801–1872), one of Her Majesty's Inspectors of Schools, and previously professor of natural and experimental philosophy and astronomy at King's College, London, writing in 1846 and quoted in E. E. Rich, *The Education Act 1870* (London, 1970).

'To meet some of the objections to compulsory attendance on the score of removing boys from agricultural labour, it has occurred to me that certain modification in the present plans for holidays and hours might be introduced e.g., if schools commenced work at 8½ a.m. instead of at 9, and at 1½ p.m. instead of at 2; and if a half instead of a whole holiday was given on Saturday, and the Easter and Whitsuntide holidays stopped, and the Christmas holidays reduced to a day or two, sufficient gain of school time would accrue, to allow boys to go to work in the spring and summer months, compelling attendance only through the winter and early spring'. Comment by the Revd H. W. Bellairs, H.M.I. of schools in Oxfordshire and Berkshire in 1870 and incorporated in *Report of the Committee of Council on Education*, P.P. 1870–71, xxii, p. 25.

At the beginning of the nineteenth century the educational facilities available to the vast majority of country children were inadequate to their needs in both quality and quantity. In some villages there was no school at all; in others an ineffective dame school kept by an elderly woman, or perhaps a Sunday school, provided the only means of instruction. A few parishes had small endowments for educational purposes which had been bequeathed by earlier generations, but for the most part day schools depended for their existence upon the initiative and interest of clergy and landowners, plus, more rarely, parents themselves. Gradually, under the pressure of changing religious and social attitudes and as a consequence of Parliamentary action, that position was to be modified.

Oxfordshire schools at the beginning of the nineteenth century

Oxfordshire was no exception to the general pattern and this Introduction seeks to trace the nature of its educational provision over the years. Evidence has been drawn from a number of parishes, although the documents reproduced relate to one specific village only — that of Whitchurch — which lies on the county's southern border.

In the early eighteenth century Oxfordshire's record in elementary education was undistinguished. The visitation articles for the Oxford diocese in 1738 show, for example, that out of 179 parishes making returns only fifty-three (or about thirty per cent) mentioned a school. And some of these were of little value. Thus at the endowed school at Bladon near Woodstock a salary of £20 per annum was payable, although in the opinion of the vicar it was 'little other than a Sine-Cure to the Master Mr Du Bois who, I think, was a French Refugee and has been admitted to degrees and Orders at Oxford'.[1] But as the appointment was the responsibility of Woodstock corporation, he felt unable to intervene.

Nor had facilities in the county improved two decades later. For of 163 parish returns which have survived from the 1759 visitation a mere forty-one (or twenty-five per cent) report a school.[2] Although such returns are not entirely reliable, depending as they do upon the interest and zeal of individual clerics, the picture they present is very different from that of the York diocese in 1743. There, at the time of Archbishop Herring's primary visitation, out of 645 returns made by the clergy, 379 (or approaching sixty per cent) reported a school of some kind.[3]

So it was only in the last decade or so of the eighteenth century — and partly under the influence of the Sunday School movement — that any real advance in Oxfordshire's position could be discerned. And even in 1808, when a survey of education in the county was undertaken at the request of the Archbishop of Canterbury, it showed that well over one quarter of the two hundred or so rural parishes submitting returns still had no day school. Sometimes, as the incumbent of Cuxham pointed out, this was because of a shortage of suitable teachers or because the children were 'required by their Parents to go so early to labour'. Elsewhere, as at Westwell, the reason lay in the opposition of local farmers and proprietors who, in the opinion of the curate of Westwell, were 'perhaps . . . of Opinion that the Education disqualifies the Poor for Labour'. He called upon Parliament to intervene 'to prescribe some Plan for the better

---

[1] H. A. Lloyd Jukes (ed.), *Articles of Enquiry Addressed to the Clergy of the Diocese of Oxford at the Primary Visitation of Dr. Thomas Secker, 1738*, O.R.S., xxxviii (1957), 19.
[2] Clergy Visitation Returns for the Oxford Diocese for 1759 in Bodl. MSS. Oxf. Dioc. Pp. d., 555–57.
[3] J. Lawson and H. Silver, *A Social History of Education in England* (London, 1973), p. 184.

Education of the Children of the Poor' and praised in particular a measure
unsuccessfully put forward by the Radical M.P., Samuel Whitbread, in
the previous year.[4] This had proposed the levying of a local rate to
provide two years' free elementary education for pupils who were unable
to afford the penny or twopence per week fee normally charged for
attendance at school. But most of Whitbread's contemporaries disliked
the idea of governmental interference in a sphere which had traditionally
belonged to charity and to the Church. They preferred to allow voluntary
effort to take its course, despite its obvious failures and weaknesses.

A further thirty or so of the Oxfordshire parishes reporting in 1808 had
dame schools only, where children were taught with varying degrees of
efficiency to read and sew, plus, in a few cases, to write and do simple
arithmetic. Typical of establishments in this category was one at Fifield
kept 'by an old woman, who teaches reading, knitting, a little sewing &
the catechism'.[5] Academic attainments in such institutions had improved
little by the 1820s when four-year-old Mary Smith, the daughter of a boot
and shoemaker at Cropredy, attended a small school kept by 'Dame
Garner'. Mrs Garner

had two little forms, which were the sum total of her school furniture; and from
these seats she called, one by one, all the little ones to her knee to read. She
sometimes pinned them to her knee for punishment, and always wore the same
hard look of stern authority . . . No smile was ever seen to illuminate her stern
countenance, from the time of our arrival at school, to the time we made our
curtsies and hurried out of it.[6]

Her pupils were taught only to read.

In a minority of the remaining Oxfordshire villages claiming educational
facilities in the early nineteenth century were schools like those at
Bletchingdon and Cassington, which were financed partly by endowments.
But far more common were ones — as at Whitchurch itself — which
depended upon the support of the clergyman and local landowners, plus
the weekly pence of the children themselves. Many of the endowments
were, in any case, too small to be effective. At Bletchingdon the figure of
£5 per annum to teach 'ten poor children of the parish' was hardly likely to
attract a master or mistress of high calibre, even when supplemented by
the small fees paid by other youngsters attending the school. At Cassington
the endowment amounted to £4 a year to instruct four boys in 'reading,
writing & arithmetic', with the master also teaching 'about thirty other

[4] Return of Schools, 1808, Bodl. MS. Oxf. Dioc. Pp. d., 707. For a general examination
of the role of the clergy in the provision of elementary schools in the early nineteenth
century see G. Kitson Clark, *Churchmen and the Condition of England 1832–1885*
(London, 1973), 99–103.
[5] Return of Schools, 1808.
[6] *The Autobiography of Mary Smith, Schoolmistress and Nonconformist* (London, 1892),
p. 16.

Children who pay him weekly'.[7] And although the master at Dr Radcliffe's School at Steeple Aston was more generously rewarded, with an endowment of £20 per annum, it was to be said of the man holding office in 1860 that he was 'neither trained nor certificated . . . [and] the school, as now conducted, was useless'.[8]

Finally, in certain parishes which were without a daily school of any kind attempts were made to fill the gap from the 1780s onwards by the establishment of Sunday Schools, where youngsters might at least learn to read and understand the Bible and the Church catechism.[9] Many regarded this as a proper limit to elementary education anyway, fearing that if children were more broadly instructed they would be unwilling to perform the necessary but mundane tasks carried out by their parents' generation. Vaughan Thomas, incumbent of Yarnton, was one who held this view, considering that the inclusion of writing and arithmetic in the curriculum of elementary school children would encourage them to leave the land for positions elsewhere: 'Reading is a key to the treasures of holy writ and . . . should be put into the hands of all. But writing and arithmetic being qualifications for particular places, services and sorts of business, should be reserved for specific purposes and particular children'.[10] Again, in 1802 John Randolph, Bishop of Oxford, considered that the aim in instructing the children of the poor should be: 'merely to give them an entrance into a life of daily labour, well fortified with the principles of duty; all beyond that may puff up their tender minds, or entice them into a way of life of no benefit to the publick and ensnaring to themselves. Accomplishments which are useful and becoming in one rank of life are neither becoming nor safe in another'.

Such ideas took a long time to die. Even in 1857, when instruction in writing and arithmetic had become generally available, Bishop Wilberforce,

[7] Return of Schools, 1808.
[8] C. C. Brookes, *A History of Steeple Aston and Middle Aston* (Long Compton, 1929), p. 310 (comment by F. O. Martin, Inspector for the Charity Commissioners).
[9] In the 1802 Clergy Visitation Returns for the Oxford Diocese, twenty-eight parishes (of 187 making returns) mentioned Sunday schools only; seventy-three claimed day schools (with over a quarter having a Sunday school as well); and eighty-six were still apparently without any provision at all. Returns in Bodl. MSS. Oxf. Dioc. Pp. d. 566–7. In the view of Joan Simon, 'Was There a Charity School Movement? The Leicestershire Evidence' in *Education in Leicestershire 1540–1914*, ed. B. Simon (Leicester, 1968), p. 94: 'it was the Sunday Schools that paved the way for the mass daily school'.
[10] Quoted by Diana McClatchey, *Oxfordshire Clergy 1777–1869* (Oxford, 1960), pp. 142–43. However, Vaughan Thomas took an interest in school provision not only in Yarnton but also in the nearby parish of Begbroke. Here, under his influence, the tenant of the parish poor house, 'Widow Parker', was set up as schoolmistress — somewhat reluctantly — in 1820. She was paid 6s. a week by the parishioners and received fees of ½d. per scholar per week — which were estimated to bring her weekly earnings up to 7s. During the harvest she was allowed to close the school for six weeks and 'to go afield' for her own profit (Bodl. MS. D.D. Par. Begbroke d. 4).

in a speech at the annual meeting of the Diocesan Association of School-masters, thought 'there was, perhaps, too much outcry against children being taken from School early to work on farms', adding frankly that they 'did not want everybody to be learned men, or to make everybody unfit for following the plough, or else the rest of us would have nothing to eat.'[11]

Nevertheless, while some clerics shared Bishop Wilberforce's doubts on the desirability of expanding the curriculum of elementary schools, others adopted a different stance, seeing a widening of educational provision as a means of inculcating correct social attitudes of obedience to authority, piety and industry into the new generation. To the vicar of Enstone, for example, schooling was a means by which 'vice is checked, industry encouraged, and property . . . improved in value', while to his colleague at Benson it gave an opportunity for instilling the 'truth and Church principles' in a parish 'over-run with Dissent'.[12] But perhaps the clearest expression of this philosophy was supplied by the Revd H. Newland in 1856 in a lecture to an educational conference of parochial clergy and schoolmasters within the Oxford diocese, when he advised the masters present:

the farmer will be more ready to engage a labourer whom he has reason to believe is steady, regular in his habits, obedient, civil; . . . When you have manufactured a steady, honest, God-fearing, Church-going population, then you have done your duty as Schoolmasters.

The role of the voluntary societies and of the state

It was partly to further this latter approach that two national voluntary societies for the promotion of elementary education were set up at the beginning of the nineteenth century. For as the first annual report of one of them openly admitted in 1812, its sole object was 'to communicate to the poor generally . . . such knowledge and habits, as are sufficient to guide them through life, in their proper stations, . . . and to train them to the performance of their religious duties by early discipline'. Each of the organizations sought to tackle the problem of mass education on an

[11] *Report of the Annual Meeting of the Diocesan Association of Schoolmasters in the Diocese of Oxford* (Oxford, 1857), p. 38. A similar view was held by the well-to-do at Adderbury as late as 1874, since it was felt that education would 'spoil the girls for domestic service'. Significantly only 51 out of 82 girls on the register had made a satisfactory number of attendances at school in that year (*V.C.H. Oxon.*, ix (1969), 41). See G. Kitson Clark, *Churchmen and the Condition of England*, for other aspects of Bishop Wilberforce's education policy — including his cautious agreement to the appointment of lay managers for church schools and his view that the children of dissenters attending such schools 'might accept as much of the education provided as their parents were prepared to allow'.
[12] Vicar of Enstone to the Dean and Chapter of Christ Church, 27 Nov. 1840, Ch. Ch. Archives MS. Estates 72, f. 207; incumbent of Benson to the Dean and Chapter of Christ Church, 11 Dec. 1849, ibid., 60, f. 237.

economical scale by adopting a monitorial system, whereby older pupils were used to instruct the younger under the general direction of the teacher. It was a pyramid-like arrangement in which the teacher taught the monitors and the latter passed on the information to their younger fellow-pupils. Dictation and open round-the-class reading were common features of the curriculum, and some of the system's most enthusiastic protagonists claimed that in this fashion one teacher could handle a thousand children.

The idea had been developed initially in India by Dr Andrew Bell, an Anglican clergyman serving with the East India Company, and for this reason was sometimes also known as the Madras system. In England it was taken up by Joseph Lancaster, a Quaker, and later by Dr Bell himself. In 1810 Lancaster and his friends formed the Royal Lancasterian Association, designed to promote the spread of schools on Lancaster's principles throughout the country. In 1814 this body changed its name to the British and Foreign School Society and in the main drew its support from dissenters. The Anglicans responded with the formation in 1811 of the National Society for Promoting the Education of the Poor in the Principles of the Established Church — usually shortened to the National Society. After its first meeting on 16 October, 1811, John Randolph, now Bishop of London, noted the importance of the step, adding: 'For if the great body of the Nation be educated in other principles than those of the established Church, the natural consequence must be to deviate the minds of the people from it or render them indifferent to it, which may in succeeding generations prove fatal to the Church & to the State itself'.[13]

In the event, thanks to the energy with which its members pursued their task, schools associated with the National Society soon outstripped their British and Foreign Society rivals.[14] Other religious denominations, like the Wesleyans and the Roman Catholics, also developed their own schools but in Oxfordshire these had little significance. (See Tables 1 and 2.)

The managers of schools in union with the National Society were required to promise that their pupils would be instructed in accordance with the liturgy and catechism of the Church of England and would attend divine service on the Sabbath. Whitchurch School managers made this promise when the school became associated with the National Society in 1819. (See Document III.)

In this fashion, therefore, educational provision was slowly extended. In 1818 the Select Committee on the Education of the Poor (England)

[13] Bishop Randolph's notes on the foundation of the National Society are in Bodl. MS. Top. Oxon. b. 170.
[14] See R. A. Soloway, *Prelates and People* (London, 1969), pp. 370–75 for a discussion of the 'defensive' motives which led to the creation of the National Society in 1811.

had revealed that of just over two hundred rural parishes and market towns within the county submitting returns, 41 had no educational provision at all — not even a Sunday School or dame school — while a further 31 relied upon Sunday Schools only. There were at this stage only nineteen schools in the county organized on the new National or British and Foreign pattern.[15] But by 1833 when a fresh Educational Enquiry was set in hand, the picture had changed dramatically. By that date only about fifteen parishes — most of them very small — were without a school at all, and the total of day schools in the county (including separate boys' and girls' departments and infants' schools) had risen to 576, as compared to a total of 312 put forward in 1818.[16] Nearly three-quarters of these were maintained primarily by the pence of the scholars, while most of the remainder depended on the subscriptions of well-wishers. But both then and later a number of schools also relied to some extent on sales of the children's work to help defray expenses. In 1815 the newly-established Bampton National School, for example, issued a printed list of 'prices for work'. These included charges of 2s. for making men's 'fine shirts'; 10d. for night shirts; 4d. to 6d. for making a pair of sheets; and 6d. to 1s. for producing a dozen pocket handkerchiefs. In all, quotations were given for twenty-five different items.[17] Similarly, at Whitchurch entries in the school accounts for the period 1829 to 1861 include payments for 'Children's Work'; in 1860 the sum of £2. 19s. 7d. was realized in this way out of total annual receipts of £83. 13s. 7½d.,[18] while as late as 22 June 1871 the log book refers to a sale of pinafores 'which the girls had made'. Shutford National School and Charlbury Board School are but two further examples of the many that could be quoted of schools which were continuing the practice even in the 1880s.

But the 1833 Enquiry did not confine itself to providing details of the number and, in some cases, the financial arrangements of elementary schools. It also revealed that twenty-five of the Oxfordshire schools had libraries attached to them — among them one at Wolvercote, where the

---

[15] *Select Committee on the Education of the Poor (England): Digest of Parochial Returns*, P.P. 1819, ix, Part 2.

[16] *Education Enquiry: Abstract of the Answers and Returns*, P.P. 1835, xlii. E. G. West, 'Resource Allocation and Growth in Early Nineteenth-Century British Education', *Economic History Review*, 2nd Series, xxiii (1970), 79 draws attention to possible underestimates of elementary school provision in the larger industrial towns in the 1833 Survey but in Oxfordshire the returns appear reliable.

[17] Return of Schools, 1815, Bodl. MS. Oxf. Dioc. Pp. c. 433.

[18] School accounts for Whitchurch at the Rectory, made available by the kind co-operation of the rector, the Revd T. B. Pelham. At Cogges school in West Oxfordshire the girls were involved in sewing for a local charity. According to Mrs Brookes, who attended Cogges school in about 1900: 'The girls made underwear, and red flannel petticoats which were given to old people each year, as part of the Blake charity. They also knitted long black stockings for old ladies' (Reminiscences at O.C.M.).

master and mistress were paid £50 per annum jointly to teach 102 pupils. But its report showed, too, that most teachers elsewhere in the county were far less generously remunerated. At Wiggington, where there were 67 children on the school books, 'the master [received] a salary of 12s. per week for the attendance of himself and wife', while at Mongewell, with twenty pupils in daily attendance, the mistress was paid a mere 4s. a week 'with coals and a house'. No doubt the quality of the teaching corresponded to these rates of pay.

However, in addition to setting in hand the Schools Enquiry, Parliament took an even more momentous step in 1833 when for the first time it made available public funds for the building of schools. The sum authorized — £20,000 — was modest and was to be divided equally between the two major voluntary societies, the National and the British and Foreign, with the pre-condition that the amount of state aid was to be matched by an equivalent effort from the societies themselves. Six years later, in 1839, came the setting up of a Committee of the Privy Council 'for the consideration of all matters affecting the education of the people' and 'to superintend the application of any sums voted by parliament for the purpose of promoting public education'. At the same time the education grant itself was increased to £30,000 and during November of that year the first of Her Majesty's Inspectors of Schools were appointed. Henceforth receipt of a Government grant carried with it the obligation to accept school inspection. Not unexpectedly, these various developments were viewed with suspicion by some churchmen. From Garsington the rector and certain other inhabitants even petitioned Parliament on the issue in 1839, expressing 'unfeigned sorrow and alarm' at the creation of the Committee of Council on Education, since this would 'place the whole Instruction of the present and future youth of the country entirely under the direction and control of an official Board of Laymen, and from which the heads of the National Church are systematically excluded'. Nine years later Bishop Wilberforce wrote to the vicar of Wantage similarly declaring: 'The only safe ground seems to me the broader one, of opposing *all* dictation emanating from the Privy Council to the founders of Church Schools'.[19] Over the course of time such hostile attitudes were to mellow.

Nevertheless, within the Church of England as a whole the appointment of the Privy Council Committee was matched by the establishment of

[19] R. K. Pugh (ed.), *The Letter-Books of Samuel Wilberforce 1843–1868* (O.R.S., xlvii, 1969), no. 190. For a more friendly attitude towards the state's role in education see also Wilberforce's letter ibid., no. 520, dated 9 Jan. 1854, to Earl Granville. A copy of the Garsington petition is in Bodl. MS. D.D. Garsington c. 4 (j). For the appointment of the first of the H.M.I's see E. L. Edmonds, *The School Inspector* (London, 1962), pp. 31 and 36. J. Murphy, *Church, State and Schools in Britain, 1800–1970* (London, 1971), pp. 27–30 and 32–34 deals with the general attitude of the Church of England towards growing state intervention in education in the late 1830s and the 1840s.

diocesan boards of education with their own inspectors. These were drawn from among the local clergy and were usually assigned on the basis of one for each deanery. The Oxford Diocesan Education Board was set up on these lines in 1839, and shortly afterwards also began to provide training facilities for teachers. Male students were catered for at a training school at Summertown until in 1853 they moved to a new college at Culham, which was financed by the Oxford and Bristol and Gloucester dioceses jointly. Women teachers were trained first at Reading and then from 1845 to 1853 in premises at Kidlington. In the latter year all facilities were transferred to the Stapleton Training Institute at Fishponds, near Bristol. Numbers were small at the beginning, with a joint total of less than twenty students being trained each year.[20] Yet their existence marked a further step in the painful process of transforming the occupation of teacher from one of last resort for the person who could earn his bread in no other way to that of a respectable profession. Most of the new generation of aspirant teachers were from modest backgrounds — the children of small farmers, tradesmen or upper servants in gentlemen's families. Of the first forty-one students admitted to Culham College in January 1853, seven were the sons of farmers, eleven of craftsmen (carpenters, wheelwrights and the like), and three were the offspring of gardeners; in ten cases no parental occupation was recorded. The same pattern persisted in succeeding years, so that of thirty-seven students admitted in January 1870, three were the sons of gardeners, three of labourers, four of grocers, and eleven of small tradespeople. With the exception of two schoolmasters and a trade instructor at Her Majesty's prison at Chatham none of the paternal occupations given was remotely academic. In 1871, nearly half of the forty-two students admitted at the beginning of the year were from tradesmen's families, while three were the sons of gardeners and three of labourers.[21]

[20] According to the *Seventh Annual Report of the Oxford Diocesan Board of Education* (Oxford, 1846), pp. 10–11, the training school for masters had in six years admitted a total of 'sixty-two pupils; of whom twenty are now employed as schoolmasters within the Diocese and nine in other places. One on the plea of health has quitted the occupation of a schoolmaster; two were unable to meet with situations, and have taken temporary employment of another kind'. Three of the rest were unemployed, eleven had withdrawn 'chiefly either on the score of health or poverty', two had been dismissed and the rest were under instruction. Among the females, twenty-eight had been trained over the course of about five years and had been sent out as qualified teachers. The records of students at the Summertown training school are preserved at Culham College. They show, for example, that among twelve students admitted in 1844, two were the sons of bedmakers at Oxford colleges, two of carpenters and one — 'very coarse in manner and appearance' — of an Enstone ragman.

[21] Details of the background of students were obtained from the Registers of Students at the Diocesan Training College, Culham; these are preserved at the College and were consulted by the kind co-operation of the librarian. Of the first forty-one students admitted in January 1853, nine obtained employment in Oxfordshire when they left.

As for unsectarian teacher training, it is worth noting that the British and Foreign School Society and its Royal Lancasterian predecessor had begun to provide a rudimentary 'training' for a few masters and mistresses at their Borough Road School in London from about 1804. However, even in the early 1830s it was admitted that most of the students remained a mere three months (paying a fee of 6s. a week) while they learnt the 'monitorial system' and improved their general education a little. But by the middle of the nineteenth century Borough Road, too, was improving the quality of its curriculum and facilities.[22]

Teacher training was one concern of the Oxford Diocesan Education Board; school inspection was another. The men selected for appointment to the diocesan inspectorate were local clergymen and were appointed on a deanery basis — so that, for example, the Revd L. A. Sharpe, rector of Tackley, inspected schools in the Woodstock deanery during the mid-1850s. Although diocesan inspectors were less severe in their criticisms of scholastic achievements than were their governmental counterparts, in the early days they, too, reported on the general efficiency of schools, as the following extract from a report on Kingsey Mixed School indicates. The inspection took place on 7 November 1854 and there were thirty-six children in attendance, aged between four and twelve years of age:

This school hitherto almost inoperative is rising into order and effectiveness under the active & daily superintendence of the Clergyman and his wife. The same Teachers an old worn out parishioner and his wife are employed but acting entirely under the clergyman's supervision their inefficiency is of less consequence. As the above change for the better has only lately been made and the thing is still in progress it was thought best to defer the examination until next year.[23]

Whereas H.M.I's would only report on schools claiming government grants, diocesan inspectors could examine and advise on the much wider

---

[22] Details of the organization of the Borough Road training school in 1833 were given by Henry Dunn, secretary to the British and Foreign School Society, in evidence before the *Select Committee on the State of Education*, P.P., 1834, ix, Qs. 215–87. In that year there were ninety-eight men and women trained at Borough Road as teachers — a total which was more than fifty per cent higher than the peak achieved in any previous year. Among those admitted, according to records still preserved at the College, was Robert Pargeter of Deddington, aged 18. In 1833 his mother, a widow, ran a bakery business in Deddington and Robert was described by his sponsor as bearing 'a good character for steadiness, sobriety & correctness of conduct. His demeanour is simple, humble & unaffected'.

[23] Diocesan Inspector's Reports on schools at Kingsey, Shabbington and Worminghall for 1854 (Bodl. MS. Oxf. Dioc. Pp. c. 450). Similar comments were made by the Revd L. A. Sharpe, inspector of schools in the Woodstock deanery during the same year (ibid., e. 51). Thus at Cassington it was noted that the former schoolmaster had been dismissed for misconduct and was now keeping a rival establishment. 'The new Master is a modest well-behaved Man, with scarcely sufficient experience & talent for his work. The Children have fallen off in Intelligence — Arithmetic &c. &c.'

group of church schools in union with the diocesan board within their area. By this means they could hope gradually to raise educational standards.

Once Parliament had become financially involved in elementary education, however, its role rapidly increased. In 1843 a new type of grant was offered for school apparatus and then in 1846, in an effort to overcome the limitations of the monitorial system, the post of pupil-teacher was created.[24] In essence this was a form of apprenticeship. In schools of which Her Majesty's Inspector approved, children of thirteen years and over could be apprenticed to the teacher for five years. During this period they received extra instruction from him and also carried out some teaching duties under his supervision. At the end of each year the pupil-teacher's work was examined by an H.M.I. and, if found satisfactory, both teacher and pupil-teacher would receive grants, amounting to £5 per annum in the case of the former and between £10 and £20 per annum for the latter, depending upon the stage of the apprenticeship reached. In addition, at the end of their training period the pupil-teachers could enter national examinations for a Queen's Scholarship to permit them to undergo a further period of formal instruction at a training college so that they might become qualified teachers. If successful they could look forward to an additional grant to supplement their salary when they took up a permanent teaching appointment, as well as a pension at retirement providing they had completed at least fifteen years' service.[25]

The effect of these and other measures, including in 1853 the introduction of special capitation grants linked to attendance for schools in rural areas, all led to a sharp rise in government expenditure on education. In Oxfordshire between 1833 and 1852 £4,373.19s. 7¼d. had been received by way of grants, of which £4,129. 9s. 10d. was paid to the National schools. Three-quarters of this latter sum was devoted to building operations, but over £81 had been allocated for books, £162. 15s. for augmentation of the salary of certificated teachers and £605. 19s. 8d. as stipends to pupil teachers.[26] Nationally by the late 1850s the education grant was topping half a million pounds per annum, amounting to £663,435 in 1858 alone.[27] The speed with which this expenditure was growing began to cause alarm in official circles. And in an effort to ensure that 'value for money' was being obtained it was decided in 1858 to appoint a Royal

---

[24] A. Tropp, *The School Teachers* (London, 1957), pp. 17–25.
[25] Male qualified teachers were to be paid a supplement of between £15 a year for one year's training and £30 for three years' training. Women teachers obtained two-thirds of these amounts.
[26] *Minutes of the Committee of Council on Education for 1852*, P.P. 1853, lii, General Report of the Rev. H. W. Bellairs, H.M.I., p. 74.
[27] *Final Report of the Commissioners appointed to inquire into the Elementary Education Acts* (England and Wales), P.P. 1888, xxxv, p. 11.

TABLE 1

TABLE OF PUBLIC WEEK-DAY SCHOOLS IN OXFORDSHIRE, 1858*

	Schools, i.e. Departments†	Number of Scholars belonging to the Schools		
		Total	Males	Females
CLASS I				
Church of England	370	17,285	8,604	8,681
British	18	1,724	926	798
Roman Catholic	5	221	96	125
Wesleyan (Original Connexion)	3	360	253	107
Congregational	4	194	94	100
Society of Friends	2	166	88	78
Primitive Methodist	1	67	31	36
CLASS III				
Workhouse	14	553	272	281
CLASS IV				
Collegiate and superior Endowed	9	583	583	—

*Compiled from the *Report of the Commissioners into the State of Popular Education in England*, P.P., 1861, Vol. XXI, Pt. I, pp. 607, 623 and 632. In 1858 Oxfordshire had the third highest proportion of public week-day scholars to total population in the whole country — at one scholar per 8.3 of the population. Only Wiltshire (one in 7.8) and Westmorland (one in 7.9) had a better record (ibid., p. 595).

TABLE OF SUNDAY SCHOOLS IN OXFORDSHIRE — 1858

	Schools, i.e. Departments†	Number of Scholars belonging to the Schools		
		Total	Males	Females
Church of England	445	16,934	8,477	8,457
Wesleyan (Original Connexion)	37	2,967	1,439	1,528
Congregational	19	1,771	828	943
Primitive Methodist	16	592	302	290
Baptist	16	1,360	670	690

† The use of the word 'department' refers to those mixed schools in which there were separate sections for boys, girls and infants, each with a head teacher of its own.

TABLE OF EVENING SCHOOLS IN OXFORDSHIRE — 1858

	Schools, i.e. Departments†	Number of Scholars belonging to the Schools		
		Total	Males	Females
Church of England	33	1,157	997	160
British	1	40	40	—
Congregational	2	69	54	15**

** The evidence of marriage registers also indicates that the improved educational provision in Oxfordshire was reducing the number of people unable to sign their name when they married. In the year ending Midsummer 1840, 37 per cent of men and 46 per cent of women were unable to sign when they married; by the year ending Christmas 1863 only 26 per cent of both sexes were still making a mark. See *Catholic Education Today*, Vol. 2, No. 5 (1968), p. 29.

Commission under the chairmanship of the Duke of Newcastle 'to inquire into the present state of Popular Education in England, and to consider and report what Measures, if any, are required for the extension of sound and cheap elementary instruction to all classes of the people'.

The Commission reported three years later and through its county statistics revealed that elementary school provision in Oxfordshire — thanks primarily to the efforts of National Society supporters — was now among the most satisfactory in the country. Only Wiltshire and Westmorland registered a higher proportion of public weekday scholars to total population. (See Table 1.) But on a broader national basis it concluded that although the grants system was working fairly well in principle it did not provide adequate assistance for the most needy areas, since they were unable to raise from voluntary sources the necessary half-cost of building and maintenance. In addition, many elementary subjects were poorly taught, while attendance, particularly in country districts, was irregular, with most boys leaving school for good at the age of ten or eleven. The Revd G. Marshall, vicar of Pyrton, in evidence to the Royal Commission concluded that the greatest obstacles to educational advance in his part of Oxfordshire were 'the want of interest felt by parents, and the value of their children's labour after the age of 10 or 11'. The situation was aggravated by the 'jealousy' of farmers when efforts were made to 'raise the standard of education among the lower orders. They remark . . . that there are far greater opportunities for the labourer's children to acquire a sound education than for their own. As a rule, farmers take little interest in the day school, and contribute nothing towards its expenses'.[28]

[28] *Royal Commission on Popular Education*, P.P. 1861, xxi, Pt v, pp. 311–12.

The Revd Charles Keene of Swyncombe House near Henley-on-Thames shared many of these concerns in his own evidence to the Commission. But he expressed special anxiety at the moral dangers of allowing young girls to work on the land, suggesting instead that they remain at school until the age of fifteen, when they could be sent straight into domestic service:

to pass from a well-ordered school with its high inculcated morals and conduct, to be associated with the uncivilized youth of the other sex, and the coarse habits too frequently incidental to the ordinary employments in field husbandry is not only undesirable but most pernicious in its effects upon the character and feelings of those, who in future are to exercise so much influence for good or bad in family life.[29]

The Revised Code of 1862 and its aftermath

It was partly to combat the weaknesses highlighted by the Commission's Report of 1861, and partly to tighten up on the financial administration of the grants, that in 1862 Robert Lowe, vice-president of the Committee of Council on Education, introduced the new and rigorous device of the Revised Code. Henceforth government grants, other than building grants, were to be calculated only on the attendance of pupils at school under a certificated teacher plus the results of an annual examination conducted by Her Majesty's Inspector and based on the three 'R's'. A grant of 12s. per child was to be offered for all pupils over six years of age, 4s. of which was determined by attendance and 8s. by passes in the annual examination in reading, writing and arithmetic. Failure in any one of the examination subjects meant a deduction of 2s. 8d. from that particular child's grant. The infants, who were exempted from the ordeal of the annual examination, could produce 6s. 6d. each (in addition to their attendance grant) provided the Inspector was satisfied that they were 'instructed suitably to their age, and in a manner not to interfere with the instruction of the older children'. The examinations for these latter were arranged in a series of Standards and each child was expected to move up a Standard every year. (See Table 4.) At the same time the teachers' annual grants, the pension scheme, the allowances for school apparatus and the pupil-teachers' stipends were all withdrawn; payments to training colleges were cut back shortly afterwards.[30] Overall, between 1861 and 1865 the education grant fell by more than twenty per cent, although by

[29] Ibid., p. 265. His view was shared by other clergymen, like Edward Coleridge, the incumbent of Mapledurham, who declared in 1866 that a serious impediment to his ministry was 'women working in the fields. This is the ruin of all the Girls'. Clergy Visitation Returns for 1866, Bodl. MS. Oxf. Dioc. Pp. c. 332.

[30] H. C. Barnard, *A History of English Education from 1760* (London, 1961 ed.), p. 112. The pension scheme for teachers was partly revived in 1875, but as early as February 1873 the Oxford and West Oxfordshire district of the National Union of Elementary Teachers had called for new pension provisions. See *The Schoolmaster*, 1 March 1873.

the end of the decade an upward movement had been resumed.

One of the aims of the Revised Code was to ensure that *all* children received attention from the teacher, not merely the brightest, since all had to succeed at the annual examination if the maximum grant were to be earned. In fact according to Article 4 of the Code, the express object of the whole exercise was 'to promote the education of children belonging to the classes who support themselves by manual labour'. In addition, general reading books had to be provided to supplement the Bible, which all too often had been used, on economy grounds, as the sole source of reading material and spelling practice as well as of religious instruction. But if these were gains, in almost every other respect the new system exerted an adverse influence on the instruction given. Because reading, writing and arithmetic were the grant-earning subjects, they were concentrated upon to the virtual exclusion of all others apart from religious knowledge and needlework, which was compulsory for the girls. Over the years efforts were made to widen the curriculum with, for example, the provision of additional grants for 'specific' subjects such as English grammar, history and geography in 1867, and eight years later the conversion of these latter to 'class' subjects, with the grant earned by the proficiency of the whole class rather than the success of the individual. By this time the range of 'specific' subjects had also been extended to cover modern languages, Latin, mathematics, science and domestic economy.

But such refinements had little impact in the country areas. The three R's examination, combined with average attendance, remained the basis of the education grant up to 1890, and the last elements of the 'payment by results' system did not finally disappear for 'specific' subjects until 1897. However, after 1890 the grant for the three R's was replaced by higher payments for attendance and an 'additional "discipline and organisation" item'.[31] Only with the Code of 1900 was the final liberation secured. This swept away all piecemeal grants. Instead schools received 'capitation grants of 17s. for infant children, and 22s. for older. The inspectors were able to reduce the grants by only a shilling for defects and the only additional payments were for cooking and manual instruction' — neither of which affected most rural schools.[32]

---

[31] Pamela Horn, *The Victorian Country Child* (Kineton, 1974), pp. 42–43; E. Midwinter, *Nineteenth Century Education* (London, 1970), p. 38. For a survey of changes in the curriculum see *Report of the Board of Education for 1910–11*, P.P. 1912–13, xxi, Survey of the Curriculum of the Public Elementary School. From 1866 the groups intended to benefit from elementary education were widened to include shopkeepers, craftsmen, policemen and others '*of the same means and social level*' as manual workers.

[32] One Oxfordshire village school which held cookery lessons for pupils was Cogges. Here, according to members of the Cook family, who attended at the turn of the century: 'Cooking was done in the evening or on Friday afternoon. On Friday afternoon they used a kitchen range and made jam tarts, sponges, etc. for sale. With the money they bought hymn books, hassocks and surplices for the church' (Reminiscences at O.C.M.).

In the meantime more than one generation of children grew up for whom learning by rote and a narrow curriculum were the order of the day. Her Majesty's Inspectors, thanks to their financial power over the schools, became feared by teachers and pupils alike, and it is possible to trace a note of desperation in school log books as the date of the dreaded annual examination drew near; the entries in the Whitchurch log book for 10 December 1869, and 21 January 1870 well illustrate this. At Claydon in the early 1880s, mock tests were held regularly for six months before the Inspector's arrival.

These difficulties no doubt stemmed in part from the wide differences in background and education of Inspectors and teachers. Most H.M.Is were from well-to-do professional families and had been educated at one of the older universities, so that of thirty-six Anglican Inspectors on the strength of the Education Department in 1860, twenty-two were graduates of Cambridge and thirteen of Oxford. The thirty-sixth came from Trinity College, Dublin. By 1870, when the total inspectorate had increased to sixty-two, fifty-one were Anglican clergymen. Although during the rapid expansion of the 1870s, with a peak of 134 Inspectors employed by 1880, the recruitment of clergymen came to an end and the age of those appointed fell, in other respects family and educational backgrounds remained unchanged.[33]

The Oxfordshire Inspectors certainly conformed to the general pattern. The Revd Henry W. Bellairs (1812–1900) was the son of a clergyman and was educated at Shrewsbury and Christ Church, Oxford, before becoming an Inspector in the county from 1844 to 1872.[34] His successor, the Revd H. A. Pickard (1832–1905) was the son of an army officer, and went to Rugby and Christ Church, where he acted as tutor from 1857 until he entered the inspectorate in 1864.[35] And in the south of the county the Revd C. D. Du Port (1836–1905) was the son of the assistant treasurer to the States of Guernsey. He graduated at Caius College, Cambridge, and after a short career in India (where he was elected a Fellow of the University of Bombay in 1863) returned to England in 1866 to enter the inspectorate.[36] In 1886, Du Port was succeeded by Seymour Greig Tremenheere (1848–1942), the eldest son of C. W. Tremenheere, an Indian army officer and Political Resident at Aden, 1870–74. He was

---

[33] Gillian Sutherland, *Policy-Making in Elementary Education 1870–1895* (Oxford, 1973), pp. 55–59. Nancy Ball, *Her Majesty's Inspectorate* (Birmingham, 1963), p. 223; J. Hurt, *Education in Evolution* (London, 1971), esp. the useful discussion on the background of some inspectors on pp. 174–85.

[34] Ibid., p. 53, note. He was a founder of Cheltenham Ladies' College (1854), and later Vicar of Nuneaton (1872–91).

[35] Ibid., p. 215, note; obituary in *The Times*, 29 Sept. 1905.

[36] J. A. Venn, *Alumni Cantabrigienses*, Part II, s.n.

another Oxford man, being educated at Lancing and New College, where he graduated in 1871. He joined the inspectorate in May 1875, and was initially assigned to its northern division.[37] Such men were 'little inclined to regard teachers as in any way their equals', even though they did recognize the pressure under which many of them laboured.[38]

Yet, the Inspectors' attitude was of overwhelming importance in deciding the future of schools, for records show that the government grant could make or break certain of the smaller establishments. Thus at Shutford during the school year 1884–85 the grant amounted to £31. 2s. 4d. out of a total school income of just over £82; a decade later this proportion had increased, so that the various grants were now providing almost three-quarters of the total income. Similarly at Whitchurch from 1869 to 1875 inclusive the school acounts show that in four out of the seven years the government grant was supplying between one-quarter and one-third of the school's income. And in years like 1869, when the payment was a mere £6. 2s 5d., the deficiency had to be met by an increase in the amount of the subscriptions from local well-wishers and the transfer of cash from a savings bank account.[39]

Even the salary of the teachers might depend in part on the success of the annual inspection. At Shutford the mistress was paid £50 a year plus one-third of the grant in the 1880s and 1890s, while at Whitchurch arrangements varied from the £70 per annum and two-thirds of the grant paid to the master and mistress from 1868 to 1870, to the £100 per annum plus half of the grant paid to their successors after 1872. Similarly, in March 1888 at Charlbury Board School the newly-appointed headmaster was paid a salary of £80 per annum plus 20 per cent of the grant; his principal female assistant received £50 per annum plus 10 per cent of the grant, and the second female assistant a mere £15 per annum and 5 per cent of the grant. In most years the extra payment to the headmaster equalled well over one-quarter of his basic salary, and in May 1891 this position was recognized when he was placed on a fixed salary of £125 per annum, but without a share of the grant.[40] The financial arrangements of his colleague at Combe Church School were, on the other hand, a good deal less generous, since in May 1889 this unfortunate's salary was set at

---

[37] Details of Tremenheere's background can be found in Burke's *Landed Gentry* (London, 1937, 15th ed.) and in B. W. I. Handford, *Lancing* (1933), pp. 116–17. In view of the great stress Tremenheere laid on Shakespearean plays in the Whitchurch curriculum, it is interesting to note that in 1862 he acted in *Romeo and Juliet*, the first school play produced at Lancing.

[38] Ball, *Her Majesty's Inspectorate*, p. 223.

[39] Shutford National School Cash Account and Fee Book 1885–1901 (O.R.O., TSB/7); Whitchurch School Accounts.

[40] Minute Book of Charlbury School Board (O.R.O., T/SM.4/i).

£25 per annum plus 'the school pence' and 'half the government grant'.[41]

In achieving a maximum grant for their school one of the most difficult problems for teachers was the attendance issue. Throughout the 1860s there was no general compulsion for children to attend school, and at a time when child labour was general, especially in agriculture, there was a constant battle to ensure that pupils made the requisite number of attendances. Youngsters working in cottage industries, like lacemaking, glovemaking and straw plaiting, were in theory at least restricted by the 1867 Factory and Workshops Regulation Act, which laid down that no child below the age of eight was to be employed in a handicraft, and between the ages of eight and thirteen he or she was to attend an approved elementary school for at least ten hours per week. In Oxfordshire the restrictions applied to the lacemaking trade of the Banbury, Bicester and Thame area, and to glovemaking around Woodstock but they had no application to those children employed in agriculture or domestic service, who together formed the largest groups of young workers.[42] For them, evening classes run by the local incumbent or village schoolmaster might provide the sole opportunity for academic instruction, and these were normally on offer during the winter months only.[43]

Education legislation from 1870

It was to deal with this broader class of youngsters that the Education Acts of 1870, 1876 and 1880 were passed. So far, all attempts at direct provision of schools by the state had foundered on the opposition and jealousies of the various religious bodies, who were each anxious to preserve their own role within the educational system.[44] Nevertheless by

[41] Minutes of Managers' Meetings at Combe School (O.R.O., T/SM.17). Bad results at the annual inspection might also lead to dismissal of the teachers — as at Bix in July, 1888, when the school board unanimously decided 'a change of teachers was necessary in the interest of the Ratepayers and children'. Both the headmistress and her assistant were given notice in this case.

[42] For a discussion of the difficulties of implementing the 1867 Factory and Workshops Act in the county see Pamela Horn, 'Pillow Lacemaking in Victorian England: The Experience of Oxfordshire', *Textile History*, 3 December 1972, pp. 108–12. As regards employment, the 1861 Census of Population suggests that there were 301 boys aged 5–9 inclusive engaged full-time in agriculture, plus 2,983 aged 10–14 inclusive. Among the girls there were 4 aged 5–9 inclusive and 734 aged 10–14 working as domestic servants; there were also 169 female lacemakers and 135 glovers in the latter age range. P.P. 1863, liii, Pt I.

[43] McClatchey, *Oxon. Clergy*, p. 159 suggests 'that out of 208 villages and market towns' in the county, 'all but forty-nine' had evening classes in 1866. See also Table 1.

[44] Needless to say this did not prevent church/chapel conflicts from taking place — as at Littlemore during 1866, when a member of New Road Baptist Chapel, Oxford, wrote to the secretary to the Committee of Council in London, complaining that the Littlemore incumbent and the mistress of the village school had '*sent word* to . . . parents, that [pupils] *must* come to the Church School on Sunday *if* they wish to come to the School during the

the late 1860s it was becoming clear that day school facilities in England and Wales were inadequate to meet the needs either of the children or of the community generally. It is likely, too, that the extension of the franchise in 1867 to the male urban householder and the influence of pressure groups like Joseph Chamberlain's National Education League, launched from Birmingham in 1869, also encouraged further state intervention.[45] In February 1870, W. E. Forster, who was now vice-president of the Committee of Council, introduced a compromise Bill designed, as he put it, 'to complete the present voluntary system, to fill up gaps'. The new legislation was to ensure that every child had an elementary school place and in areas where the voluntary schools were unable to meet this need local ratepayers must form an elected school board, financed partly out of the rates, to fulfil the obligation. Boards were permitted to make bye-laws forbidding the employment of children below the age of ten and requiring attendance at school at least part-time up to the age of thirteen unless the pupils could pass an appropriate leaving examination — usually the Fourth Standard. Attendance officers could be appointed to pursue those who were evading the regulations.[46]

In Oxfordshire, as in most rural areas, the measure was of limited *direct* importance only, since voluntary schools continued to supply the bulk of school places. (See Table 2.) Indeed, on a national basis some writers, including E. G. West, have argued that voluntary effort was already meeting the deficiencies in school provision without the need for state intervention.[47] But whilst it may be true that 'the Forster Act did not significantly hasten the spread of literacy', it did ensure 'that the rate at which literacy had increased in 1851–71 would be maintained'. In short, the Act was 'responsible for the mopping-up operation by which the very poor children, living in slums or remote country regions were taught to read'. It also helped to raise accommodation standards in existing schools; a survey of elementary accommodation in the county published in 1874 revealed that in sixty-four grouped parishes and eight-five single parishes, provisions were inadequate, while in 130 they were 'sufficient'.[48] *Indirectly,*

---

[45] Gillian Sutherland, *Elementary Education in the Nineteenth Century*, Historical Association Pamphlet G.76 (1971), pp. 27–28.
[46] Sutherland, *Policy-Making in Elementary Education*, p. 83
[47] E. G. West, *Education and the Industrial Revolution* (London, 1975), Chapters 2, 3 and 8.
[48] P.P. 1874, xviii. The earlier quotations are from Richard D. Altick, *The English Common Reader* (Chicago, 1967), pp. 171–72.

---

week, or if they go to our School on Sunday they cannot have them at their Day School (the *only* school in the village for the children to go to)'. These charges were strongly denied by the incumbent, the Rev. G. W. Huntingford, and his position was upheld by the Committee of Council. See uncatalogued Papers re Littlemore School 1838–1947 in Bodleian Library.

then, the 1870 legislation did useful work in forcing the voluntarists to improve their standards if they wished to preserve their independence. At Epwell, for example, building extensions took place in 1873 'to meet the requirements of the 1870 Education Act', while at Mollington a new National school was built in 1872 for the same purpose. Several similar examples could be quoted.[49]

These efforts were made because many clergymen regarded the establishment of a school board in their parish, with its attendant electoral contests, as a threat both to their own position and to general 'good feeling' within the village, and they fiercely opposed all attempts to introduce one. Among those feeling in this way was the rector of Whitchurch, the Revd Edward Moore, and by dint of voluntary effort, a government grant and a little help from the National Society, he was able to extend the Church School so that it could cater for 152 pupils. As he pointed out to the National Society when appealing for assistance in November 1870, he was anxious to avoid the appointment of a school board 'which in [my] opinion the circumstances of the Parish make it most desirable to avoid'. His counterpart at South Stoke was still more emphatic, writing to the Education Department in London and his local H.M.I. in a vain attempt to 'avoid the vexation of a School board'. The dispute dragged on for some time until eventually on 26 April, 1875, Du Port visited the school at Woodcote within South Stoke parish which was the particular bone of contention and sealed its fate when he reported that its walls were 'built of such a faulty clay brick that the room is simply

---

[49] V.C.H. Oxon., x (1972), 206, 258. Almost thirty years earlier a Church School Enquiry instituted by the National Society had revealed that in 1846–47 of 395 day and Sunday schools in Oxfordshire, 64 were held in rooms in 'dames' cottages' and 33 in 'portions of Church, including Vestry-room'. See report at National Society headquarters in London. However, even in the early twentieth century some school accommodation of dubious quality was still in use, as records at Oxfordshire Education Office make clear. Thus at Mixbury the school was built over cart sheds leading into the rectory drive and had first been opened in 1838, while at Nether Worton instruction was given in a room built on to the Church. The construction of new schools was a remunerative exercise for builders and architects, both before the 1870 Education Act and afterwards. At Deddington, where a new National school was built in 1853, the cost amounted to £1,244. 14s. 7d., including the gift of a site by Mr W. C. Cartwright, at a value of £150. A Government grant of £400 was also received. William Hambley, a London architect, was paid £56. 2s. as his fee, while Robert Franklin, builder, secured £626. 18s. 8d. and James Hopcraft, mason, £311. 14s. 6d. See Deddington School Buildings (pamphlet, Deddington, 1854), pp. 9 and 13 at Bodl. MS. D.D. Par. Deddington c. 20(j). Among other architects benefiting in this fashion were William Wilkinson (1819–1901) and his nephew, Clapton Crabb Rolfe (1854–1907). Wilkinson, the son of a carpenter-cum-auctioneer and builder of Witney, joined his father's auctioneering business in 1838, but commenced his architectural career in 1841. He designed new schools at Bampton in 1863 and at Minster Lovell and Clanfield in the early 1870s. See A. Saint, 'Three Oxford Architects', Oxoniensia, xxxv (1970), 71, 74.

TABLE 2

ELEMENTARY DAY SCHOOLS IN OXFORDSHIRE ON THE
ANNUAL GRANT LIST ON 31 AUGUST 1899*

	No. of Schools	Accommo- dation for scholars	No. of scholars on register	Average no. of scholars in attendance†
National or Church of England	199			
Wesleyan	2			
Roman Catholic	5			
British and other Schools	10			
Total Voluntary Schools	216	32,071	24,032	20,440
Total Board Schools	25	3,510	2,704	2,365
Grand Total	241**	35,581	26,736	22,805

* Compiled from a *Return of the Number of Public Elementary Day Schools on the Annual Grant List on 31 August 1899*, P.P., 1900, lxv, Pt. I, pp. 12–13, 24 and 32.
† Average attendance figures throughout the year were estimated at about 85 per cent of those on the register. This was one of the highest county averages in the country and compares, for example, with a mere 76.6 per cent achieved in Monmouth and 78.2 per cent in Cornwall over the same period.
** By 1899, 104 of the schools had libraries attached to them.

not habitable, reeking damp'.[50] By June 1875 a board had been elected and two years later a new mixed school was opened to cater for eighty children. But other incumbents were more successful in their opposition and even in the mid-1890s only about twelve per cent of Oxfordshire villages had fallen under the jurisdiction of a school board. Some clerics, indeed, used financial as well as religious arguments to sway reluctant voluntary subscribers, by pointing out that school boards, with their triennial elections, would prove an expensive luxury. So when an appeal was launched at Caversham in 1892 to provide extra accommodation at the local church schools, it was stressed that according

[50] South Stoke file at P.R.O., Ed. 2. 366. However, some of the school extensions were over-ambitious, and this became increasingly the case as migration from the rural areas was stepped up in the final quarter of the nineteenth century. At Tadmarton, where a new school was opened in 1876 to cater for 84 children, average attendance up to 1906 was only about 44. Similarly at Wigginton the accommodation had increased to 89 by 1894, although attendance 'barely reached half the capacity'; in 1894 there were only about 30 day pupils. *V.C.H. Oxon.*, ix, 159, 170.

to the latest calculations the average cost of a scholar educated under the Voluntary system is £1 16s. 11½d. per annum, while the cost per scholar under the Board system is £2 5s. 11½d.; and it ought to be generally known that in the event of the formation of a School Board at Caversham it has been estimated . . . that the annual rate would scarcely be less than 11d. in the pound . . . We are confident that on due consideration you will on the score of economy, as well as in the interests of religious education, see the advisability of continuing the present system . . .

The arguments proved persuasive, for within two years the 'friends of Church schools' in the parish had rallied round and the financial crisis was at an end.[51]

Yet though school boards aroused such deep emotions in many villages, an examination of the membership of some of those elected in Oxfordshire leads to the view that they differed little in character from the management committees of voluntary schools. On both, farmers, landowners and clergy were prominent, while successful 'working men' or 'radical' candidates were few and far between. Of seven school boards investigated — at Bix, Brightwell Baldwin, Enstone, Milton-under-Wychwood, Stadhampton, Tetsworth and Watlington — no less than 56 per cent of the members were farmers or landowners-cum-farmers, while about 10 per cent were clergymen. Landowners or gentlemen of independent means made up a large part of the remainder, contributing 16 per cent of the total. In voluntary Church of England schools, on the other hand, the managers normally consisted of the principal minister of the parish, his curate and some lay subscribers to the school. Though in a few villages, management of non-Anglican schools might devolve on a single landed proprietor if he were the principal financial backer. The small Roman Catholic school at Mapledurham, which functioned during the third quarter of the nineteenth century, was financed and managed by the squire, who was himself a Roman Catholic. While at Spelsbury, where the parish school was under the control of Viscount Dillon, the incumbent plaintively observed in 1888 that his lordship would allow 'no clerical teaching' in the school; even the holding of a Sunday school was prohibited and '[he] will not let me even go inside the building'.[52]

[51] Correspondence on Caversham schools in Ch. Ch. Archives, MS Estates 66, ff. 184, 190.

[52] For details of the situation at Spelsbury see correspondence ibid., MS. Estates 82, f. 200. Details of the situation at Mapledurham are in P. L. R. Horn, 'Education in an Oxfordshire Village: 1800–1870', *Catholic Education Today*, Vol. 2, No. 5, Sept.–Oct. 1968, pp. 28–29. P. Gordon, *The Victorian School Manager* (London, 1974), pp. 9–15 discusses voluntary school managers. School board minute books examined are all at O.R.O.; the years considered for each board were as follows: Bix 1876 and 1879 elections, T/SM.2/i; Brightwell Baldwin 1895, T/SM.19/i; Enstone 1872 and 1875, T/SM.8/i; Milton-under-Wychwood 1874 and 1877, T/SM.9/i; Stadhampton 1877 and 1880, T/SM.11/i;

But these were private idiosyncracies. The significant factor was that school boards and voluntary school managers were recruited from roughly the same sectors of rural society. Yet, despite that, distrust of school boards remained strong, especially in the early days — so much so that Bellairs could report gloomily of Oxfordshire and Berkshire in 1871:

Compulsory attendance will probably for a long time be confined to the towns. The proprietors in many of the agricultural parishes dislike the idea of school boards. The tenant farmers object to the removal of juvenile labour from their fields, and the parochial clergy cannot bear any interference with the assumed right of sole management, denominational influence, and exclusive superintendence which they have hitherto enjoyed.

Hence in those places where the managers and teachers have for so long ridiculed all attempts at real efficiency without compulsory attendance, they now refuse the very means of securing it, and so in rural districts we shall have, with irregular or non-attendance, ignorance with its concomitant vice.[53]

It was an attempt to control the still large and unregulated child work-force engaged in agriculture, therefore, that in 1873 Clare Sewell Read, Conservative M.P. for South Norfolk, introduced a Private Member's bill seeking to prevent the employment of children on the land below the age of eight and requiring a specified number of attendances for those between eight and twelve. Although the Agricultural Children Act was passed and came into operation on 1 January 1875, its failure to nominate an enforce-ment agency soon led to widespread evasion. On 24 April 1875, for example, the Oxfordshire magistrates reported that 'children of the prohibited age are, more or less, employed in agricultural labour, and . . . no instance has yet occurred of a prosecution for this breach of the law'.[54]

So it was only following these earlier failures that the 1876 Education Act imposed full-time attendance at school on all children from five to ten years of age, with a minimum of 250 attendances a year for those aged between ten and twelve and 150 attendances for those between twelve

---

[53] *Report of the Committee of Council on Education for 1870–71*, P.P. 1871, xxii, Report by H.M.I. Bellairs, p. 23.

[54] *Return to the House of Commons on the Operation of the Agricultural Children Act*, P.P. 1875, lxi, p. 12. Significantly the magistrates added that 'in their judgment the police ought not to be employed' for the purposes of enforcement.

Tetsworth 1889 (existing board) and 1890, T/SM.12/i; Watlington 1873 and 1876, T/SM.14/i. Some of the farmer members were very large employers of labour, as at Milton-under-Wychwood, where the 1877 chairman, William Mace, farmed 830 acres and employed 21 men, 9 boys and 3 women at the 1871 Census, while his vice-chairman, Robert Craddock, farmed 740 acres and employed 21 men and 9 boys. See Census Return at P.R.O., RG.10/1456.

and fourteen.[55] Permanent *legal* exemption before fourteen could be achieved only if the child passed an approved leaving examination in the three 'r's' (often known as the 'labour certificate'), or by making the required number of attendances for five years he or she might qualify for the so-called 'dunce's pass' and be permitted to leave at thirteen. In order to make effective the compulsory provisions of the Act a new type of local authority — the attendance committee — was introduced to cover those school districts which were still without a school board. Parents neglecting to send their children to school could now be fined, and despite the laxity of some attendance officers and magistrates, a number were. In 1879 and 1880, for example, magistrates at Henley petty sessions (which covered the Whitchurch area) heard about twenty prosecutions a year for breaches of the attendance regulations; fines averaged about 2*s*. 6*d*. for each offender.[56] At Watlington, similarly, between 1880 and 1882 school attendance cases accounted for nearly one-quarter of the cases heard. Nevertheless teachers complained of the weaknesses of the system and the vagaries of the attendance officers. This was perhaps not surprising since the latter appointment was normally a part-time one only in country districts, and the rate of pay for the job was poor. At Enstone school board in 1881 a new attendance officer was appointed at £3 per annum, for example, while at Charlbury in July 1888 the annual sum was set at £5, and rates of £3 or £5 a year were common in many parts of the county.[57]

The need to enforce attendance regulations was further underlined in 1880, when a fresh Education Act made the adoption of attendance bye-laws mandatory for all education authorities, since some had failed to take action under the 1876 legislation. (At Marsh Baldon, for instance, attendance bye-laws were only adopted in 1881.) By the early 1880s, therefore, the case had theoretically been established that attendance was compulsory for every child. But a further problem was that school fees were still payable. Normally these amounted to 1*d*. or 2*d*. per child per week only, though some parishes adopted a sliding scale based on parental income. At Milton-under-Wychwood from the mid-1870s the children of labourers paid only 1*d*. a week, but those belonging to tradesmen paid 3*d*. each per week and to farmers, 6*d*. Similarly, at Adderbury in 1877 the rate varied from 1*d*. or 2*d*. for labourers' children (according to family size) to 4*d*. for a tradesman's child or for the offspring of farmers cultivating under 50 acres; those cultivating over 50 acres were expected to pay a weekly fee of 6*d*. per child. Not until 1891 was attendance made virtually free, as an extra government grant of 10*s*.

---

[55] Horn, *Victorian County Child*, pp. 59–60.
[56] Ibid., p. 63. From 1880, however, Whitchurch school attendance cases were transferred to Reading petty sessions.
[57] See Minute Books for Enstone and Charlbury School Boards at O.R.O., T/SM.8/i and T/SM.4/i, respectively.

per pupil per annum led to the abolition of fees in most elementary schools. Three years later the *minimum* school leaving age was raised from ten to eleven, and in 1899 from eleven to twelve, although in most rural areas eleven still seems to have been accepted.[58]

The problems of school attendance

Despite this theoretical framework, problems of securing satisfactory attendances persisted. Sometimes they arose from the ill-health of the pupils or their lack of adequate clothing. Footwear was a particular problem. In June 1866, the master of Launton school recorded in his log book that a Mrs Sansome, the wife of a local labourer, had informed him that she had been unable to send her seven-year-old daughter to school or to Church on Sunday, 'because her shoes were so very bad'. She appealed to the master to let the girl 'come to school this week [and] she would try to get her some new ones for next'. But sickness was a still greater cause of absenteeism and occasionally — as at Steeple Aston in the autumn of 1863 and the early months of the following year, or at Whitchurch in the winter of 1887–88 — epidemics would cut sharply into attendances. At Whitchurch the problem was an outbreak of mumps, while at Steeple Aston an epidemic of scarlet fever was followed by measles. By the end of January 1864 more than half of the Steeple Aston scholars were away with the latter disease and one unfortunate child had died of it. Once such illnesses came to a village the unhygienic living conditions of the inhabitants and the low resistance to infection caused by poor feeding meant that many youngsters were vulnerable to attack. Even milder disabilities, like colds or chilblains, could lead to absence. At Asthall School, the mistress noted on 1 March 1895: 'The attendance this week not so good as last. Several of the elder children at home with chilblains, *"can't get their boots on"'*.

Nevertheless, alongside these unavoidable causes of absence, child employment was an even more common reason for non-attendance, as the mistress at Kelmscott (then in Oxfordshire) recorded during October 1895: 'The Attendance has not been good this week, several children

[58] For details of school fees see Minute Book of Milton-under-Wychwood School Boaru, O.R.O. T/SM.9/i and *V.C.H.*, *Oxon.*, ix, 42. From 1876 poor law guardians were explicitly authorised to pay the fees of children whose parents were too poor to pay in the ordinary way, but not all guardians interpreted these provisions generously. At Cropredy and Bourton School, the master sadly noted on 25 April 1880, that they had decided 'not to allow payment of school fees of any scholar who had passed the third standard'. See Horn, *Victorian Country Child*, p. 67. Under Section 5 of the 1891 legislation every parent had an absolute right to demand free education 'and if no existing local school gave it and refused to provide it', a school board must be set up. Nevertheless by 1895 around 800,000 children still paid school pence — as opposed to almost 4m. who received their education free. B. Simon, *Education and the Labour Movement 1870–1920* (London, 1965), p. 141 gives details of the school leaving age position.

being needed at home to pick up potatoes'. In June and July of that same year she had even altered the hours of attendance in order to fit in with the children's work plans. An entry for 19 June reads: 'This afternoon and the remaining afternoons of this week the registers will be closed at 1 o'clock to allow the children to leave at 3 o'clock as they are needed in the hay fields'. Work on the family's allotment garden was another cause of truancy, but it was at the time of the corn harvest that the greatest gaps were likely to appear in the school ranks. In many villages the exact timing of the summer or 'harvest' holiday would be decided by the ripeness of the corn. At Sydenham on 6 August, 1884, the mistress noted that the school was 'very thin; harvest was ready to gather in sooner than expected, children away from School in consequence. School closed till Sept. 15th'. Similarly at Asthall in 1898 the school was closed on 4 August, a Wednesday, because the children were no longer attending; the log book entry reads: 'Fully two-fifths of the children have been in harvest field all this week'.[59] The youngsters were engaged either in looking after younger brothers and sisters at home whilst their mother went to help with the harvest or they would themselves work, leading the horses, carrying food and drink to the harvesters, or perhaps helping to bind the corn into sheaves. At a time when an adult male farm worker might be earning a basic wage of a little as 10s. to 12s. per week the 4d. or 6d. a day that a child could obtain was a valuable addition to family resources.[60] Arthur Wilkinson of Bladon, who was born in 1884, remembers that he started work at the age of about nine, helping in the harvest field during his summer holidays:

I used to have to go with my Father and lay bands for him, then I used to tie the Shaves [sic] up and then shock them up, and then rake up between the rows of shocks from 6 o'clock in the morning until 9 or 10 o'clock at night . . . When I was eleven years old I passed the 4th Standard and I left school and went to work on a farm: wages 2/6d. a week.[61]

Once the corn had been carried a mother and her children would go out gleaning, or leazing as it was called in North Oxfordshire.[62] This too kept the children away from school for a further two or three weeks; but from

[59] Asthall School Log Book at O.R.O.
[60] Flora Thompson, *Lark Rise to Candleford* (Oxford 1963 ed.), p. 6, recalls that even in the 1880s farm workers at Juniper Hill earned only 10s. per week as their basic wage. In 1892 Mr Cecil M. Chapman reported for the *Royal Commission on Labour* that in the Thame Poor Law Union day men earned on average 12s. or 13s. per week during the summer months and 11s. or 12s. in winter. But at Great Haseley, Great Milton, Chalgrove and Worminghall the basic weekly wage was 11s. all the year round. P.P. 1893–94, xxxv, Mr Chapman's Report, p. 54.
[61] Reminiscences of Mr Arthur Wilkinson of Bladon at O.R.O.
[62] Thompson, *Lark Rise to Candleford*, p. 14, describes the scene at Juniper Hill.

the stock of corn thus gathered a family's supply of flour could be secured for the winter.

It is, indeed, an indication of the priorities of education and agriculture in the Oxfordshire villages that the return to school was delayed until the end of the harvest season. Typical was the entry at Sydenham School on 20 September 1886: 'School reopened, but closed again by order of the Vicar, the harvest being not quite finished'. Again, in villages where the school managers were themselves farmers or were related to them there was sometimes a reluctance to prosecute either the parents of those who worked illegally or the men who employed them. In 1882 H.M.I. Pickard complained that 'a former board at Claydon prosecuted a parent and obtained a conviction against him for not sending his boy to school, but they did not prosecute the farmer who was illegally employing the lad, for he was a member of the school board'. Small wonder that on 31 October 1885, the head of this school should write despondently: 'The attendance of some of my pupils is most distressing'. Worse still, at Hornton two successive school boards managed for more than ten years to avoid altogether their basic obligation to provide school places. Although children were working 'at any Age', it was not until 1882 that Government pressure at last led to the opening of a school. In the Oxford area as a whole Pickard concluded that while 'some progress' had been made on the attendance issue, there was still 'ample room for improvement'.[63]

In fact it was in the following year that Pickard was to have one of his severest struggles on this issue, at the small parish of Tadmarton. Here the school board declined to prosecute either the parents of a boy illegally employed or his employer because the latter was a brother of a member of the board. The affair came to light when Pickard attended for his annual inspection at Tadmarton school on 9 January 1883 and found the boy, Albert Coxe, absent. The incumbent, who was chairman of the board, informed Pickard that he had been to the employer and had 'begged him to allow the boy to attend the examination but the employer said he could not spare [him]'. Pickard pressed the Education Department in London for action, claiming that the Banbury School Attendance Committee were 'stirring themselves up to put the Act in force and if a farmer is allowed to set the law at defiance because his brother is on the School Board there will be a good deal of annoyance felt'.[64] The affair dragged on until April, with the board still refusing to prosecute, and in the end the Education Department had to intervene. The existing board was

---

[63] *Report of the Committee of Council on Education for 1882*, P.P. 1883, xxv, p. 413. The Hornton children eventually attended a rebuilt National School under the aegis of the school board. See *V.C.H., Oxon.*, ix, 139.

[64] Tadmarton School File at P.R.O., Ed.2.366. The Tadmarton children attended a church school under the aegis of the school board.

deposed and a new one appointed which, it was clearly hoped, would pursue attendance defaulters with the necessary zeal.

By contrast, a few schools — despite the pressures of agriculture — offered rewards for good attendance, as at Charlbury Infants' School where an entry in the school board minute book for 3 July 1896 notes that 'a prize be given for the greatest number of attendances in each class made during the past year'. This practice was adopted by the newly established Oxfordshire Education Committee early in the twentieth century, and Mrs Margaret Watson, who attended Whitchurch School around the turn of the century, recalls that she was one of the virtuous few who won a handsome bronze medal supplied by the Education Committee and inscribed with the words: 'Never Absent — Never Late — 1905–6'.[65]

The end of the Victorian era

So the attendance battle was slowly won. Thanks in part to the influence of education legislation (including the abolition of fees in many schools from 1891) and in part to other factors, by the 1890s comments about poor attendance had ceased to be the major preoccupation they once were for Oxfordshire teachers. Among the additional influences at work were the improvement in the money wages of many farm labourers which took place following the establishment of the first agricultural trade unions in the county in the early 1870s and, even more importantly, the sharp fall in food prices in the last quarter of the century, as cheap imported wheat and frozen meat became available. Farmers, too, under the influence of agricultural depression cut back on their juvenile work force, either by doing without or by substituting machinery for labour where possible. So although families continued to live 'near the bone', most now allowed their children to attend school for the greater part of the year. (See Table 2.)

Within the schools themselves facilities likewise gradually improved, while literacy rates — as shown by the number of people able to sign their name when they married — shared in the general advance. By the 1890s only 5% of men and 2.7% of women marrying in the county were unable to sign the marriage registers, as compared to 30.5% of men and 28.3% of women making a mark when they married in 1860. (See also Table 1.) On a broader front, Object Lessons were introduced for infants and younger children, to increase their perception of the world around them, and in

---

[65] Mrs Margaret Watson in correspondence with the editor, September 1975. The staff of the Chief Education Officer for Oxfordshire believe that the issuing of medals was discontinued in the early 1930s. During the First World War by-laws were again eased, to permit children to work in agriculture — a policy which became apparent from the autumn of 1914. *Returns on School Attendance and Employment in Agriculture*, P.P. 1916, xxii, show that on 31 May, 1916, eight boys aged 11 and 199 aged 12 were granted special exemption in Oxfordshire.

1895 were made compulsory for these groups. Drawing also became a subject for which grants could be earned (this time from the Department of Science and Art rather than the Education Department) and from 1890 it became compulsory for boys to learn to draw 'unless it was certified impracticable, for them to do so'.[66] Reading books, too, improved in quality, with the sickly moral tracts in general use in the first half of the century giving way to livelier texts. Indeed, in order to meet the provisions of the 1870 Education Act that 'no child was to be compelled to attend religious instruction' in any elementary school (Church or otherwise) in receipt of a government grant, religious texts had to be omitted from school readers. But in earlier years, as one critic has put it:

To instruct in religion and in morality was the entire preoccupation of every writer for children . . . The exhortation, the sermon, the Bible quotation, the hymn, fable and moral tale were the vehicles. They exhalted obedience to teacher, parent, minister; respectfulness to one's betters; industriousness, neatness, cleanliness; kindness to animals. They castigated fighting, quarrelling, lying, stealing, begging, drinking, swearing, gambling, playing cards, keeping bad company and telling tales.[67]

Although such objectives may appear laudable in themselves, when translated into written form they often made very dull reading, as a brief examination of early nineteenth century textbooks will soon confirm. As late as 1875 another H.M.I. (T. W. Danby) could condemn a high proportion of the older school reading books as 'of a dryness so repulsive that the notion of regarding a book as a source of pleasure can never for one moment occur to the readers in class'.[68] But by the 1880s and 1890s other books were becoming available. At Cottisford school, Flora Thompson remembered with pleasure the *Royal Reader* which was in general use: 'There was plenty there to enthral any child: "The Skater Chased by Wolves"; "The Siege of Torquilstone", from *Ivanhoe*, Fenimore Cooper's *Prairie on Fire*; and Washington Irving's *Capture of Wild Horses*'.[69]

[66] R. R. Sellman, *Devon Village Schools in the Nineteenth Century* (Newton Abbot, 1967), p. 115. For literacy figures see Twenty-second and Sixty-third *Annual Reports of the Registrar-general for Births, Deaths and Marriages in England*, P.P. 1862, xvii (for the 1860 figure) and 1901, xv, for the 1890s figure. The national average for men making a mark when they married in the 1890s was 4.6% and for women, 5.3%. In 1860 the rates had been 25.5% for men marrying in England and 36.2% for women.
[67] J. M. Goldstrom, *The Social Content of Education 1808–1870* (Irish University Press, Shannon, 1972), pp. 25 and 28.
[68] Horn, *Victorian Country Child*, p. 27 (Danby was reporting on Schools in Suffolk and Essex). See also Pamela Horn, *Labouring Life in the Victorian Countryside* (Dublin, 1976), p. 53 for the views of another H.M.I. on the widespread use of collections of extracts — 'scissor-and-paste compilations', as he called them.
[69] Thompson, *Lark Rise to Candleford*, p. 193. The extracts were from Vol. v of T. Nelson & Sons Ltd., *Royal Readers*, first published in 1872.

Various forms of physical activity, such as marching and drill, were also introduced from the 1870s, and their advent met with the enthusiastic approval of Her Majesty's Inspectors. In 1871 Bellairs felt constrained to criticize the poor standard of drill in Oxfordshire and Berkshire schools, adding:

I should like to see a regular system of military drill introduced, with marching tunes and, where practicable, with drum and fife bands. Arrangements with the adjutants of the militia and volunteers for providing the necessary teaching might easily be made, and the expense of it by employing drill serjeants would not be great.[70]

Twelve years later some progress had been made, and his successor, Pickard, particularly praised the high standard of military drill at the small school at Kingham. Here 'a corps of some 30 or 40 boys . . . will go through everything required from a volunteer corps to prove itself efficient, including skirmishing drill'. At Whitchurch, a log book entry reveals that 'Military Drill' was introduced 'in playground for the boys' on 15 April 1872.

Along with other changes, school treats became more widely available in the second half of the nineteenth century. Sometimes they took the form of annual teas and magic lantern shows held after a prize-giving, as occurred at Whitchurch on 4 February 1869. On other occasions there were May Day processions or concerts or perhaps Band of Hope festivals organized to wean the younger generation from 'the demon drink'. Many children were invited to an annual 'treat' in the grounds of the local manor house or other large property, and at Stonesfield Miss M. Thornett (b. 1896) remembered the regular invitations received by members of her school to visit Blenheim Palace early in the present century. 'A Stonesfield farmer let his carter drive us there in a four-wheeled wagon drawn by two cart horses'. Once they had arrived there was tea, followed by games, a walk round the grounds 'and then, before coming home, the Duchess of Marlborough would come out in front of the palace. Each girl in turn would walk up the steps, curtsy and would then be given a present'.[71]

At a few schools clothing was presented to the pupils, although this was more characteristic of the early nineteenth century than the later. Nevertheless at Mapledurham, the incumbent, Lord Augustus FitzClarence, continued to provide a uniform of green tunics with black buttons and corduroy trousers, plus peaked caps, for the boys and green frocks with white straw poke bonnets for the girls, until his death in 1854. At Kidlington, the distribution of clothing coincided with the school children's annual treat. According to *Jackson's Oxford Journal* of 7 January 1871, each girl

---

[70] *Report of the Committee of Council on Education for 1870–71*, P.P., 1871, xxii, Report by H.M.I. Bellairs, p. 26.
[71] *Oxford Times*, 7 Jan. 1971.

attending the National school was presented with toys and 'a nice comfortable garment' by local well-wishers, after a substantial tea. At Whitchurch, smocks, cloaks, hats and bonnets were regularly supplied to the children until the latter part of 1868, according to the school accounts. The phasing out of this scheme seems to have coincided with the appointment of two new and more highly paid teachers, but occasional gifts of clothing were still being made in the 1880s, as an entry in the school log book for 3 January 1881 shows.

Within the rural community itself, late Victorian schools likewise played a part in creating fresh social attitudes — and in undermining the old, firmly structured, village society. At Cottisford, Flora Thompson remembered the schoolmistress instructing her charges that 'on the material plane people need not necessarily remain always upon one level. Some boys, born of poor parents, had struck out for themselves and become great men . . .'. She sought to inspire the children with a like ambition, and it is significant that Flora's own brother subsequently announced that he did not want to become a country carpenter or mason when he grew up, as his parents had planned: 'what he really wanted was to travel and see the world'. For as the youngsters' knowledge of outside events increased, so they became unwilling to accept the low pay and limited prospects that all too often still went with rural employment. At Great Rollright, indeed, the schoolmaster, Frank Dormer, informed Rider Haggard at the turn of the century that in his parish 'three-quarters of the young men and all the young women left the village at nineteen or twenty years of age, only the dullest staying at home'.[72]

On another level many schools also acted as entertainment centres for adults in the evenings, with penny readings, concerts and dances held in them from time to time.

Yet, despite the overall advances, even in 1900 problems remained. All too frequently lessons were boring and repetitive. In arithmetic, for example, Edwin Burden of Chipping Norton (b. 1890) remembered that each child was issued with cards: 'there were five sums we had to do from each of these cards'. The virtues of perseverance and determination were instilled, too, for a failure to reach the answer on the first occasion meant that the sum had to be worked over and over again until success was achieved. Others, like William Breakspeare of Church Hanborough (b. 1893) and George Swinford of Filkins (b. 1887), recalled the strict discipline, with canings administered to those who transgressed. But even in these conditions rebellions could occur. According to Swinford the master 'used to glory in giving me a good thrashing for the least thing, but when I got older, I turned on him and kicked his legs, then he used to send my

---

[72] H. Rider Haggard, *Rural England* (London, 1902), ii, 114; Thompson, *Lark Rise to Candleford*, pp. 200–1 and 429–30. See also Horn, *Victorian Country Child*, p. 92.

mother [a] note, [and] I had another good hiding'. In the end he proved too unruly for the master to handle and was allowed to leave school at the age of twelve even though he had not passed his 'labour certificate'. At Filkins the older boys were expected to make themselves useful around the school, and according to Swinford they 'were appointed each week to light the fire in winter, and sweep and dust the rooms. This meant an hour before and after school, and we received twopence a week for our work'.[73] The use of pupils to clean the premises was a common — and economical — practice in other schools, too.

William Breakspeare, who confessed to being 'always worried and perplexed in school . . . I was always very embarrassed because I seemed so stupid', was, like Swinford, encouraged to leave without having reached the appropriate standard, because he was regarded as 'a bad influence in the village'. Thanks to the efforts of the vicar he obtained work as a kitchen boy in the parish of Sandhurst, where it was presumably hoped he could make a fresh start.[74]

The Teachers

Some of the discipline difficulties in schools may, however, have been due to the youth and inexperience of the teachers. In 1871, more than one in three of the male teachers and schoolmasters employed in Oxfordshire were under the age of twenty-five, while among the females the proportion was not far short of one in two. Thirty years later the proportion of young male teachers had declined a little — to about one in four — but among the women those under twenty-five still formed almost one-half of those employed. By contrast, female teachers over forty-five were a mere one-eighth of the work force, although among the men that age group accounted for around one-quarter of the total.[75]

Part of this weighting in favour of youth was a result of the large-scale employment of pupil-teachers and monitresses. Typical of the youngsters so engaged was Flora Thompson's fictional character Charity Finch, the daughter of a North Oxfordshire village carpenter. At the age of thirteen and a half Charity was appointed a monitress

with a salary of two pounds ten a year and, as her badge of office, a short, light cane, known as a pointer, officially intended for pointing out the letters of the alphabet on the big wall card to her class of infants, but equally useful for banging the desk to give emphasis to her instructions. To help her support the dignity of

[73] G. Swinford, MS. History of Filkins (c. 1958) in Bodl. MS. Top. Oxon. d. 475, pp. 26 and 41.
[74] Transcript of an interview with William Breakspeare at O.C.M.
[75] At the 1901 Census there were in Oxfordshire 595 male teachers, schoolmasters, professors and lecturers, plus ten 'others concerned with teaching'. The women numbered 1,344 and ten, respectively, in the same two categories; 1,219 of all the females were unmarried and 661 of them were under twenty-five. 1901 Census Report, P.P., 1902, cxx.

her new position, her hair, which had hitherto hung loose about her shoulders, was plaited into a long thick pigtail. Her skirts were brought down from her knees to her ankles and, over them, instead of a white pinafore, she wore a small black, or coloured apron. Instead of as 'Charity' or 'Cherry', as formerly, the children of her class were told to address her as 'Teacher', and this trifling rise in status gave her great satisfaction, for she felt she had taken the first step towards realizing her long-cherished ambition of becoming the mistress of a village school . . .'[76]

Charity took up her appointment as monitress at the school she had formerly attended as a scholar — a not uncommon arrangement. Later, with the approval of the Inspector, she became a pupil teacher.

But if monitresses and pupil teachers were one group of youthful instructors, even among school heads there was a surprisingly high representation of young people. Among them were men like John George, who left Culham College in 1854 at the age of nineteen to take up the headship of Wolvercote National School, although in the opinion of the principal: 'His teaching power [was] low. His command of numbers also very low'. A colleague, who became head of Cowley National School at Christmas 1855, when he was aged only eighteen, was described in equally unenthusiastic terms: 'He is as yet nervous, shy, timid in his school keeping'. While in July 1863, when George Jefferies left Culham to become headmaster of Ramsden School at the age of nineteen, the principal considered him to be 'youthful in appearance & manner. Too much so to take a school on his own account'. However, he seems to have made a success of the job; others were less fortunate. It was in these circumstances that Bellairs complained in 1868 that one cause of failure in the county's elementary schools was 'the unskilfulness as well as the comparative youth and inexperience of the teachers'. It is worth remembering, too, that despite the development of training colleges, even in the mid-Victorian years many teachers were still being recruited locally — as a brief examination of the 1871 census returns will confirm. Thus of fifty schoolmasters and mistresses in the county whose place of birth has been investigated, only about one-third had originated outside Oxfordshire. In fact, according to the census, almost half of the thirty-eight school mistresses considered had been born in the parish where they were employed.[77] Many would have had no formal training and would

[76] Flora Thompson, *Still Glides the Stream* (Oxford, 1948), pp. 83–84.
[77] The census returns for the parishes investigated are at the P.R.O.: R.G.10/1277 for Whitchurch; R.G.10/1444 for Newton Purcell; R.G.10/1445 for Fringford, Hethe, Cottisford, Stoke Lyne, Bicester; R.G.10/1446 for Steeple Aston; R.G.10/1448 for Bladon, Combe, Kidlington and Stonesfield; R.G.10/1449 for Wolvercote, Woodstock, Wootton, Yarnton; R.G.10/1450 for Eynsham, the Hanboroughs and North Leigh. For Mr Bellairs's comments see *Report of the Committee of Council on Education*, P.P., 1868–69, xx, Mr Bellairs's General Report for 1868, p. 23.

perhaps also face discipline problems caused by over-familiarity with their pupils and their pupils' parents.

On the other hand, for those young teachers who were recruited from a distance, village life could often prove very dull and isolated, with few congenial companions. For this reason Bellairs advised parish clergy to show 'little acts of hospitality and kindness. These will help a young teacher to dissipate many a train of sad or homesick recollections, and to bear with contentment, if not with cheerfulness, a more than ordinary lonely life'.[78] At the same time, the youthfulness of the teachers may have made them vulnerable to pressure to engage in the varied out-of-school activities which were expected of many of them, especially in Church schools. These included playing the organ in Church on Sundays, training the choir and teaching at Sunday School. Some accepted the extra duties willingly — like John Knight, who was appointed master at Wheatley in 1880, when he was aged twenty-three. He informed the incumbent that he had 'been used to large organs, and to taking any kind of service', adding subsequently: 'With regard to the Sunday School, it would give me great pleasure to assist'. Similarly, Miss Kate Daniels of Deddington, far from resenting clerical interference in the running of her school, only deplored the fact that 'the vicar [was] not taking interest'. But others shared the embittered views of a Buckinghamshire schoolmaster, when he wrote that the rural teacher was all too often regarded as 'the parson's fag, squire's door-mat, church scraper, professional singer, sub-curate, land surveyor, drill master, club collector, parish clerk, letter writer, librarian, washerwoman's target, organist, choir master, and youth's instructor'.[79] Not surprisingly, as the status of teachers became more assured towards the end of the century, attempts to impose such tasks were resisted with increasing success. Indeed, teachers' agreements signed in the county early in the twentieth century include the following clause: 'The Teacher shall not be required to perform or abstain from performing any duties outside the ordinary School hours, or unconnected with the ordinary work of the School.[80] This was in accordance with the provisions of the Elementary School Code of 1903, which regulated the position of teachers in voluntary schools on this issue.

---

[78] H. W. Bellairs, *The Church and the School, or Hints on Clerical Life* (London, 1868), pp. 120–21. See also Pamela Horn, 'Oxfordshire Village School Teachers: 1800–1880', *Cake and Cockhorse*, Vol. 7, No. 1, Autumn 1976, p. 15.

[79] E. Richardson, *Cloddy in Bucks.* (pamphlet, London, 1872), p. iv. Similar views were expressed in *The Schoolmaster* of 23 and 30 July 1881. For details of John Knight see Bodl. MS. D.D. Par. Wheatley c. 13 — letters dated 20 and 23 August 1880. Miss Daniels's letter to the Wheatley incumbent about Deddington, dated 24 June 1872, is also preserved at this reference.

[80] See Teachers' Agreements at North Leigh School, O.R.O., NS. II/iii–vi.

In other spheres, too, progress was being made. Slowly the State was groping its way towards the creation of a network of publicly financed elementary and secondary schools by the close of the Victorian era. That aim was largely achieved by the 1902 Education Act, which abolished school boards, designated borough and county councils as the basis of the new local education authorities which were to replace them, and made rate aid available to *all* elementary schools, including Church ones. This was a decision which pleased Anglicans and Roman Catholics, whose schools were its main beneficiaries, but angered some Nonconformists — as well as school board supporters — even at that late stage. In addition, for the first time local authorities were authorised to set up their own secondary schools, financed partly out of the rates. As H. C. Barnard has written: 'By the Act of 1902 a co-ordinated national system of education was at last introduced and the "confusion arising from lack of organisation" was ended'.[81]

Yet, despite the benefits bestowed by the 1902 legislation, the situation still remained unsatisfactory in some respects. This was particularly true of *secondary* education and some critics have blamed the 1902 Act itself — coupled with the various regulatory Codes subsequently issued — for its slow growth. For it was from the start accepted in official circles that the majority of children would receive elementary schooling only, and that secondary provision would be restricted to youngsters who showed 'promise of exceptional capacity' or whose parents could pay fees. These were normally fixed at a minimum of £3 per child per annum, and given the economic circumstances of the time, even such a comparatively modest sum as that inevitably excluded most working-class children, other than scholarship holders, from secondary education.[82] Although the number of scholarships was increased from 1907, under the 'free place' system, as late as 1924 it was estimated that 'less than 5 per cent' of those in Oxfordshire's elementary schools were being selected 'as capable of profiting by secondary education'. Similarly, only forty out of 212 of those schools had in 1924 sent scholarship or free place pupils to the county's six secondary schools at Banbury, Bicester, Burford, Henley, Thame and Witney. With such a limited provision it is scarcely surprising that Oxfordshire's proportion of secondary scholars to total population

---

[81] Barnard, *English Education from 1760*, p. 211. At national level three years earlier the Board of Education had been established as a replacement for the Committee of the Privy Council on Education, which had acted as the supervisory body for education for just sixty years.
[82] See, for example, Simon, *Education and the Labour Movement*, pp. 238–46.

was well below the average for English counties as a whole.[83] Even for those who were successful, family poverty might mean a constant struggle by parents to maintain their children at a secondary school despite local authority financial assistance.

In the elementary field, also, much remained to be done at county level after 1902. A surviving list of elementary schools and staff taken over by Oxfordshire County Council indicates the continued predominance of the *untrained* certificated head teacher in the early twentieth century. In March 1904, over fifty years after the first Queen's scholarships were offered, about 60 per cent of the county's elementary schools had untrained heads, that is, those who had passed the relevant qualifying examination without receiving formal instruction at a training college. Even more surprisingly, all but 7 per cent of the schools were overstaffed according to the Council's reckoning.[84] This overstaffing was partly a product of the widespread rural depopulation which took place, particularly among younger people, in the later nineteenth century, but it owed something, too, to the haphazard method of recruitment and management which had existed under the old school board and voluntary systems. Among the worst examples was Worton, where with an average attendance of only eighteen children, the headmaster was paid £76. 17s. 6d. per annum, plus free fuel, and was aided by a paid monitress and a sewing mistress. Similarly, at Minster Lovell there was sufficient staff for 185 children but an average attendance of only seventy-nine; the headmaster received £95 a year. At Whitchurch itself, the staff of headmaster, one certificated assistant, two uncertificated assistants, and a paid monitress was considered sufficient for 170 children, although the average attendance in 1904 was only ninety-eight.[85] But perhaps most disturbing of all was the

[83] K. Lindsay, *Social Progress and educational Waste* (London, 1926), p. 136. Mr Lindsay (pp. 117–44) discusses in considerable detail secondary education in Oxfordshire during the 1920s, and he classes the county as 'a poor country; its rateable value is lower than surrounding counties; its occupations are limited mainly to agriculture and domestic work' (p. 117). J. Graves, *Policy and Progress in Secondary Education, 1902–1942* (London 1943), pp. 132–33 notes that as late as 1938 there were still forty-three all age schools in the county, the descendants of the old nineteenth century elementary schools. This situation was said to be largely due to the 'widely scattered population' of the county.

[84] This was no doubt based on the Board of Education's Code for 1904 which, in parishes where the population was 500 or less, allowed one head teacher or one certificated assistant for forty children, one uncertified assistant for thirty children, and one supplementary, provisional or pupil teacher for every twenty scholars. In larger communities, like Whitchurch itself, staffing ratios were less favourable, e.g. one head to fifty pupils and one certificated assistant for sixty. The Whitchurch log book contains several examples of mistresses qualifying themselves for certification through the relevant examinations whilst still working at the school.

[85] Files Reports of Oxfordshire Education Committee, 1 March 1904, CER/I/1 at O.R.O. The overstaffing problem was reported as much in former board schools as in voluntary ones. Council, i.e. ex-board, schools were found in the following parishes in 1904:

ubiquity of paid monitresses, particularly for infant teaching. These girls were recruited directly from the class room, without training and, many of them, unlike Charity Finch, had no serious intention of making teaching a permanent career. Yet they comprised 24 per cent of all assistant teachers in Oxfordshire in 1904, whereas pupil teachers were only around 7 per cent of that total.[86] Such girls provided little more than a cheap and convenient child minding service, with some, as at Shipton-under-Wychwood and Sibford Gower, paid as little as £2. 2s. 0d. per annum. Gradually under the new local education authority these weaknesses and anomalies were to be eliminated.[87]

Perhaps less desirable was the fact that these improvements were accompanied by the closure of some of the smaller village schools. Although such closures were justified on grounds of economy, as rural depopulation and a falling birth rate led to a drop in the number of pupils, with the disappearance of a village school a focal point of community life was lost. This, to some, was a cause of serious regret. Although the bulk of the closures took place after 1945, there were thirty-six before 1939, beginning with Newington School in 1903, Cornwell School in 1904, and Alkerton School in 1905.

[86] By comparison, an analysis of the county staffing records for Devon in 1903 shows that there 30 per cent of all assistant were monitors and another 12 per cent were pupil teachers (Sellman, p. 84).
[87] The *city* of Oxford had its own education authority, of course, under the 1902 Education Act.

Ambrosden, Arncot, Bix, Blackthorn, Brightwell, Brize Norton, Burford, Chalgrove, Charlbury, Church Enstone, Claydon, Eynsham, Great Tew, Hanwell, Lyneham, Milton-under-Wychwood, Mongewell, Neat Enstone, Nettlebed, Nuffield, Over Norton, Salford, Shorthampton & Chilson, South Stoke, Spelsbury, Stadhampton, Tetsworth, Watlington, Wendlebury, Wolvercote and Woodcote.

TABLE 3

SALARIES OF HEAD TEACHERS IN OXFORDSHIRE SCHOOLS ON
1 MARCH 1904*

Salary†	Council		Voluntary	
	Men	Women	Men	Women
£150 and over	—	—	10	—
£125–£149	2	—	26	—
£100–£124	9	—	51	11
£90–£99	5	—	18	9
£80–£89	1	3	8	30
£70–£79	1	9	9	42
£60–£69	1	4	—	22
£50–£59	—	4	—	6
£40–£49	—	—	—	3
£30–£39	—	—	—	1

* Calculated from Filed Report of Oxfordshire Education Committee, 1 March 1904, CER/I/1 at Oxfordshire Record Office. In two schools there were vacancies for head teachers.
† The highest salary — £232. 4s. — was paid to the headmaster of Witney Wesleyan Mixed School; he was the only elementary school teacher in the county to earn over £200 per annum at this date. The lowest salary — £32 — was secured by the headmistress of Waterstock National School. By comparison, the Royal Commission on Popular Education (England) had suggested that in Oxfordshire the average remuneration of certificated masters in *grant-aided* Church of England schools in the late 1850s was around £89. 16s. 5d. per annum; for uncertificated men it was £58. 5s. For certificated mistresses in *grant-aided* Church schools the average rate was about £58. 16s. 10d. a year and for uncertificated women, £33. 19s. 0d. Certificated infants' mistresses obtained £57. 8s. 9d. on average in *grant-aided* schools and uncertificated mistresses £32. 16s. 1d. However, in schools visited 'for simple inspection only', the average rate for male teachers was around £44. 10s. per annum only, and for females, £26. 9s. 9d. See *Report of the Royal Commission on Popular Education (England)*, P.P., 1861, xxi, Pt I, p. 641.

TABLE 4

REQUIREMENTS FOR THE ANNUAL EXAMINATION UNDER THE REVISED CODE OF 1862
(Arranged in Standards)

Standard I
Reading: Narrative in monosyllables.
Writing: Form on blackboard or slate, from dictation, letters, capital and small, manuscript.
Arithmetic: Form on blackboard or slate, from dictation, figures up to 20; name at sight figures up to 20; add and subtract figures up to 10, orally, from examples on blackboard.

Standard II
Reading: One of the Narratives next in order after monosyllables in an elementary reading book used in the school.
Writing: Copy in manuscript character a line of print.
Arithmetic: A sum in simple addition or subtraction and the multiplication table.

Standard III
Reading: A short paragraph from an elementary reading book used in the school.
Writing: A sentence from the same paragraph, slowly read once, and then dictated in single words.
Arithmetic: A sum in any simple rule as far as short division (inclusive).

Standard IV
Reading: A short paragraph from a more advanced reading book used in the school.
Writing: A sentence slowly dictated once by a few words at a time, from the same book, but not from the paragraph read.
Arithmetic: A sum in compound rules (money).

Standard V
Reading: A few lines of poetry from a reading book used in the first class of the school.
Writing: A sentence slowly dictated once, by a few words at a time, from a reading book used in the first class of the school.
Arithmetic: A sum in compound rules (common weights and measures).

Standard VI
Reading: A short ordinary paragraph in a newspaper, or other modern narrative.
Writing: Another short ordinary paragraph in a newspaper, or other modern narrative, slowly dictated once, by a few words at a time.
Arithmetic: A sum in practice or bills of parcels.

In the course of time the Code was amended somewhat, so that writing was tested in Standard I by a ten-word spelling text, in Standards II, III and IV by a prescribed number of lines of 'dictation,' and in Standard V by the reproduction of a short story read twice by the Inspector. In 1882 Standard VII was introduced, requiring pupils to 'read passage from Shakespeare or Milton, etc., or from a History of England: write theme or letter: work sums in averages, percentages, discount or stocks'. But very few country children reached the heights of Standard VII.

TABLE 5

THE GRANT SYSTEM: EXTRACTS FROM THE CODE

1871 Edition (P.P., 1871, xxii, p. cviii):

Grants to Day Schools
19. The managers of a school which has met not less than 400 times, in the morning and afternoon, in the course of a year, as defined by Article 13, may claim at the end of such year —

A. The sum of 6s. per scholar, according to the average number in attendance throughout the year (Article 26).

B. For every scholar, present on the day of examination, who has attended not less than 250 morning or afternoon meetings of the school:—
   1. If above four, and under seven, years of age at the end of the year (Article 13), —
     (a) 8s., or
     (b) 10s. if the infants are taught as a separate department, in a room properly constructed and furnished for their instruction.
   2. If more than seven years of age, 12s., subject to examination (Article 28), viz. —
     4s. for passing in reading;
     4s. for passing in writing;
     4s. for passing in arithmetic.

20. 150 attendances (Article 23) qualify for examination —
   (a) Scholars attending school under any half-time Act.
   (b) Boys above 10 attending school in a rural district.

21. If the time table of the school, in use throughout the year, has provided for one or more specific subjects of secular instruction beyond Article 28, —
A grant of 3s. per subject may be made for every day scholar, presented in Standards IV–VI (Article 28) who passes a satisfactory examination in not more than two of such subjects.
No grant may be claimed under this Article on account of any scholars for whose proficiency, in the same subject, grants are made by the Department of Science and Art.

1883 Edition (P.P., 1883, liii, pp. 11–13):

Grants to Day Schools
106. Infant Schools or classes
(a) A *fixed grant* amounting
(i) to 9s. if the scholars are taught as a separate department . . .
(ii) to 7s. if the scholars are taught as a class of a school, suitably to their age, and so as not to interfere with the instruction of the older children.
(b) A *merit grant* of 2s., 4s. and 6s., if the Inspector reports the school or class to be fair, good, or excellent . . . No merit grant is made unless the report on the instruction in the elementary subjects is satisfactory.
(c) A *grant for needlework* of 1s. if the scholars are satisfactorily taught needlework according to the Third Schedule . . .
(d) A *grant for singing* amounting (i) to 1s. if the scholars are satisfactorily taught to sing *by note*, . . . (ii) to 6d. if they are satisfactorily taught to sing *by ear*.

109. The grants to schools or classes for older scholars are as follows:
(a) A *fixed grant* amounting to 4s. 6d.

(b) A *merit grant* amounting to 1s., 2s., or 3s., if the Inspector, allowing for the special circumstances of the case, reports the school to be fair, good or excellent in respect of (1) the organization and discipline; (2) the intelligence employed in instruction; and (3) the general quality of the work, especially in the elementary subjects.

(c) A *grant for needlework*, amounting to 1s. if the girls are satisfactorily taught needlework according to the Third Schedule . . .

(d) A *grant for singing* amounting (i) to 1s. if the scholars are satisfactorily taught to sing *by note* . . . or (ii) to 6d. if they are satisfactorily taught to sing *by ear*.

(e) A *grant on examination in the elementary subjects* determined by the percentage of passes in the examination at the rate of 1d. for every unit of percentage . . .

(f) A *grant on examination in class subjects* amounting to 1s. or 2s. for each subject, if the Inspector's report on the examination is fair or good.
(i) The recognised class subjects are:
1. English
2. Geography
3. Elementary science
4. History
5. Needlework for girls (according to the Third Schedule).
(ii) For the purpose of examination in class subjects a school is considered as made up of two divisions.
(iii) The lower division must contain the scholars presented for examination in the elementary subjects in the standards below the fourth, and the upper division those in the standards above the fourth . . .

(iv) No more than two class subjects, of which one must always be English, may be taken by either division . . .

(v) If two class subjects are taken, the second must be, in the lower division, either geography or elementary science; in the upper division, geography, elementary science, or history . . .

(vi) Girls may take needlework as their second class subject; but in this case the school cannot receive the grant of 1s. under Article 109 (c) . . .

(g) A *grant on the examination of individual scholars in specific subjects** amounting to 4s. for each scholar passing in any subject . . .

---

* The 'specific subjects' at this stage comprised: Algebra; Euclid and Mensuration; Mechanics; Chemistry; Physics; Animal Physiology; Botany; Principles of Agriculture; Latin; French; Domestic Economy. Under Article 104 it was also noted that: 'Except where it is specially provided otherwise, the sum mentioned is the amount of a year's grant for each unit of average attendance'. This applied to the overall grant position.

WHITCHURCH PARISH AND SCHOOL

Whitchurch is a straggling parish lying on the border of Berkshire and Oxfordshire, about 6½ miles north-west of Reading and 22 miles south-east of Oxford. In 1843 it was romantically described in *The Environs of Reading*, edited by J. G. Robertson (p. 29) as a

quiet and shadowy spot, removed from the noise and feverish excitement of cities and towns, and where nature throws out in profusion her floral beauties, and spreads before us her sylvan scene.

Something of that serenity still survives in the later twentieth century, especially along the banks of the river Thames, which borders the parish on the west and separates it from Pangbourne.

The population of Whitchurch rose from 577 in 1801 to a peak of 893 fifty years later; from this it fell back to 836 in 1871, before resuming its upward trend, to reach 946 at the end of the century. Agriculture provided the main employment, but a number of workers were also engaged in basket-making as well as in the usual rural trades of smithing, baking, shoemaking and the like, while many of the unmarried women and girls were domestic servants.

The parish was selected as a case-study to illustrate trends in village education during the nineteenth century in one 'typical' Oxfordshire rural community. The Whitchurch school log book, which runs from 1868 to 1893 and is by far the longest of the documents reproduced, is one of the few surviving in this county which begin in the years before the Act of 1870; it deals with a village and school of considerable size; and its value is increased by the survival of the Whitchurch School Accounts.[88] The log book gives an idea of the dulling and repetitive routine which all too often comprised elementary education in mid- and late-Victorian England. But it indicates, too, the importance of seasonal employment on the land in the general scheme of school life. It is significant that the summer holidays are referred to as 'harvest holidays' and that the school ranks are thinned as soon as employment opportunities offer themselves.

[88] Other Oxon parishes for which early school log books have survived at O.R.O. include Ardley (1863–1891); Steeple Aston (1863–1892); Beckley (1863–1888); Benson (1863–1888); Burford (1863–1873); Drayton St Leonard (1863–1898); Clifton Hampden (1865–1889); Launton (1865–1879); Noke (1864–1892); Shutford (1869–1895); and Souldern (1869–1892). Of these Benson and Burford were slightly more populous parishes than Whitchurch; the remainder were much smaller.

Whitchurch School itself was situated in the upper part of the parish, being located, most unsuitably, at the base of a disused chalk pit, the sides of which rose steeply to its immediate rear. The building was solidly constructed of brick, with a slate roof and wooden floors, but its amenities were poor. Even in 1910 the Medical Inspector reported: 'Pails of water to wash in . . . Rain water for washing. No drinking water — Bad'. When the log book begins the school was still being held in what H.M.I. Du Port called 'one low & narrow room', but in 1871 extensive alterations were carried through, and as a result one room, measuring 48' 9" × 17' was allocated to accommodate the children of the mixed school, and another, measuring 26' × 16', to cater for about fifty infants. Inside, the bare walls were adorned with a few pictures and maps, while the rooms were sparsely furnished with long desks and, for the infants, a gallery as well. When the school was taken over by Oxfordshire County Council in 1903, the premises were described as 'dark, the walls need recolouring and the rooms should be divided by partitions'. It was also noted that there was one teacher's desk — 'deal antiquated' — while the musical instrument(s) comprised one 'harmonium very ancient and wormeaten'.[89] It was in these rather depressing conditions that teachers and pupils laboured to perform their daily duties.

In its early days Whitchurch school depended heavily (as the extracts from the School Accounts at the end of this volume make clear) upon the interest and energy of the incumbents and upon the generosity of some of the leading inhabitants. In order to make identification easier the names of the incumbents (who were all graduates of Oxford), of some of the principal supporters of the school, and of the teachers, are listed below.

Nineteenth-century rectors of Whitchurch[90]
HUGH MOISES (Rector 1806–22), a son of the headmaster of Newcastle-on-Tyne Grammar School, was educated at University College, Oxford. He was rector of Whitchurch and vicar of East Farleigh, Kent, from 1812 until his death in 1822 — an example of plurality not unusual in the Church at that time.

W. A. HAMMOND (Rector 1823–40), son of George Hammond of Philadelphia, was educated at Christ Church, Oxford. He was rector of

---

[89] Information on the school building has been obtained from typescript 'Notes on Whitchurch' at the Rectory, and also from the records of the premises at Oxfordshire Education Office. Plans of the school, dated c. 1871, are at O.R.O. (T/S Plans 60). In 1872 Du Port classed the accommodation as sufficient for 152 scholars. See Whitchurch file at P.R.O., Ed. 21/14578.

[90] All are listed in J. Foster, *Alumni Oxonienses* (London, 1888); details about various curates at Whitchurch are given in notes to the text of the log book.

Whitchurch until his resignation in 1840, and died at Naples on 29 November 1844.

EDWARD MOORE (Rector 1840–80), son of a Lancashire clergyman, was born in 1792 and educated at Brasenose College, Oxford. He was rector of Gisleham, Suffolk, from 1817 to 1840, and of Whitchurch until his death on 11 February 1880. In the late 1840s he was described by Bishop Wilberforce as a 'painstaking Churchman', although by 1855 the Bishop was adding the less favourable comment: 'Has little hold on the Parish'.[91]

JOHN SLATTER (Rector 1880–99), eldest son of the Rev. William Slatter of Iffley, Oxfordshire, was born in 1818 and educated at Lincoln College, Oxford. Before coming to Whitchurch he had been curate of Sandford-on-Thames and then vicar of Streatley, Berkshire, from 1861 to 1880. He became an Honorary Canon of Christ Church in 1876 and was the author of a book on Whitchurch entitled *Some Notes of the History of the Parish of Whitchurch, Oxon.* (London, 1895). He was a friend of C. L. Dodgson (Lewis Carroll).

HENRY E.TROTTER (Rector 1899–1914) was educated at Christ Church, Oxford, and became an Honorary Canon of Christ Church. Trotter enlarged the rectory, making a total of twenty-two rooms, to accommodate his large family and numerous domestic staff. This included three or four gardeners.

Principal Inhabitants of Whitchurch

WILLIAM FANNING (b. c. 1817) of Hardwick House and later of Bozedown, was a landowner and former Australian merchant. In 1871 he farmed 250 acres of land and employed eight men and two boys. He was a school manager in the 1870s.

ALEXANDER C. FORBES (d. 1901, aged 77) of Swanston House, was a retired barrister, justice of the peace and landowner. Forbes was also a school manager. In 1871 he employed a large staff of ten resident female domestic servants and two males.

CAPTAIN R. DASHWOOD FOWLER, R.N., and his wife regularly supported the school.

SAMUEL GARDINER (d. 1827, aged 71), was a former West Indian merchant, who purchased the estate and manor of Whitchurch in the late eighteenth century. Shortly after the purchase he built a new residence at Coombe Park in the parish. His son, RAWSON GARDINER, also supported the school, and was father of CHARLES GARDINER, who provided land for the school extensions in 1871 and also acted as a

---

[91] Bishop Samuel Wilberforce's Diocese Books for 1845–50 and 1854–64, Bodl. MSS. Oxf. Dioc. Pp. d. 550, d. 178. Moore is listed in *Brasenose College Register 1509–1909* (O.H.S., lv, 1909), p. 430.

school manager. Charles' brother was the historian, Samuel Rawson Gardiner.

WILLIAM B. WOOD (1796–1879) of Uplands was of independent means and a school supporter.

Principal teachers at Whitchurch School[92]

MRS DAVIS held office from 1829 to 1839, and was initially paid £20 per annum and then from 1835 until her retirement at rates ranging between £21 and £25 per annum. She received a retirement pension of nearly £10 in the first year of her retirement. In the second year it was cut to £6. 6s. and by 1841 it had been reduced to £1 per annum 'according to promise'. After this it appears to have been discontinued.

CHARLES SOPER and his wife, Eliza, who served from 1839 to the mid-1840s, received a joint salary of £50. 8s. per annum, rising to £54. 12s. by 1841. At that date Soper was aged 32 and his wife was 30.

FREDERICK OGILWY and his wife, Sarah, were at Whitchurch from the mid-1840s until 1859. They were paid a joint salary of £54. 12s. per annum. Ogilwy had been born at Windsor in Berkshire and his wife came from Colnbrook in Buckinghamshire; at the time of the 1851 Census they were aged 45 and 49 respectively. Mr Ogilwy died in 1859.

MRS OGILWY was employed at a salary of £27. 6s. per annum from 1859 to 1861.

FREDERICK T. W. BATSON was in charge from 1861 to 1866; he and his wife, Damaris, were paid a joint salary of around £63 per annum. Batson was aged 28 at the time of his appointment and his wife was one year his senior. They had two children — a girl aged 6 and a boy of 5 — who had both been born in the father's home parish of Kingswinford in Staffordshire. Mrs Batson was born at Hagley in Worcestershire.

MISS COOKE was employed at a salary of £50 per annum in 1867 and 1868.

JOHN EASTMAN and his sister, Clara, were engaged at a joint salary of £70 per annum plus two-thirds of the government grant. With their appointment (1868) Whitchurch School became subject to government inspection for the first time. Miss Eastman was responsible for teaching the infants and for needlework. They left in September 1870.

---

[92] Information on the teachers has been obtained from the Census Returns (P.R.O. H.O. 107/882 for 1841; H.O. 107/1691 for 1851; R.G. 9/744 for 1861; and R.G. 10/1277 for 1871) and from the school accounts. In the case of Mr and Mrs Winchester, birth, marriage and death certificates have been used, as well as the reminiscences of Mrs Margaret Watson of Reading, a pupil at the school from *c.* 1901, and an account in the *Reading Mercury* (1 March 1930) at the time of Mr Winchester's death. Details of assistant mistresses who stayed only a short time are given in footnotes to the text of the log book. It has not been possible to trace the names of the teachers before 1829.

BARNABY BROWN and his wife, Jane, were paid at the rate of £70 per annum during the period October 1870 to November 1871. Brown had been born in Lancashire and was aged about thirty-seven when he took up his appointment. His wife, who was eight years his junior, had been born at Lampeter in Cardiganshire. At the time of the 1871 Census they had five children, the youngest, Edgar Griffith, being only one month old. Although the Browns were paid such a modest joint salary, they nevertheless managed to employ a fourteen-year-old general servant and a twenty-six-year-old nursemaid to look after the household and family.

THOMAS WARNER, a temporary teacher (December 1871 to April 1872), was paid £1. 1s. per week.

THOMAS LITCHFIELD and his wife, Sarah, were at Whitchurch for seven years (1872–79). They received £100 per annum jointly, plus half of the government grant — except in their first year, when the share was one-third only.

HERBERT W. WINCHESTER (b. 1854; d. 1930) and his wife, Henrietta (d. 1920) were paid £100 per annum, plus half of the government grant. Like their predecessors they had a free house as well. Mrs Winchester retired from teaching in January 1884 and from then onwards Winchester, as the school log book makes clear, was aided by a procession of assistant mistresses, pupil teachers and monitors. A list of school staff prepared in 1903,[93] when Oxfordshire Education Committee had assumed overall control of the county's elementary education, under the 1902 Education Act, shows that Winchester was paid £142 per annum (with a deduction for superannuation of £3 per annum). He was at that time assisted by three mistresses and a monitress. The most senior of the mistresses earned £55 a year, and the two juniors (who included Lilian Winchester, one of Winchester's daughters) were paid £26 a year. The monitress received £6. 10s. per annum. Winchester himself was described as 'certificated but not trained' by qualification; this meant that he had passed the relevant certificate examination held each year at one of the training colleges but had not received formal instruction at the college itself.

Herbert Winchester was born on 25 May 1854, at Salehurst in Sussex, the son of Isaac Winchester, a 'wheeler' (or wheelwright) and his wife, Caroline, and was married at Lambeth on 23 March 1878 to Henrietta Rowe, the daughter of a mercantile clerk. Henrietta was one year her husband's junior, and so both were still young when they moved to Whitchurch in 1879. Mrs Margaret Watson, who attended the school at

[93] See Whitchurch School Log Book, Vol. 2, T/SL 58/ii, f. 258, at O.R.O. For details of the staffing of the school in 1903, when it came under the jurisdiction of the Oxfordshire Education Committee, see Reports of Teachers' Salaries, CER I/i at O.R.O.

the turn of the century, remembers Winchester as 'always smartly dressed and very strict'. He had a cane on his desk which he used 'when needed'. For a time, between February 1899 and June 1905, Mr Winchester was assisted by his daughter, Lilian, who was approved as an 'Article 68' teacher, i.e. as 'a woman over eighteen years of age approved by the Inspector, who is employed during the whole of the school hours in the general instruction of the scholars and in teaching needlework'. She was responsible for teaching the youngest children, but following a Report by Sub-Inspector Butler in December 1904 that the teacher of the lowest class of infants 'should undergo a period of observation and training in a good Oxford school', she left Whitchurch approximately six months later. Her colleague, Edith M. Ashby, another 'Article 68' teacher and a former scholar at the school, by contrast continued to be employed there until the school closed in 1947.

Herbert Winchester's own career ended some ten years after his daughter's move. In December 1914 he became seriously ill and in February 1915 a temporary head was appointed. He finally retired on 30 June in that year, when he was replaced by a headmistress, Miss F. E. Gwinnell. A former pupil at the school believes that he then left the parish, with his wife, to live with one of his daughters at Portsmouth. If this were the case, the move was a temporary one only, for by 1920 he and his wife had returned to Reading, and it was there that Mrs Winchester died in the early part of that year. Winchester himself survived to 21 February 1930, when he died as a result of an accidental fall. At that time he was living with one of his daughters, Mrs Louisa A. M. Short, of 5 Sherwood Street; the accident occurred whilst he was returning from a visit to his other daughter, Lilian, who lived in George Street, Reading.

After Winchester's years of toil at Whitchurch school it is sad to read the comment of the General Diocesan Inspector of Schools in July 1917: 'This school has, since I saw it, made a fresh start under a new Head Teacher. The results are at present incomplete; but they are very encouraging, & full of promise which, I feel sure, will be abundantly fulfilled in the near future'. No mention was made of Winchester's own contribution to the school over more than thirty-five years: however, the Inspector's remarks may in part reflect difficulties caused by Winchester's illness.

I

RETURN OF WHITCHURCH SCHOOLS
IN 1808

[In 1808 the Bishop of Oxford (Charles Moss)[1] approached his clergy for information on schools within each parish, in response to a request by Charles Manners-Sutton, Archbishop of Canterbury from 1805 to 1828. In the previous year the Archbishop had strongly opposed Samuel Whitbread's proposals that local rates might be levied in England and Wales by vestries or magistrates to finance the elementary education of poor children. The measure proposed the provision of two years' free schooling for children aged from seven to fourteen who could not afford fees. In a debate on Whitbread's Bill in the House of Lords the Archbishop had emphasized that neither he nor the Church as a whole 'should be considered hostile to the principle of diffusing instruction among the poor', but the Bill if passed, would 'subvert the first principles of education in this country, which had hitherto been . . . under the control and auspices' of the Church of England.[2] It was no doubt partly as a result of this debate that the 1808 inquiry was set in hand, for the Archbishop had observed that he intended to follow the subject up 'to a certain extent'. In the Oxford Archdeaconry some two hundred rural parishes submitted returns, now Bodl. MS. Oxf. Dioc. Pp. d. 707. In about a third of the sample there were schools which, unlike those at Whitchurch itself, taught at least two of the three 'R's — reading, writing and arithmetic.[3] Answers were sought to the following queries:

1. Have you any Schools in your Parish and how many?
2. Are they endowed Schools, or supported by Voluntary Subscriptions, and what is taught in them?
3. Are there any Sunday Schools, and what is taught in them?
4. How many Children receive Instruction in each School?
5. Are any of the Schools supported or kept by Dissenters, and by

---

[1] Charles Moss (1763–1811) was Bishop of Oxford from 1807; in 1801 he had published an anonymous pamphlet in favour of the education of the poor.
[2] *Hansard*, 1 Ser., ix, 1177.
[3] Stone, 'Literacy and Education in England 1640–1900', *Past and Present*, 42 (1969), p. 112.

what Denomination of Dissenters and of what Number does such
School or Schools consist?
The incumbent of Whitchurch replied:]

My Lord,
The following is the best answer which my knowledge & experience
enable me to give to the several Queries submitted by your Lordship
relative to the Schools — public & private in the Parish of Whitchurch.

In the Village there are two day Schools consisting of Boys & Girls.
To one the Rector sends 14 Children — eleven of which are (at present)
Girls & three Boys. These are paid for out of the Sacramental money. In
the same School are also 4 Boys, & 4 Girls put to School by their Parents
or Friends in the Parish — at 4d. aweek for the Girls & 3d. for the Boys.
The former are taught plain needlework & reading. The latter reading
only.

This School is visited occasionally by the Rector, who hears them
read the Scriptures, & rehearse their Catechism.

The second School is of the same description at which ten Girls are
placed by their Parents. There is a small School upon the Common
consisting of seven very young Children.

There is also a private Day School of 16 Girls supported at the expence
of Mrs Gardiner — & exclusively under her direction.[4] On Sundays they
join the Rector's School — & are catechised & examined by the Rector —
who can conscientiously attest to their proficiency. They attend Church
twice every Sunday — & are under the inspection of the Rector's
Schoolmistress along with the Children of her School.

There are two Sunday Schools — one for Boys — the other for Girls.
The first consisting of 34 — the second of 30.[5]

The Boys Sunday School is visited by Gentlemen of the Parish in
rotation. The Girls School is not visited. The Mistress is merely qualified
to teach them to read.

The Boys with their Master attend Church twice every Sunday — &
are catechised Publicly with the other Children at stated periods.

The Girls with their mistress being situated at the eastern extremity
of the Parish attend the Chapel at Goring Alms House.

---

[4] Mrs Gardiner was the wife of Samuel Gardiner, lord of the manor of Whitchurch. See
J. H. Baker, *Whitchurch-on-Thames: The Story of a Thames-side Village* (Reading, 1956),
p. 28; and above, p. lv.
[5] In 1802 John Lichfield, the then curate, had reported to the Bishop of Oxford that the
two Sunday Schools were supported by voluntary contributions. 'Here the Children are
instructed in the Church Catechism, in the Summer at Church after Evening Service, in the
Winter at School; on this occasion a Form is used entitled the Ch. Catechism broke [*sic*] into
Short Questions, printed for the Society for the promotion of Christian Knowledge' (Clergy
Visitation Returns for 1802, Bodl. MS. Oxf. Dioc. Pp.d. 567).

None of the Schools are supported, or kept by Dissenters.
Total number daily instructed   55
Boys Sunday School   34 ⎱
Girls   do.   do.   30 ⎰ 64

I have the Honor to be
my Lord
Yr. Lordships most obedt Sert
H. MOISES

Whitchurch Ap. 6th
1808

II

RETURN OF WHITCHURCH SCHOOLS
IN 1815

[This enquiry was issued following the establishment in 1811 of the Church of England National Society for Promoting the Education of the Poor in the Principles of the Established Church, usually known as the National Society; the General Committee of the National Society on 13 July 1814 resolved to ask the Bishops to inquire, '1st What Schools are now established or establishing upon the Plan & Principles of the National Society. 2dly Whether any & what causes are likely to prevent the further establishment of such Schools, in order that this Society, so far as depends upon its own means, may co operate in removing impediments to such extension'. The Whitchurch return, required by the Archdeacon before 20 Aug. 1815, is Bodl. MS. Oxf. Dioc. Pp. c. 443, f. 221:]

1st What is the number of Day Schools in your Parish; and what number of Children attend them, distinguishing Boys and Girls?   Ans. There are 3 day schools, containing 98 children all together: of whom 69 are girls & 29 are boys.

2nd What Sunday Schools, and what number of Children are collected in them, distinguishing Boys and Girls?   Ans. There are two Sunday Schools *one* containing 43 boys — and *the other* 38 girls.

3rd Are they conducted in whole, or in part, on the National Society's Plan of instruction?   In part only.

4th When where [*sic*] they established, and how are they supported? They have been established about 20 years. The Sunday Schools are supported by private Subscription. The Day Schools partly by monies appropriated by the Rector, partly by private benevolence, and partly by the parents of the children.

5th If on the old Plan, are the present Teachers likely to be induced to learn and practice the new method?

6th In that case, what number of Children are capable of being collected for instruction, within a walk of two miles?

7th What causes operate to prevent the adoption of the method of instruction recommended by the National Society — and how can they best be removed? With any general remarks that occur.

In answer to these 3 last questions — it is to be observed that the Teachers would have no objection to learn & practise the new method — but it is thought that it would be impracticable to collect the children into one Day School, from the extent and peculiar situation of the Parish; part of it being upon high hills at a distance too great for little children to go and return. By being distributed into three schools conveniently situated in different parts of the Parish, it is found that nearly all the children have the benefits of instruction from some one of these Schools: but the numbers in each are presumed to be too few to admit wholly of the Arrangements of the National Schools.[6]

[?] W. PAGE

Officiating Minister of Whitchurch, Oxon.[7]

---

[6] In 1817, however, the incumbent noted that at that date one of the three day schools was being conducted 'on Dr. Bell's plan', i.e. in accordance with National Society policy. The total number of pupils in attendance at the three schools was put at 98. (Clergy Visitation Returns for 1817, Bodl. MS. Oxf. Dioc. Pp.d. 577).

[7] Possibly William Page (1778–1819), Vicar of Steventon, Berks., 1812–17.

III

PROPOSAL FOR UNION OF WHITCHURCH SCHOOL WITH THE NATIONAL SOCIETY, 1819

[From the Whitchurch National School File at the headquarters of the National Society in London; written c. 1819.]

It is the wish of those who have the management of the School at Whitchurch in Oxfordshire that the same should be united to the National Society.

In this School the National system of teaching is to be adopted: the Children are instructed in the Liturgy & Catechism of the Established Church and do constantly attend Divine Service at their Parish Church under the Establishment as far as the same is practicable on the Lords days; unless such reasons for their non-attendance be assigned as shall be satisfactory to the persons, having the direction of the School.

No Religious Tracts shall be used in the School but which are or shall be contained in the catalogue of the Society for Promoting Christian Knowledge.

Signed

H. Moises   Rector

George Hunt M.A.   Curate

Lydia Prescott

Saml Gardiner

Frances Prescott[8]

---

[8] The statement was not dated by the signatories but on the reverse side it has been endorsed in another hand with the words 'September 1819' and 'Withdrawn'. However, Whitchurch did become associated with the National Society in 1819, and according to the *Ninth Annual Report of the National Society* (London, 1820), p. 109, at the time of union the Daily and Sunday School had 67 pupils — 37 boys and 30 girls — plus 30 pupils who attended the Sunday School only (i.e. 10 boys and 20 girls). The *Thirteenth Annual Report of the National Society* (1824) shows that following the issue of the King's Letter in 1823, directing the parochial clergy 'to promote contributions throughout their parishes in aid of the Society's funds', the contribution from Whitchurch amounted to £13 7s. 0d.; this was the sixth largest parish total for the whole Archdeaconry. Spelsbury came first with an amazing £57 6s. 6d. In all, over £28,000 was eventually collected throughout the country as a result of this appeal (*Fourteenth Report of the National Society* (1825), p. 7).

IV
RETURN OF WHITCHURCH SCHOOLS
IN 1833

[*From Education Enquiry: Abstract of the Answers and Returns* for 1833 in H.C. 62 (1835), xlii, p. 757. This enquiry, discussed in the Introduction, revealed that in Oxfordshire as a whole there were 510 daily schools (including separate girls' and boys' departments) and 66 infant schools.]

Whitchurch Parish (Pop. 745). *One Infant School*, containing about 12 children of both sexes, whose instruction is paid for by their parents. *One Daily School*, supported by a gentleman of the parish, contains 12 females. *Two Day and Sunday Schools* attended by 44 males and 41 females daily, and by 3 of the former and 23 of the latter in addition on Sundays: these Schools are supported by voluntary contributions.[9]

---

[9] In 1834 the incumbent, the Rev. W. A. Hammond, informed the Bishop of Oxford that children were admitted to the two day schools at the age of five and that they left 'as soon as they can get work or about 11 or 12'. Fees were fixed at 1*d.* a week 'but they receive clothing to more than the amount of their payments'. (Clergy Visitation Returns for 1834, Bodl. MS. Oxf. Dioc. Pp.b. 39.) This claim is borne out by the school accounts: thus in 1834 — and typically — whilst the children's pence yielded just over £12 8*s.*, subscriptions to the clothing account amounted to £17 5*s.*; among the items purchased were 20 cloaks, 20 smock frocks, 39 girls' bonnets and 38 boys' hats.

V

EXTRACTS FROM THE WHITCHURCH INCUMBENT'S ANSWERS TO THE BISHOP OF OXFORD'S VISITATION QUESTIONS, 1854–75

[In their triennial visitation returns incumbents were asked to comment upon educational provisions within their parish. There are gaps in the returns for the Oxford Diocese between 1838 and 1854 and again between 1860 and 1866. However, the following extracts, for the years 1854 to 1875, show developments during the period immediately before and after the commencement of the school log book. They also indicate the response of the incumbent, Edward Moore, to the 1870 Education Act. The earlier returns were requested by Samuel Wilberforce, Bishop of Oxford from 1845 to 1869, and the two last by his successor J. F. Mackarness; the questions and answers reproduced are the only ones having direct relevance to general elementary education.]

Questions of 1854, 1857, & 1860

Q.15 What Schools are there in your parish; distinguishing daily schools for Adults, for Children, and for Infants under six years of age, and Sunday schools; how are they supported, and how many scholars are there in each?

Q.16 Are you able to retain your young people in your Sunday School after they have ceased to attend the Daily School?

Answers of 1854

Q.15 The National school for boys and girls from five or 6 years to 12 or 13 comprising about 70 children, supported by subscription and the children's pence. And a girls school of about 12 children supported by Mr Powys.[10]

Q.16 They do not attend after they cease to attend the Daily School. (Bodl. MS. Oxf. Dioc. d. 701.)

---

[10] Henry Philip Powys (1791–1859) of Hardwick House near Reading.

Answers of 1857

Q.15 A boys school   29 } supported by subscription
      A Girls' do.   31 }
      A Mixed School boys & girls — 16 Supported by Mr Powys.
Q.16 In a very few instances & only for a very short time. (Ibid., d.179.)

Answers of 1860

Q.15 The Whitchurch National School, supported entirely by subscriptions & the children's pence, has in it 59 scholars.
Q.16· The school children assemble on Sunday, but no others are inclined to attend. (Ibid., d. 180.)

Questions of 1866 & 1869

Q.15 What Schools are there in your Parish; distinguishing daily Schools for Adults, for Children, and for Infants under six years of age, and Sunday Schools; how are they supported, and how many Scholars are there in each? In the case of Sunday Schools; specify how many of the Children attend also the daily School, and how many attend only the Sunday School?

Answers of 1866

Q.15 Our schools have within a few months been for children of all ages — at present the Infants are seperated [*sic*] from the others. The schools are supported by Subscriptions — and we have one hundred on our Books. The Children meet on Sundays — and are expected to attend the Parish Church Morning and Evening. (Ibid., c. 332.)

Answers of 1869

Q.15 We have only a Mixed School under Government & Diocesan Inspection — but no regular Sunday Schools, but the children are assembled to go to Church — the average attendance 70.[11] (Ibid., c. 335.)

Questions of 1872

Q.12 What schools are there in your Parish; distinguishing daily Schools for Adults, for Children, and for Infants under six years of age, and Sunday Schools; how are they supported, and how many scholars are there in each?
Q.13 Are you able to retain your young people in your Sunday School after they have ceased to attend the Daily School?
Q.15 Is a School Board, under the Education Act 1870, elected, or about to be elected, in your Parish, or District? Is it proposed to make

---

[11] According to the school accounts, the first Government grant was only paid over in 1869 — following the appointment of new teachers, Mr and Miss Eastman.

over any Church School to such Board? If so, give the date of the erection of such School, and of any grants made to it (1) by the Diocesan Education Society, (2) by the National Society.

Answers of 1872

Q.12   The schools of the Parish are National Mixed schools supported by Voluntary contributions aided by Government Grants.

Q.13   At present we have no Sunday School.

Q.15   Ours is a Church of England according to the late Act — has received Grants. (Ibid., c. 338.)

Questions of 1875

Q.15   Is religious instruction given in your Day Schools by the Clergy? Do the Clergy take part in the religious instruction of Pupil-Teachers?

Q.18   Is a School Board, under the Education Act 1870, elected, or about to be elected, in your Parish, or District? Is it proposed to make over any Church School to such Board? If so, give the date of the erection of such School, and of any grants made to it (1) by the Diocesan Education Society, (2) by the National Society.

Answers of 1875

Q.15   Religious instruction is given by my curate in the Day School.

Q.18   We have no School Board nor do we intend to have one. (Ibid., c. 341.)

VI

THE WHITCHURCH SCHOOL LOG BOOK
1868–93

[In accordance with the Revised Code of 1862 all elementary schools open to public inspection — and thus eligible for Government grants — had to maintain a regular record of school activities. The Whitchurch log book, bound in green and black imitation leather, is preserved at the Oxfordshire Record Office, T/SL.58/1. Presumably no earlier record was maintained because the school was without a certificated head teacher — an essential pre-requisite for qualifying for a grant. The log book is paged from 1 to 498; a few pages (107–10, 131–4, and 179–80) are missing, and a few are blank. Log books contained at the beginning the following instructions on the methods by which they were to be kept:

Extract from the Revised Code of Regulations for 1862

The Principal Teacher must daily make in the Log Book the briefest entry which will suffice to specify either ordinary progress, or whatever other fact concerning the School or its Teachers, such as the dates of withdrawals, commencements of duty, cautions, illness, &c., may require to be referred to at a future time, or may otherwise deserve to be recorded.

No reflections or opinions of a general character are to be entered in the Log Book.

No entry once made in the Log Book may be removed nor altered otherwise than by a subsequent entry.

The Inspector will call for the Log Book at his annual visit, and will report whether it appears to have been properly kept throughout the year.

The Inspector will not write any report on the good or bad state of the School in the Log Book at the time of his visit, but will enter therein, with his own hand, the full name and standing (*certified Teacher of the ____ Class, or Pupil Teacher of the ____ Year, or Assistant Teacher*) of each Member of the School Establishment. The Inspector will not enter the names of Pupil Teachers, respecting whose admission the Committee of Council has not yet pronounced a decision.

11

The summary of the Inspector's Report, when communicated by the Committee of Council to the Managers, must be copied into the Log Book by the Secretary of the latter, who must also enter the name and description of all Teachers to be added to, or withdrawn from, those entered by the Inspector, according to the decision of the Committee of Council upon the Inspector's Report. The Secretary of the Managers must sign this entry.

The Inspector before making his entry of the School Establishment in the following year will refer to his own entry made in the preceding year, and also to the entry which is required to be made by the Secretary of the School, pursuant to Article 62, and he will require to see entries in the Log Book, accounting for any subsequent change of the School Establishment.

Extract from Instructions to Her Majesty's Inspectors upon the Administration of the Revised Code

The Diary or Log Book requires no special Ruling. An outer margin for the date is all that needs to be observed. One such book should be kept by each principal teacher having charge of a school or separate department of a school. These books will not only furnish valuable records of school-keeping, but will (it is hoped) in the course of a few years save much of the registration which has to be performed at this office for the identification of teachers.

Extract from a Letter dated 20th November, 1862, from R. R. W. LINGEN, ESQ. [Secretary to the Education Office]

With regard to a Diary or Log Book, beyond the matter referred to Articles 61–63, my Lords are of opinion that a zealous and intelligent teacher will not be at a loss to make other entries, and will not find that the term 'ordinary progress' expresses the whole of his experience from year's end to year's end.

Log Books and Diaries are kept in other employments that offer no greater variety of observation.

If it were necessary to specify entries of importance, one that might be named would be the record of each occasion when the Managers examined the several classes of the School, in what subjects, and with what result.

If such examination were periodical, the record would be still more valuable, and would tend to maintain the recurrence of them.

The extent to which the superintendence of the School was maintained by visits of the Managers would also appear.

In the working of the School, most days would suggest some indication to an observant teacher, as to whether this or that class, this or that subject, this or that method, was all that it ought to be; or not, and why. Similarly, fluctuations of attendance, co-operation of parents, and the rates of and modes of taking school-fees, are so many heads under which facts worthy notice are constantly occurring, and of a different kind in towns and in the country.

The Log Book is not meant to contain essays on these or similar subjects, but to collect the items of experience. A teacher who performs this duty simply, regularly, and with discrimination, will find it a powerful help in mastering his profession, as well as an honourable monument of his labours.

The practice of the Whitchurch teachers varied. Eastman (1868–70) and Brown (1870–1) made entries every day; but Warner (1871–2) made one longer entry each week (on Fridays), except during two weeks when visits were made by the H.M.I. and by the rector. Litchfield (1872–9) often made only one entry each week, at first usually on a Monday, but after mid-1875 on either Monday or Friday. Winchester (1879–1914) varies in his practice.

[The entries have been printed in weekly paragraphs.]

1868

Nov. 2 Whitchurch School, Oxon. Commenced duties at this school Oct. 5. Examined the children. In arithmetic the children know very little. Gave to first class the following. Take 79 from 601. Result 3 boys did it right. Not a girl attempted it. Neither boy nor girl set about it in second class. JOHN EASTMAN **3** Attendance today 29 Boys & 23 Girls. **4** Wet day. Much better attendance than last wet day. Heard Standard II. Arithmetic. Had to teach several boys to count with beads. **5** Standard III. Arith. The children can now write down any numbers containing the figures. **6** Scripture with Stand. III & IV was parable of the Sower.

Nov. 9 Admitted Charles Terry, seven years old. **10** Found the bigger children had forgotten all about the parable of the Sower. **11** Heard the children sing the hymns for Sunday. **12** Nearly all in Standard II wrote all the numbers up to 20. **13** Only 1 boy Wm Wallis absent today.

Nov. 16 Parable of the Tares to 1st & 2nd Classes. **17** Scripture to Standard II. Found they knew nothing connected with our Lord's life. **18** The Rector came to the school today. **19** Standard II seem to show very little memory. Know very little of Tuesday's Scripture. **20** Ordinary progress.

Nov. 23 Admitted William Cross & Alfred Cross. **24** Scripture with 1st & 2nd Class was parable of the Ten Virgins. **25** Scripture for Stand. II. 1st & 2nd Commandments. **26** Mr Moore came this morning. **27** Stand. III Arith. Boys write numbers much better than girls.

Nov. 30 Sent word to father of Wm Wallis that his son's name would be taken off the books if he were not here next Monday. **Dec. 1** Usual progress. **2** Began Simple Addition with Standard II. **3** Nothing to record.

Dec. 7 Wm Wallis's name taken off. **8** Find great difficulty with Multiplication Table for Standards II III IV. **9** Gave Stand. II Twice times to write & learn for Home lesson. **10** Cannot make much progress with the Scripture. **11** Cannot get any intelligent answers. 11th Ordinary progress.

Dec. 14 Mrs Moore sent for patterns of cloaks for girls.[12] **15** Taught Standard II Subtraction for first time. **16** Heard the children sing their hymns. **17** Mistress taught the girls to gather. **18** Taught Standard III Multiplication by 2 figures.

Dec. 21 Monday. Very Wet day. 37 in attendance. **22** Scripture to Standard III IV duty to neighbour. **23** Singing. Taught the children 'The bell doth toll Round'. **24** Scripture. Began the Sermon on the Mount.

Dec. 28 Emily Cook's name taken off. **29** Very Wet. 15 in attendance this morning. **30** Mistress taught the little ones the hymn 'Children never tell a lie'. **31** Last day of school year. **Jan. 1** Made out new registers.

1869

Jan. 4 Thomas & Charles Tayler admitted.[13] **5** Very Wet day. 14 children this morning. **6** Finished the 5th Chap. St Matthew. Have taken first three classes together. **7** Examined the children today. Result not very satisfactory. **8** 1st & 2nd Class Home Lesson learn the desire.

Jan. 11 Thomas and Henry Burgess admitted. **12** Scripture — Parable of the Labourers in the Vineyard. **13** Scripture. Matthew VI to Lord's prayer. **14** Arithmetic to Standard III. Multiplication with noughts in the multiplier. **15** Scripture to end of Matthew VI.

Jan. 18 Daniel Lewendon, Mary Knight admitted. **19** Gave the girls arithmetic part of the afternoon. **20** Got some of the school subscriptions today.[14] **21** Mrs Fowler gave each of the children a pair of cuffs & an orange. **22** Finished Form IX for meeting of managers tomorrow.

[12] An entry in the school accounts for 1868 records that 'Material & making frock[s] cloaks &c.' cost £13 5s. 4d. According to the accounts this was the last occasion on which clothing was bought for the children.
[13] Thomas and Charles were the sons of James Tayler (or Taylor), one of the Whitchurch carriers. Thomas was aged about seven at this time and Charles about five (1871 Census Return for Whitchurch at P.R.O., R.G.10.1277, hereafter cited as 1871 Census).
[14] In all subscriptions of £75 6s. were secured during this year. The rector and four others each provided £10, while four more, including Alexander Forbes and Captain Fowler, subscribed £5 each (School Accounts).

Jan. 25 Admitted Geo. & Emily Wells, readmitted William Wallace [*sic*]. **26** Examined the children on the Sermon on the Mount. **27** Examined the children on the few parables taught them. **28** John Eastman, Certfd. Teacher of the Upper Grade of the 4th Class, and Clara Eastman described as Probationer, C. D. Du Port H.M. Inspr. **29** Mr Forbes came to learn the result of the examination.

Feb. 1 Received the following from H.M. Inspector.

'In schools where no other system of religious instruction has been arranged and appointed to the Teachers by the managers I will examine as nearly as possible in accordance with the accompanying Schedule.

C. D. Du Port

4th or lowest division Say elder infants & Stand. I	Easy hymns & texts Creation, Fall — Noah. Birth & Boyhood of Xt.
3rd Division Say Stand II & Part of III	*Add* early Catechism and the Commandments intelligently. Events in Xt's life, e.g. Baptism, Temptation, Transfiguration, Passion &c. The teacher choosing & keeping mainly to one of the Gospels.
2nd Division Say part of Stand. III and Stand. IV	*Add* Catechism — Moses, Joshua, Christ's chief parables & miracles. Teacher again keeping mainly to one Gospel.
1st Division	*Add* chief Judges and early Kings fuller knowledge of Xt's teaching (again taking one Gospel) first 12 Chapters of Acts.

N.B. Prayer book lessons of a more exclusively Pastoral character will doubtless be given to the elder classes.'

Copied & returned to the Rev. C. D. Du Port, H.M. Insp. of Schools, 2 Albion Place, Reading

2 Began Simple Multiplication with Standard III. **3** Ordinary Progress. **4** Heard the singing today having no books yesterday. **5** Rev. E. Moore & Mr Forbes came today heard the children read & distributed prizes to

Robt Goodall	Robinson Crusoe
Chas Pocock	Arabian Knights [*sic*]
John Holmes	Swiss Family Robinson
James Guttridge	White's Selborne
Joseph Martin	Sanford & Merton
Thos. Goodall	Book of Birds
Ann Allright	Stories from Eng. History
Henrietta Simmonds	Pitcairn
Emma Kent	Animal World
Sophia Rogers	Manners & Customs
	& pictures to little ones.

Tea & Magic Lantern in evening.

Feb. 8 Put the best children from lower classes to higher.   **9** Began Addition of Money with Standard IV.   **10** Mistress unwell not able to come to school. **11** Ditto.   **12** Began the history of Abram with the first class.

Feb. 15 Alf. Lewendon Admitted.   **16** Mistress gave Stand. I a lesson on the Deluge.   **17** Life of Abram. Standard III, IV. (Journey to Egypt).   **18** Standard III. Taught them to write numbers to one figure in thousands.   **19** Nothing to record.

Feb. 22 Standard II. Addition to one figure in thousands. Think it best to divide thousands from units by a dot as 6.021.   **23** 1st Class Scripture parable of the Tares.   **24** Report received from the Council Office:

Mixed. The plan of working two distinct departments, one for Infants and the first standard, and one for a Mixed School of the other standards, is wise; to work well the Mixed School should be provided with a good room and class room, instead of the one low and narrow room now used. Porches or vestibules for hats and cloaks should be added to both schools. Desks and apparatus for the elders and a gallery for the Infants' School are wanting.[15] Three months very effective grounding work has been done. Of course the intelligence and Religious answering is [sic] still imperfect, and the Standards occupied by the Children are low for their ages. Some progress has already been made in sewing; cutting out should be taught: and equal supervision from the Teacher will be received by the Girls individually if they are taken in two divisions each for half the afternoon only.

Infants. 'A fair three months' work has been done in the Infants' School in Writing very specially. Attainments are of course still imperfectly grounded and oral answers whether in Scripture or other subjects not very accurate or intelligent.'

H.M. Inspector also states that the school premises require to be more effectually railed off from the neighbouring cottages, and that separate offices are needed for the Girls and Infants.

My Lords trust that these defects will be remedied with as little delay as possible (Art. 52(a)).[16] A new school room for the elder Children seems much wanted.[17]

---

[15] A gallery, or raised platform, was a standard feature of infants' schools, planned so that the teacher could see clearly what each infant was doing.

[16] Under this Article of the Revised Code the grant to a school could be reduced by 'not less than one-tenth nor more than one-half in the whole, upon the inspector's report, for faults of instruction or discipline on the part of the teacher, or (after one year's notice) for failure on the part of the managers to remedy any such defect in the premises as seriously interferes with the efficiency of the school, or to provide proper furniture, books, maps and other apparatus of elementary instruction'.

[17] The alterations and additions were completed by the end of 1871 at a cost of £1,435 15s. The site, valued at £530, was given by Charles Gardiner, the lord of the manor and a major landowner in the parish; a goverment grant of £178 11s. 10d. was secured; £50 were given by the Diocesan Board of Education; £35 by the National Society; and the rest of the money — £642 3s. 2d. — was raised by 'subscriptions and collections raised in the Locality or otherwise' (Whitchurch School file at the National Society headquarters in London).

A much larger proportion of the children qualified by Attendance should be presented for examination.

25 Heard the singing today.   26 Standard IV. Dictation from Reading book (Nelson's IV Book) page 22.[18]

Mar. 1 Hon. and Rev. Henry Bligh Diocesan Inspector visited the school. Gave a prize to John Holmes.[19]   2 Gave the children Half holiday yesterday. 3 1st Class & 2nd. Scripture. Jacob robs Esau of his blessing.   4 Subtraction of Money to Standard IV.   5 Ordinary Progress.

Mar. 8 John Wells admitted.   9 Gave Standard III a lesson on the I & II Commandments.   10 The Mistress taught Stand. IV to make a seam. 11 Stand. IV Dictation page 35 Average 5 mistakes in 10 lines.[20]   12 Heard the singing for Sunday.

Mar. 15 Thos Wallis Readmitted.   16 Scripture to 1st Class. Page 47. 17 Arithmetic for Standard III. Multiplication with a cypher in multiplier as 504. 18 Ditto.   19 Wet Afternoon. Attendance 44.

Mar. 22 12 Girls absent. Girls as a rule attend badly.[21]   23 Scripture to 1st Class. Parable of Ten Virgins. 2nd Class. Birth of Christ.   24 Gave 1st Class a lesson on the Cardinal Points.   25 Broke up for Easter Holidays.

Apr. 12 Opened School after 2 weeks holiday. Admitted Kate & Alice Pocock, Em. Cooke, Jas Kent. Left Sam and Harriet Bunting & Sar. Thorpe. 13 The Mistress gave the girls their first lesson on button holes.   14 Nothing to record.   15 1st Class Reading & Dictation page 38. Dictation Average 5 mistakes in 10 lines.   16 Average for the week 51.

Apr. 19 Elizabeth Wells admitted.   20 Mistress gave Standard II a lesson in stitching.   21 Scripture to 1st Class. Migration of Jacob & his family to Egypt. Page 67.   22 Usual Progress.   23 Average for past week 62.

Apr. 26 Fortescue Martin admitted. Mary & Kate Godfrey admitted and Mary & E. Wallis.   27 Left Henry, Mary & Rosa Knight & Ellen Weller left. 28 Taught the elder children the round 'A southerly wind'.   29 Scripture to 1st

---

[18] Probably Thomas Nelson & Sons Ltd., *The Progressive English Reading Books*, first published in 1862.

[19] John Holmes, aged 9, was the son of one of the Whitchurch blacksmiths (1871 Census).

[20] If this, too, were taken from Nelson's *Progressive English Reading Books*, it was an extract from the Rev. Newman Hall's *Dignity of Labour* and included such sentences as: 'Labour seizes the thoughts of genius, the discoveries of science, the admonitions of piety, and, with its magic types impressing the vacant page, renders it pregnant with life and power, perpetuating truth to distant ages, and diffusing it to all mankind'. One wonders how the Whitchurch scholars greeted these impressive phrases.

[21] Many girls were kept at home to help their mothers with household chores; absence on Mondays — as on this occasion — probably meant they were helping with the family wash.

Standard 'The birth of Christ'.   **30** Arithmetic to Standard III Short Division. Find the need of a thorough Knowledge of the Multiplication Table.

May 3 Kate Hine admitted. Left F. Martin & Sam. Smith.[22]   **4** Very wet. 29 in morning. 30 in afternoon.   **5** Heard the singing for Sunday next.   **6** The Mistress taught Standard II the marking stitch.   **7** Dictation to Standard page 52. 9 lines average 7 mistakes.

May 10 F. Martin readmitted. Left Kate Lewis.   **11** Think John Holmes and Thos Kent will be able to miss one Standard next examination.[23]   **12** 1st Class Girls were taught to cut out a gusset.   **13** Lesson on the Lord's Prayer to 3rd Class.   **14** Only 28 boys today.

May 17 Six New Desks arrived from Windsor.   **18** Carpenters came to fit up new desks. The Rector came to see them.   **19** Very wet. Only 14 in morning. None in the Afternoon.[24]   **20** Mistress taught the little ones the song 'The rain is falling'.   **21** Average for the week, 43.

May 24 Jane, Henry & George Lowman admitted.   **25** Scripture to 1st & 2nd Class. Parable of the Labourers in the Vineyard.   **26** Cannot yet get many of Standard II to do subtraction properly.   **27** Dictation to 1st Class page 57. 6 lines Average 5 mistakes.   **28** Wet day 33 in morning 32 in afternoon.

May 31 Ann Lyford admitted.   **June 1** Nothing to record.   **2** Heard the Children their singing for Sunday, and the song of the Cuckoo.   **3** The mistress is not satisfied with the children's progress in Arithmetic.   **4** Average for past week 65.

June 7 Geo. Lambourne was admitted.   **8** Scripture to 1st & 2nd Class the 'Birth of Moses'.   **9** Gave the 1st & 2nd Classes their first lesson on England. Want the New Maps.   **10** Usual Progress.   **11** Average for this week 67.

June 14 Admitted Geo. Fuller. Left Alf. Lewendon and Mary Lewis. **15** Needlework. Taught cutting out of a baby's pinafore.   **16** Taught the song 'Never look sad' today.   **17** Dictation page 66. Seven lines Average 2 mistakes. Easy passage.   **18** Parable of the Ten Virgins. Find very little remembered from last lesson on same subject.

June 21 Nothing to record.   **22** Mistress taught first class girls to cut out a shirt sleeve.   **23** Scripture to Standard II Baptism of Xt.   **24** Gave Joe

---

[22] Entries such as 'Left F. Martin' probably mean that the boy in question failed to attend for one week — perhaps because his family were without the necessary school fees. The following week he is readmitted. Fortescue Martin was aged about 3 at this time and was the grandson of a widow, Sarah Smith, with whom he lived (1871 Census).
[23] Thomas Kent was the son of a farm labourer and was aged about 7 at this time (ibid.).
[24] Low attendance on wet days was partly due to the fact that there were no proper drying facilities for clothes at the school. Poor quality footwear was another factor.

Lewendon the stick for breaking a window with a stone.   **25** Average for week 69.

June 28 Visit to Purley Park in the afternoon.[25]   **29** Standard II Scripture heard the Catechism.   **30** Arithmetic to Standard V. Taught them Dry Measure. **July 1** Seventeen late this morning. Want a bell for assembling.   **2** Looked at the Girls needlework think it greatly improved.

July 5 The Rector paid me last month's salary.   **6** Dictation to Standard IV & V, page 129. Very fairly done.   **7** Gave 1st & 2nd Class a lesson on the scale of Do [*sic*].   **8** Home Lesson of 3rd Class was very badly done.   **9** Received a parcel of Maps & books from the National Society's Depository.

July 12 Readmitted Mary Lewis. John Turner & Emily Tayler left. **13** Used the New Map of Palestine with the scripture lesson today.   **14** Arithmetic to Standard II Subtraction. Better working but notation very faulty. **15** Scripture to 1st Class. The Plagues of Egypt.   **16** Nothing to record.

July 19 Heard the 3rd Class Catechism today. Not very intelligent. **20** Geography of England Mountains.   **21** Gave a lesson on the scale today. Told Dan Lewendon he might join the choir.[26]   **22** Dictation to Stand III. Page 10 (Stev. & Holes).[27]   **23** Set Standard III to learn the words at the head of their reading lesson before dictation.

July 26 Usual Progress.   **27** Ditto.   **28** 20 Girls absent this afternoon. **29** Geography of England Mountains.   **30** Closed school for harvest holidays.

Aug. 30 Admitted Fred Lewis and Mary Wells.   **31** Began all the lessons as at the Commencement of the School year.   **Sept. 1** The Arithmetic of Standard II is very bad.   **2** The Mistress finds the Girls needlework has retarded. **3** Average for this week 61.

Sept. 6 Charles Ashby admitted. Jane Cooke & Emma Kent left.   **7** Gave 1st & 2nd Class lesson on Uses of Mountains.   **8** Scripture to 1st & 2nd. The

---

[25] Purley Park was the property of Major Anthony M. Storer, J.P., who was lord of the manor of Purley. Later entries in the log book — e.g. for 28 June 1871 — indicate that the celebrations were held in connexion with the Purley Band of Hope. The Band of Hope was a temperance organization for children first established in Leeds in 1847; see B. H. Harrison, *Drink and the Victorians* (London, 1971), pp. 192–4.
[26] Dan Lewendon was the eleven-year-old son of a builder's labourer (1871 Census).
[27] This refers to E. T. Stevens and Charles Hole, *The Grade Lesson Books* (Standards I–VI), which were first published in 1863. Stevens and Hole were two schoolmasters and they claimed that the grading of the extracts was carefully undertaken; in order to avoid the necessity for purchasing arithmetic books, arithmetical exercises were put at the back of the individual volumes. These books were the first of many designed to meet the requirements of the Revised Code.

Call of Abram.   **9** Applied Tuesday's lesson (as far as possible) to Europe.
10 Looked at the Girls' needlework and told them of its importance in after life.

Sept. 13 Emily Tayler readmitted.   **14** Cannot get Standard II to recollect or
understand their Religious Instruction.   **15** Music today on the scale of Do.
16 Dictation to Stand. III page 26 last 8 lines spelling very fair.   **17** 20 Girls
absent this morning.

Sept. 20 John Turner, Fred Guttridge admitted, Geo Simmonds, T. Wallis
left. Emily & Morse Cooke & Jane Lowman left.   **21** Gave a lesson on the
Pump to 1st & 2nd.   **22** Mistress gave a lesson to Stand. IV on Gathering.
23 Dictation to Standard IV, 8 lines Page 89. Capital letters wanting.
24 Average for the past week 69.0.

Sept. 27 Repeated the lesson [on] the Pump and found more remembered
than I expected.   **28** Mistress taught the little ones to sing March Away.
29 Standard II Scripture David & Goliath.   **30** Standard V Dictation Page 92,
2 verses. 'Suppliant' only word spelt incorrectly.   **Oct. 1** Taught the fresh
Chants for Sunday next.

Oct. 4 Kate Hine left.[28]   **5** Nothing to record.   **6** 14 Children late this
morning.   **7** Lesson on Duty to Neighbour to 1st Class. Particularly the Golden
Rule.   **8** Gave all the children an examination today. Passed 52 per cent.

Oct. 11 Reading today from Nat. Society's Stand. IV book. Think it too
difficult for ordinary use.   **12** Geography on the Manufacturing Towns taking
Cotton & Wool.   **13** Arithmetic to Standard III Divisor 7 & 8. Very well done.
14 Parable of the Sower to 1st Class today.   **15** Average for this week 67.

Oct. 18 Kate & Mary Godfrey left.   **19** Needlework. Mistress taught girls
whipping.   **20** Geo. of England today on the Manufacture of Iron.   **21** Singing
today instead of yesterday having no list of Lines yesterday.   **22** Examination
today. Passed 60 per cent.

Oct. 25 Mistress gave a lesson on the Crucifixion.   **26** Geography on the
Coal districts. Think I shall be able to present for the minute of the 28th Feb. 67.[29]
27 Music as usual today.   **28** Examined Stand. I. The Arithmetic is the weakest
part.   **29** Examination today badly done only 47 p.c. Must give more
Arithmetic to Stand. II.

Nov. 1 Fred Guttridge left.   **2** Arithmetic for Stand. II Notation to Tens of

[28] This would appear to be yet another example of the practice mentioned above, p. 18,
n. 22. Kate Hine was the daughter of John Hine, a shoemaker, and was aged about five at
this time (1871 Census).
[29] The entry relates to changes in the Revised Code which permitted grants to be paid for
additional 'specific' subjects, including English, Geography and History. The grant
amounted to '3s. per subject . . . for every day scholar, presented in Standards'IV-VI' who
was successful in the examination.

Thousands. Fairly Good.   **3** Dictation to Stand. IV. 'Snatched' & 'possessed' spelt very badly.   **4** Geography of Palestine. Places mentioned in St Matthew's Gospel.   **5** Average for the week 68. Number on the Registers 73.

Nov. 8 Average progress.   **9** Geography of England Manufacture of Lace, Jewellery, Boots & Shoes.   **10** Scripture to Stand. II on The Temptation of Christ.   **11** Standard 3 Arithmetic from Reading Books. Page 43(A). Very well done.   **12** Examination today much better than the last 2 or 3 weeks.

Nov. 15 Amelia Messenger admitted.   **16** Cannot get Geo. Wells to understand Division at all.   **17** Old Testament Scripture to Passage of the Red Sea.   **18** Gave Subtraction to Stand. II from page 82 in Reading books of Standard III.   **19** Examination today. Passed 78 per cent.

Nov. 22 Geo. Simmonds & Jane Lowman were readmitted.   **23** Home Lesson today. To give the names of Manufacturing Towns with their manufactures.   **24** Home Lesson today very well done.   **25** Standard V. Taught them Long measure. Showed them a Gunter's Chain & explained it. **26** Examination today. Dictation very faulty. Cannot get some to spell correctly at all.

Nov. 29 Very little pence brought this morning. Impressed upon children the necessity of keeping rules.[30]   **30** Heard Stand. V in afternoon read the poetry in Nat. Society's Reading Book.   **Dec. 1** Mr Wood came to tell me to caution the children about opening his gate on a/c of his horse.   **2** Nothing to record. **3** Gave 1st & 2nd Examination in Geography instead of Reading today. Consider it fairly good.

Dec. 6 Mary Fuller admitted, John Turner & Ann Lyford left.   **7** Mistress taught the girls to cut out a wristband.   **8** Heard the scale again today. Think I must give it up till after examination.   **9** Mistress taught the little ones the Carol 'While I'm at school' from Hullah's Manual.   **10** Examination to[day] dictation very faulty. Must ascertain the number of mistakes allowed by H.M. Inspector.

Dec. 13 Arthur Weller readmitted.   **14** Usual Progress.   **15** Scripture to Stand. III, IV, V. Parable of the Mustard seed & The Leaven.   **16** Standard III Afternoon Dictation Page 99. 8 lines. Average of 5 mistakes.   **17** Examination today Stand. III much better. Arithmetic of Stand. II very well except Multiplication Tables.

Dec. 20 Heard the Collect for next Sunday scolded several for not knowing it. **21** Very wet 40 in attendance.   **22** Ditto. 37 in attendance.   **23** The Rector gave me H.M. Inspector's notice of examination &c.   **24** Examination today in

[30] During the late autumn and winter months, when work on the land was in short supply, many families found difficulty in providing their children with the weekly school fees. In all, during 1869 'school pence' amounted to £19 11s. 1d.; this compares with £75 6s. obtained from subscriptions, plus £6 2s. 5d. from the government grant and £16 8s. withdrawn from a savings bank account (School Accounts).

Geography (Definitions of Land & Water) in writing very well done excepting spelling.

Dec. 27 Amelia Messenger withdrawn. **28** Examined the girls' marking found it very good. Standard II beginning to make letters. **29** The rector came to baptize F. Martin in one of the neighbouring cottages & spent 10 minutes in the school. **30** Geography of England Rivers. **31** Last Day of School year.

1870

Jan. 3 Geo., Clarance [*sic*] & James Butler admitted.[31] **4** Geography of England today the Fisheries. **5** Found Geo. Butler very troublesome & little accustomed to discipline. **6** Examined Stand. II in the Multiplication Table and gave them 9 times for Home Lesson. **7** Examination of Standard I, passed 80 per cent.

Jan. 10 Geography. Manufacturers of England. **11** Ditto. Rivers & Fisheries. **12** Dictation to Standard IV. Page 145 8 lines. 'Article' 'Superintending' & 'Portion' spell wrong [*sic*]. **13** Punished Geo. Butler today continued playing. **14** Examined Stand. II. Jane Reeves absent. Will Lyford will not pass before H.M. Inspec.[32]

Jan. 17 Wrote out the Schedule today. Not presented 5 who are eligible but who will not get three passes out of the fifteen. **18** Capes & Bays of England to 1st & 2nd Classes. **19** Heard the Singing today as usual. **20** The Dry Measure of Standard V was done very well. **21** Examination not done so well as last week. Told the children they had only one more week to prepare for it.

Jan. 24 Geo. Fletcher admitted. **25** All the work carried on today as for an examination. **26** Geo. Wells will not pass in Arithmetic. **27** Examined old Testament History from the Giving of the Law to the taking of Jericho. **28** Examination 44 Eligible Present. Gave 103 passes as a minimum.

Jan. 31 John Eastman, Certfd. Teacher Upper Grade, 4th Class,[33] Clara Eastman, described as probationer. C. D. DU PORT H.M. Inspr. **Feb. 1** Spoke to the Children about yesterday's work praised their writing & sums & censured their reading. **2** Mr Forbes came today to decide about the magic lantern & treat for Friday next. **3** Took the 1st of Acts for Scripture lesson to 1st Class. **4** The Rector & Mr Forbes came & distributed Prizes today: to

[31] George, Clarence and James Butler were the sons of Henry Butler, gamekeeper, of Coombe Lodge (1871 Census).
[32] Will Lyford, aged nine, was the son of William Lyford, a shepherd (ibid.).
[33] Eastman's certificate was of the lowest class issued. According to Tropp, *The School Teachers*, p. 95, Robert Lowe, the Vice-President of the Council for Education, had created a fourth class certificate in 1862 'especially suitable for "younger and humbler classes of candidates"'. Any acting teacher over twenty-two years of age, having obtained two favourable reports from H.M.I., could be presented for an examination in elementary subjects and might then obtain a certificate'.

Chas. Pocock	Our Dumb Companions
John Holmes	Joyce's Scientific Dialogues
Robert Goodall	The Young Pilgrim
Ann Allright	Pitcairn
Henrietta Simmonds	Shepherds of Bethlehem
Jas. Guttridge	The Sea & Her Famous Sailors
Thos. Kent	Boys' Own Book of Birds
Henry Burgess	Horses & Donkeys
Will Wells	Brave Bobby
Ellen Martin	Little Woodman
Hannah Wellman	Harry & Archie
Thos. Lewendon	First Book of Birds
Annie Goodall	Mother's Last Words (Illustrated)

Tea & Magic Lantern in the evening.

Feb. 7 Wet day 43 in the morning & 42 in the afternoon. **8** The first load of Gravel was brought today for the playgrounds. **9** Mr Forbes brought a gentleman to the school who heard the children read & asked a few general questions.[34] **10** Heard the singing today instead of yesterday. **11** Average for the week 53.8.

Feb. 14 More gravel brought today making in all 14 loads. **15** Geography today. Boundaries & Islands of Europe. **16** Scripture today. Acts II. The Coming of the Holy Ghost. **17** Geography today The Countries of Europe. **18** Explained the use of the Five lines used in Music. [?**19**] Copy of the Inspector's Report on the School — dated Council office 19th February 1870:

There has been good progress in Writing and in Sums, but reading shews no sign of skill. It is unintelligent and inarticulate. The tone of teaching and prayers is too loud and wants refinement. Excepting the old Testament of the Upper Division, there is no proper Scripture Knowledge in the School classes. Geography is very fairly started, but the class wants more thoroughness and more intelligence. The Registers are evidently correct, but very untidily kept. In the junior room there is good Writing and Sums in the first Standard, but much more should be made of the oral answering and intelligence, especially of the children under six years.

The children presented for examination under Article 54 did not satisfy H.M. Inspector.[35]

My Lords trust that the Managers will rectify the points marked as requiring improvement by H.M. Inspector.

[34] This unannounced visiting of schools by outsiders was encouraged by the National Society as a means of arousing interest in schools, but it must have disrupted the daily routine seriously.

[35] Article 54 of the Revised Code of 1868 stated: 'The grant is increased at the rate of 1s. 4d. per examination satisfying the inspector (*pass*) in reading, writing or arithmetic . . . on the following conditions, viz:— (a) the number of teachers must have allowed . . . at least one certificated or one assistant teacher for every 80 scholars . . . (b) the number of passes in reading, writing, and arithmetic must . . . exceed 200 per cent of the annual average number of scholars in attendance . . .'

The Religious Knowledge requires great attention.

The issue of Mrs [*sic*] Eastman's Certificate should be deferred in H.M. Inspector's opinion, until she shews more special skill and thoroughness as a Teacher of Infants.

A.C.

Feb. 21 Scripture to the 3rd Class. The 3rd Answer in the catechism. **22** Taught Standard V Long Measure.   **23** Read Iceland & its Wonders from Nat. Soc. 4th Book.   **24** Mr Forbes came to see the Report.   **25** Usual Progress.

Feb. 28 Bricklayers commenced a wall in the Girls' Playground.   **Mar. 1** Mrs Forbes sent some needlework for the girls.   **2** Heard the singing for Sunday next.   **3** Usual progress.   **4** Average for the week 55.5.

Mar. 7 Gave 1st, 2nd & 3rd Class a short examination today.   **8** Hon. & Rev. H. Bligh, the Diocesan Inspector examined the school today.   **9** Scripture to 1st Class. First 3 Judges.   **10** Gave a short account of the Britons as a dictation lesson to 1st Class.   **11** The gravelling of the girls' playground was finished today.

Mar. 14 Mary & Ellen Wallis left.   **15** Geography, Rivers of England. **16** Standard IV. Dictation page 67. Nelsons 4th book. Badly done.   **17** Lessons progressed as usual.   **18** 3rd Class Scripture offering up of Isaac.

Mar. 21 Sent Jane Lowman home for the school money.[36]   **22** Mountains of England today for 1st & 2nd Class.   **23** The mistress taught Standard II to stitch.   **24** Nothing to record.   **25** The singing as usual.

Mar. 28 Edward Wells admitted.   **29** Began Multiplication of Money with Standard IV.   **30** Mistress taught the little ones some texts and explained their meaning.   **31** Geography to 1st & 2nd classes the River Thames.   **Apr. 1** Average for past week 60.4.

Apr. 4 Admitted Tryphena Tyrrel & Ann Lyford.   **5** Scripture to 1st Class Acts V.   **6** Mistress gave Standard I a lesson on the Crucifixion.   **7** Scripture to 1st & 2nd the seven deacons.   **8** Scripture to 3rd Class The Beatitudes.

Apr. 11 Number present morning and afternoon Boys 47 Girls 22 — Total 69. **12** Geography today. The great railroads from London.   **13** Lessons as usual. **14** Broke up for Easter holidays.

May 2 Admitted Charles Sargeant, Charles Lewendon and Rose Lambourn. **3** Moved Standard II into the mixed school.   **4** The Creation was the Scripture lesson to Standard II.   **5** 1st Scripture lesson Acts II.   **6** Weekly average 59.

---

[36] A note by the Rev. E. Moore in the school accounts indicates that when Eastman left at the beginning of September 1870 he failed to hand over £13 11s. 9p. in school pence which he had collected during the year. In the previous year school pence had yielded £19 11s. 1d.

May 9 Dan Turner returned to school after making 17 attendances this year.[37] **10** History of Eli to 1st Class. **11** Read to 1st and 2nd class a short account of the Great Plague and they produced **12** it on their slates. **13** Nothing to record.

May 16 Admitted Frederick, Frank, & James Tuffnell. **17** Received a parcel of slates &c. from National Society.[38] **18** Dictation to Stand. III & IV Boys was Page 84 Nelson's 4th Book. Very well done. **19** Taught the children Keble's Hymn 'New every morning is the love'. **20** Heard the above with the singing for Sunday next.

May 23 Took John Turner's name off. His mother saw me a fortnight ago and promised faithfully to send him regularly.[39] **24** Dictation to Stand. IV. Page 96 Nelson's: Spelling bad. **25** Arithmetic to Stand. V. Division Long Measure. **26** Scripture to Standard III Healing the leper St Mark I. **27** Usual progress.

May 30 Cautioned Emily Tayler against irregular attendance. **31** Scripture to Standard II. the Fourth Commandment. **June 1** Usual Progress. **2** Fifteen children late this morning. **3** Punished Charles Cooke for coming dirty this morning.

June 6 Holiday today. Whit Monday. **7** Collected school pence this morning. **8** Lessons as for Tuesday. **9** Heard the singing today. **10** Nothing to record.

June 13 Charlotte Simmonds left. **14** Scripture to First Class 'Famine in Samaria'. **15** A Book Hawker came to the school today. **16** Progress as usual. **17** The Rector came today and gave a few prizes to the choir boys and spoke to the children respecting their absence on Sundays.

June 20 Elizabeth Bailey & Eliza Dicker admitted. Charlotte Simmonds readmitted. **21** Duty to God with Scripture proofs to First and Second. **22** Home Lesson for Stand. III. Division. Divisors 17 — 28 — 39. Averaged 2/3 Correct. **23** Nothing to record. **24** Ditto.

June 27 Emily Cross admitted. **28** Geography, Mountains of Europe. **29** Scripture to 1st and 2nd Classes Matt. V 38–48. **30** Ditto — Matthew VII 21–29. **July 1** The Rector came today.

July 4 Scripture to Stand. II. Matthew III. **5** Standard V. Arithmetic. Troy Weight. Told the children there would be holiday in afternoon. **6** Simple subtraction. Standard II is very poor. **7** Several little ones late this morning. **8** Weekly average Boys 50 Girls 19.

[37] Dan Turner, aged ten, was the son of a sixty-five-year-old agricultural labourer (1871 Census).
[38] £1 11s. 6d. was paid to the National Society to cover these items (School Accounts).
[39] John Turner, aged seven, was the brother of Dan, for whom see above, n. 37.

July 11 The Mistress unwell and unable to attend school today. **12** Geography. The capital cities of Europe. **13** Taught the tune Litany[?]. Redhead. **14** Words and tune of 'God Bless the Prince of Wales'. **15** Spoke to the children about their attendance at Church.

July 18 Henrietta Simmonds left. **19** Catechism to Stand. IV, III Belief with proofs. **20** Taught the tune St Gregory — Horsley. **21** Dictation Stand. III. Page 78. **22** Broke up for harvest holidays.

Aug. 22 Joshia Tayler was admitted. **23** Gave the 1st & 2nd Class a short account of the Continental War. **24** Taught the tunes Dundee and Moravia. **25** Mr Forbes came to the school today. **26** Cautioned the boys against talking in Church on Sunday.

Aug. 29 Jas Lewendon admitted. **30** Professor Oliver, Royal Conjuror &c. &c. brought some tickets for the Children's admission to his entertainment. **31** Hen. Knight & Hen. Lewendon were punished for climbing the school wall. **Sept. 2** Duties end here.

J. Eastman

Oct. 17 Whitchurch School Oxon. Commenced duties at this school today Oct 17th found 42 children & found them very rude in their behaviour. Barnaby Brown. **18** The Revd E. Moore called today. **19** Gave a lesson on the life of Joseph. **20** Dictation to 1st and 2nd Class. **21** Punished James Guttridge and William Lyford for swearing in the play ground.

Oct. 24 Admitted Wm Martin & Mary Cooke. **25** Scripture to 1st & 2nd Class. The temptation of Jesus Christ. **26** 14 Children late this morning gave them a lesson for it. **27** Number of children to-day 71 punished a boy for swearing. **28** The Revd E. Moore came and talked to the children — Duty to each other.

Oct. 31 Wet Morning — Gave a lesson to III Standard. Arithmetic found them rather dull. **Nov. 1** Readmitted Charlotte Simmonds. **2** Cannot make much progress with Scripture lessons. **3** Gave a dictation lesson today, and find the children improving. **4** Lesson (the Sugar Maple) (to Standards V, VI).

Nov. 8 The Revd E. Moore and Mr Withers came to school to-day. **9** Punished Alf Cross, Clar. Butler and Thos Kent for getting on the chalk. **10** Gave lesson on the giving of the law. **11** Dictation to 1st Class.

Nov. 14 Mr Forbes, Mr Fanning & Mr Morris came to school to-day.[40]

[40] The visit was no doubt connected with the building alterations at the school: J. Morris of Reading was the architect employed on this work. The building work itself was carried out by Benjamin Briant, a young master builder and brickmaker in Whitchurch. At the time of the 1871 Census he employed 24 men and 2 boys. See also entry in log book for 29 Nov. 1870 ('Mr. Bryant').

15 Admitted George Ridge. **16** The Rector called and spoke to the children for a short time. **17** Mr Gardiner called today. **18** Scripture lesson to Standard IV, V the overthrow of Sodom.

Nov. 21 Taught IV, V Standard the life of Isaac. Admitted Ann Eliz. Wallis. **22** Taught reduction to Standards IV, V. **23** Gave a lesson on the first four commandments to III, IV, V Standards. **24** Very wet, only 58 children. **25** Dictation to Standard III.

Nov. 28 Had to punish three boys for talking in Church. **29** Mr Dodd, Mr Morris & Mr Bryant [*sic*] called at School today. **30** Taught Standard I the first commandment. **Dec. 1** Gave a lesson to IV, V Standard on letter writing. **2** Scripture — The good shepherd.

Dec. 5 Had to punish two boys for using bad language in playground. **6** Heard the tables to-day. **7** Arithmetic to Standard II — multiplication. **8** Lesson the call of Abram. **9** The Life of John the Baptist.

Dec. 12 Gone to Culham to sit for certificate came home on Saturday 17 Decr.[41]

Dec. 19 Had again to punish the children for talking in Church. **20** Gave a lesson on numeration to Standard I. **21** Scripture Lesson to Standard III. **22** Gave a lesson to Standard VI on proportion. **23** Mrs Willan called today about the children she pays for, to know if they attended regularly.

Dec. 27 Readmitted Tho. & George Bushnell. **28** Gave another lesson on numeration to Standards I, II. **29** Gave a lesson to Standard VI on interest. **30** Last day of the school year.

1871

Jan. 2 Taught Standards II, III compound addition. **3** Examined the children on yesterday's lesson and found that they did not remember it. **4** Life of Abraham to Standards IV, V. **5** Dictation to Standards IV, V, VI. **6** Gave a lesson on the mountains of England.

Jan. 9 Very stormey [*sic*] day very few children. **10** Received a quantity of books for the School today.[42] **11** Had to punish the first class for throwing snowballs. **12** Examined III & IV and found them not so well up as I could wish. **13** Examined Standard IV in proportion & found they did their work well.

Jan. 16 Lesson the plagues of Egypt. **17** Lesson I, II, III standards birth of Christ. **18** The exode [*sic*] of Israel out of Egypt. **19** The wandering of the

---

[41] Brown was no doubt taking advantage of the provision of the Revised Code which allowed practising teachers to become certificated — in a new fourth division — merely by answering 'plain and simple questions, specially noted for them', and without attending a course at a training college. See above, p. 22, n. 33, for Eastman (31 Jan. 1870).

[42] 'Books from National Society for the year 1871' cost £4 9s. 10d. (School Accounts).

Israelites in the wilderness. **20** Examined the school on the above lessons. **21** George Lewendon William Kent Whitchurch Grammatical Educational course.

Jan. 23 Barnaby Brown candte for Certificate. C. D. Du Port H.M. Inspr Government examination today. **24** Lesson to Standards I, II. **25** Mr Forbes called today. **26** The Revd E. Moore & Mr Forbes came today and gave the following prizes

John Holmes	Wispering [*sic*] Unseen
Charles Pocock	Crown of Success
Robt. Goodall	Golden Year
Walter Lambourne	Lay of the Last Minstrel
Henry Burgess	Haunted House
Charles Ashby	Self Knowledge
George Fuller	Peter's £ became a penny
Charles Taylor	Paul's penny became a £
George Butler	Nine lives of a Cat
Kate Pocock	Basket of Flowers
Emily Wells	Amy's Wish
Jane Bushnell	How I became a gover[ne]ss
Annie Goodall	Always Happy
Louisa Cooke	Every day Things

Evening Xmas Tree and School Treat.
27 Had to punish nine boys for running out of the playground during play time.

Jan. 30 Admitted Thomas Hine & George Fletcher. **31** Gave a lesson on coal to Standards IV, V, VI. **Feb. 1** Examined the children on the above lesson. **2** Taught reduction to Standards IV & V. **3** Wet day few Children in school.

Feb. 6 Numeration to Standards I. II. **7** Admitted Eliz. Paynter. **8** Taught the creed to the lower classes. **9** Wet day few children this morning.

Feb. 13 Dictation IV, V, VI standards. Ten lines from page 79. **14** Heard III, IV classes Catechism, find they know very little of it. **15** Lesson. The creation of the world until the flood. **16** Had to punish Thomas Tayler and other for having so many mistakes in dictation (by keeping them in and making them rewrite the mistakes ten times over). **17** Sophia Rogers left school to go to service to Mrs Trummers.

Feb. 20 Admitted William Fletcher. **21** Taught the commandments to Standards IV, V. **22** Mistress Taught the belief to the infants. **23** Had to punish Henry Guttridge for swearing. **24** Gave a lesson on the rivers of England.

Feb. 27 Admitted Jane Paynter. **28** Standards IV, V, VI, ten lines of dictation. **Mar. 1** Recd my month's salary today. **2** Nothing to record. **3** Heard Catechism, Standards III, IV, V, IV [*sic*].

Mar. 6 Admitted Herbert John Bushnell, James Hine & Thomas Edward Pocock — today. **7** Taught the life of Joseph. **8** Taught the life of Moses. **9** The life of John [the] Baptist. **10** Dictation 6 lines to Standards II, III, found them better than I expected.

Mar. 13 Admitted James Lewendon & George Lewis. **14** Life of John [the] Baptist to Standards II, III, IV. **15** Warned Kate Lewis about being absent so very often. **16** Proportion to Standards IV & V. **17** Do not find much improvement in Arithmetic in Standards I & II but think that there is an improvement in reading and writing.

Mar. 20 Admitted Harriett Hine. **21** Admitted James Strike. **22** Gave first lesson on fractions today. **23** Mr Forbes called today. **24** Had to punish some boys for throwing stones into Mr Wood's garden.

Mar. 27 Admitted John & David Turner. **28** Taught the III & IV Standards the commandments. **29** Gave a lesson on the Wars of the Roses to V, VI Standards. **30** Mr R. Briant came to me finding fault about the boys drawing figures of men on the gate and was very angry with them for so doing had to punish 7 boys & I hope they will not do so any more. Hit Clarence Butler harder than I intended.[43] **31** Received my month's salary today.

Apr. 3 Heard today that the Hon. & Revd H. Bligh will visit this school April 26. **4** Admitted Alfred Whiting to-day, he never has been at school before. **5** Dictation to Standards III, IV. **6** Life of Moses to Standards IV, V, VI. **7** Good Friday.

Apr. 10 Holiday Easter Monday. **11** Cannot get Standard II to understand religious instruction at present but hope they will soon. **12** Gave Standard 3 arithmetic from Reading books pretty well done. **13** Gave a lesson on the giving of the law. **14** Gave Standard 6 a lesson on double proportion think they will soon learn it.

Apr. 17 Spoke again to the boys & girls about their behaviour in Church. **18** Taught the life of Joshua. **19** Taught the life of Samuel. **20** Very wet — few children only 31. **21** Very wet only 33 children today.

Apr. 24 The Hon. & Revd H. Bligh Inspected the children today and was well pleased with them. Gave the prize to Frederick Tuffnell.[44] **25** Admitted Mary & Sophia Wells today. **26** Division to Standard III I think they understand it pretty well. **27** Reduction to Standard IV. **28** Gave the children a lesson on the giving of the law from Mount Sinai.

---

[43] Robert Briant was a plumber and glazier, employing two men in 1871; for Clarence Butler see above, p. 22, n. 31.
[44] Bligh was the Diocesan Inspector, and for this reason was less feared than the H.M.I., who had considerable financial power over the school. He was also vicar of Nettlebed.

May 1 Admitted Jane & Annie Linfield also Kate Hine and Edith Mary Cross.[45] **2** Taught Standard VI addition of Fractions. **3** Spoke to the children about coming regularly to School. **4** The children do not progress as well as I could wish to see them. **5** The number present today 80.

May 8 Admitted Geo., Emily Ashby & Eliz. Fabry. **9** Had to punish Thos Tayler for not learning his lessons: he is a very idle boy. **10** Scripture lesson today the life of Elijah. **11** The life of Ahab. **12** The number present to-day 82.

May 15 Admitted Sarah Cross. **16** Received a parcel of slates &c. from the National Society today. **17** Kate Lewis left School today. **18** Nothing to record. **19** Taught the song the cuckoo.

May 22 Admitted Ellen Lewis. **23** Two builders from Reading called today to look at the School and School house. **24** Mr Bryant [sic] and Mr Withers called today to see the School and School house. **25** Mr Wood called today to tell where the boys and girls had to sit in Church on Sundays. **26** Progress as usual.

May 30 Holiday yesterday. **31** Recd from the Revd E. Moore my month's salary. **June 1** Life of Joseph. **2** Very few children today.

June 5 Mr Fanning Revd E. Moore and others met here today to take into consideration the building [of] a new boys school. **6** Find load of bricks came today for the new school room. **7** Nothing to record. **8** Had to punish some boys for coming dirty. **9** Taught Standard VI division of decimals.

June 12 Admitted Frederick W. Gutteridge & Eliza Dicker. **13** Admitted Alfred Squires & Jane Bishop. **14** Revd E. Moore called today. **15** Mr Morris came to see the foundations and to measure the playground off from the Garden.[46] **16** The number present today 86.

June 19 Had to punish the boys for inattention in Church on Sunday. **20** Gave Standard VI a lesson in decimal fractions. **21** Had to punish some boys for going to play in the new building. **22** Sold three pinafores which the girls had made. **23** The Revd E. Moore & W. Fanning Esq. called at school today.

June 26 Admitted William Ridge. **27** Received my month's salary from the Revd E. Moore. **28** Took 81 children this afternoon to Purley Band of Hope Fete.[47] **29** The Revd E. Moore called today and stayed a half-hour.

[45] In practice these were probably re-admissions; e.g. see entry for 4 Oct. 1869, concerning Kate Hine.

[46] Brown was paid 15s. compensation for 'Damage done to his Garden by Builders' (School Accounts).

[47] These visits to Purley continued into the early twentieth century, as Mrs Watson of Reading recalls in a letter to the editor dated Sept. 1975: 'we would meet at Sellwood shop & pay 2d. or 3d. for a ride in farm carts to go to Purley Park fair, 2 days. We sang the songs of the Band of Hope & 2 days' enjoyment we had there'.

30 Mrs Willan payed [*sic*] for the schooling of four children today for the last quarter.[48]

July 3 Mr A. C. Forbes and the Revd Cambell [*sic*] called to look at the school.   **4** Examined the children and think that they are progressing favourably.   **5** Some of the Children went to Englefield Fete in consequence of which we had few children in the afternoon.   **6** Taught the children the song 'Come boys be merry time is on the wing'.   **7** Had to punish Joseph Martin, Thos Kent, Henry Knight & Henry Lewendon for going to bathe in the river after telling them not to go.

July 10 Admitted Mary Ann Hutt.   **11** Arithmetic to Standard II short division.   **12** Ditto.   **13** Dictation to Standards IV, V, VI 10 lines of milkmaid.   **14** George Ridge one of my pupils was drowned last evening and his father in crossing the river the boat upset and both were drowned; spoke to the children this morning about it.[49] Showed them that in the 'midst of life we are in death'.

July 17 Mr Morris called today about the desks for the new schoolroom.   **18** Admitted John Wallis, Rosa & Charlotte Knight.   **19** Gave Thomas Tayler another lesson in long division but do not think he will ever learn.   **20** Mr Wood and others from the Uplands called today.   **21** Nothing to record.

July 24 Admitted Joseph Lewendon.   **25** The Rector and others called.   **26** Dictation on paper to Standards IV, V, VI.   **27** The above Standards worked sums on paper.   **28** Broke up for harvest holidays.

Sept. 25 Opened the school after eight weeks holiday not a window in the boy's [*sic*] school.   **26** Very few children.   **27** Had to go in the boys school with the children owing to the varnishing the girl's [*sic*] school.   **28** The workmen are filling the frames in the windows in boy's [*sic*] school.   **29** Got two windows in today.

Oct. 2 More children today think the[y] will soon come to school now.   **3** Mr Moore called today.   **4** Geography the coal fields.   **5** Mistress taught the first class of girls.   **6** Heard catechism this morning.

Oct. 9 Better school to-day but will not be able to teach well while the workmen are so near.   **10** Mr Morris came to-day to see how they were getting on with the school.   **11** Examined the children (Standards IV, V) in proportion find they remember very little of it.   **12** Found fault with the men for throwing dirt at the children as they were going into the playground.   **13** Mistress taught the girls a scripture lesson this morning.

---

[48] The school accounts show that Mrs Willan regularly subscribed £5 per annum towards the school. The Willans lived at Thames Bank House, Whitchurch.

[49] George Ridge was the son of the lock-keeper, William Ridge. George was aged about 9 and his father 39 (1871 Census).

Oct. 16 Admitted Aur. Weller today.   **17** Admitted Sarah & Jane Lewendon to-day both very backward for their age.[50]   **18** Taught Standard III reduction of money.   **19** The Rev. E Moore & W. Fanning Esqr called to-day. **20** Average progress.

Oct. 23 Admitted George Kent.   **24** Dictation to Standards IV, V, VI. The piece By me that holy office were profaned &c. average number of mistakes 1½. **25** Had to punish all the first class for being careless during arithmatic [sic] lesson.   **26** B. Bligh Esqr called and wished me to sent [sic] the children to practice.   **27** The Rector & Gardener [sic] Esqr called to see the new school.

Oct. 30 First load of gravel came today to put in the girls playground.   **31** The Rector payed [sic] me my month's salary this morning.   **Nov. 1** More gravel came today for the boys play-ground.   **2** The Rector called today to see if the School was nearly completed.   **3** Taught the Second Standard a lesson on The Flood.

Nov. 6 Began the lessons again as I did on the first of Feby of this yr.   **7** Admitted Frederick Warner.   **8** Finished gravelling the boys [sic] play-ground. **9** Geography to the first class.   **10** A. C. Forbes Esqr & F. Willan Esqr came to see the new school.

Nov. 13 A man from London came to repair the fire grate.   **14** Mr Withers & Mr Morris called to examine the new school building.   **15** Geography to the first Class (Turkey).   **16** Repeated the above lesson.   **17** Arithmetic to Standard III small bills as what is the price of 12 eggs at 4 for 5d. and 5 lbs. of meat at 7½ per lb.

Nov. 20 Nothing to record.   **21** Ditto.   **23** Saw the Rector about leaving on Decr 1st got no answer.   **24** Geography to the first class (Turkey).   **25** Miss Sykes came to the schoolhouse and gave me some Band of Hope Almanac's [sic] for the children. Lesson kindness to animals.

Nov. 27 Spoke to the children about talking in church on a Sunday.   **28** Usual progress.   **29** The Rev. E. Moore paid me my month's salary.   **30** Duties end here.[51]

Dec. 8 The School, Whitchurch, Oxon. I, Thomas Warner, commenced duties at this School, as temporary master on Dec. 4th. Examined the children, some part of each day, during the week, in subjects usually taught in a parochial School, &, with the exception of John Holmes, found their attainments exceedingly low. The discipline is very lax. The Rev. E. Moore visited the School this morning.

[50] Sarah and Jane Lewendon, aged 11 and 7 respectively, were the daughters of Thomas Lewendon, a wood sawyer. Sarah had been born in Pangbourne but Jane and a younger sister had both been born in Reading (ibid.).
[51] An allowance of £2 was made to Mr Brown in respect of his 'journey from Whitchurch' (ibid.).

Dec. 15 School work carried on as per Time Table, except a deviation on Tuesday, Wednesday, & Thursday, for extra drilling in Dictation & Spelling. Thursday, & to day examined all classes in Arithmetic; the result is far from satisfactory. Noticed this week a slight improvement in writing throughout the School; but many cannot yet write their letters, either capitals or small.

Dec. 22 Special attention has been given, during the week, to Mental Arithmetic; to each class in the time allotted on the Time Table for Arithmetic. Dictation lesson to the 1st class, written on paper each day. The writing improves, but the spelling is very bad. Examined the four classes to day, separately, in Reading & Spelling; the Reading is not given with expression, the meanings of words are not understood, & my previous remark on Spelling may be implied [*sic*] throughout the School with very few exceptions.

Dec. 29 Christmas week — Holidays.

1872

Jan. 5 Admitted on Jan. 1st Maria Day, Sarah Ann Day, & George Day, who had previously been to School at Mapledurham. In the afternoon of the same day the Rev. E. Moore, & one of H.M. Inspectors came to inspect the School buildings & House. The Rev. E. Moore again visited the School to-day, Friday. The 1st class reading lesson each afternoon in this week has been from the Geography of England & Wales. Examined each class in Arithmetic, found their knowledge of numeration sadly deficient.

Jan. 12 Gave particular attention to numeration in the Arithmetic lessons this week, & Have found the result *more* encouraging, but *not* satisfactory. Instead of Dictation to the first class on Tuesday & Wednesday, I told them to write themes — 1st subject the 'Cow', 2nd subject 'Whitchurch', & on Thursday requested them to write a letter. The letters throughout were failures, the themes showed thought. The Rector visited the School.

Jan. 19 Lessons each morning this week except Friday, on the Parables & Miracles recorded in St Matthew's Gospel; to the 1st & 2nd Classes. To the 1st Class special attention has been given to mental arithmetic, & Bills of Parcels. To the other three classes notation. Examined each class separately in the latter subject & think there is a slight improvement. Home Lessons, on Slates, each fine evening this week, Tables, Transcribing, or Arithmetic. Several children have been absent at times owing to wet weather, or illness. Miss Beecher & the Misses Baker visited the School on the 18th inst. The Rev. E. Moore & W. Fanning, Esq. came today to examine the annual accounts & the registers & appointed another meeting for auditing them on Jan 29th.

Jan. 26 During the School-week ending at this date, more time has been given to Reading in each class. Dictation & Arithmetic, on paper, to the 1st Class, Wednesday, Thursday & Friday; & found the Spelling, in the first-mentioned, very defective; & in the latter, the results were far from satisfactory. Home

Lessons — Tables, Arithmetic, & finding out passages in the Old Testament, typical & prophetical of our Saviour. The Rev. E. Moore visited the School to-day, heard the 1st Class read, in the Acts of the Apostles, & gave a Lesson thereon. The weather has been very wet, causing several to be absent, many have also been absent through ill-health. Examined each class, & think there is progress, but most particularly in writing. Admitted on Jan. 22nd Alice Turrell.

Jan. 29 Examined the 1st & 2nd Classes, in Arithmetic. Other work carried on as usual. **30** Dictation on Paper to the 1st Class; & extra time given to Spelling in each class. **31** The Rev.C. D. Du Port, Inspected the School today. **Feb. 1** Commenced teaching the children Singing. Several were late, the weather being wet. Cautioned the children about sliding down the bank, opposite the School & cottages adjoining. **2** Examined in the Church Catechism. I have been accustomed to do so every Friday, but have made no previous entry to that effect in the Log Book. Geography lesson 'England & Wales' to the 1st Class. In Writing & Spelling, there is improvement. George Butler, Clarence Butler, and James Butler withdrawn; their parents leaving this neighbourhood.

Feb. 9 Friday — School Work as per Time-Table. Examination in Arithmetic to-day.

Feb. 16 The Rev. E. Moore visited the School & heard the Boys in the first Class read a Lesson from the Fourth Standard Reading Book (Revised Code). School Treat to-day, at which the Rector; W. Fanning Esq.; Miss Fanning; Miss Wood; other ladies & Gentlemen, & a few of the children's parents were present. Rewards were given to the children for punctuality, regular attendance, cleanliness, & good conduct. All the visitors expressed their satisfaction with the children's conduct & appearance.

Feb. 23 Home lessons during the week — The 'Church Catechism'; & 'Tables'. Gave 4 lessons in Mental Arithmetic. Some children give more expression in Reading. Writing is done better but not with such accuracy as ought to be. Dictation on Paper (to the 1st Class); noticed improvement. Examined each class in Arithmetic this week.

Feb. 26 Admitted Kate Cook. Home Lessons, Catechism; & Tables. Extra time given to Reading & Spelling. **27** Reading, extra time. Other work as usual. **28** Having previously omitted to make the entry, that Exercise Books, for transcribing, have been introduced by me, I make this note, because those children who have them, viz. the First Class, are much pleased with them. The Exercise Books, & Copy Books are used, (during the writing lesson), alternately. Miss Sykes called this morning. **29** School work as per Time Table Home Lesson — Tables. **Mar. 1** Heard the Church Catechism this morning, as usual, & explained many words therein. Examined the Home Lessons done on Slates, & for the most part they were improved in neatest [*sic*], & distinctness. The Rev. E. Moore visited the School this afternoon, heard the first class read in the Fourth Standard Reading Book, & explained the meanings of the words in the lesson. Afterwards he asked questions relating to the Church Catechism &

Liturgy, but was not satisfied with the answers. There is gradual improvement. Seventy-seven children in attendance.

Mar. 8 School work as usual during the week. Mental Arithmetic to all the classes separately each day.

Mar. 15 Bills of Parcels, on Paper each day this week, to first class. Other lessons as usual.

Mar. 22 Each day Dictation on Paper in the First Class — noticed improvement in writing & spelling. Examined each Standard in Arithmetic.

Mar. 28 More improvement in writing Reading & Arithmetic, but *now very* deficient. Examined each class in all three subjects. My duties as temporary Master in this School terminate to-day.[52]

THOMAS WARNER

Apr. 8 We Thomas Litchfield and Sarah Litchfield commenced duties in this School on this day. **11** Examined all classes in Reading Writing and Arithmetic. Reading very poor in the lower classes. Dictation in the Second class not at all satisfactory & Arithmetic generally they know but little about.

Apr. 15 Admitted several fresh children arranged a Time Table. Introduced Military Drill in playground for the boys, & gave the two upper classes home lessons. Commenced with Jarrolds Comprehensive Registers as we found them preferable to those formerly in use. Revd E. Moore visited & heard the 1st Class read. Girls recommenced needlework which had been neglected altogether for several months.

Apr. 22 Admitted several fresh children. Visit from the Revd E. Moore who took the first class during the reading lesson. Taught the first class Tables Weights & (Measures) 2nd Class Multiplication tables of which they seem to know nothing.

Apr. 29 Slight improvement in Reading & Dictation in Second Class.[53] First class do their home lessons better. Commenced Addition of Weights & Measures with them. Visit from Mr Fanning who advised other Standard reading book than those in use.

May 6 Sent an absence enquiry card to parents of the absent children which seems to work well. First Class improve in their Arithmetic. Visit from Revd E. Moore. **9** The Upper classes attended church in the morning and the registers were not marked. The younger children stayed at school and received the usual lessons.

[52] Mr Warner was paid £1 1s. a week, in arrears. His last payment was made on 20th April and covered eight weeks. He was also paid 7s. 5d. for 'cleaning school & materials' (ibid.).
[53] All the Whitchurch head teachers denigrated the standards which they found on taking up office, and all claimed to note an improvement within weeks.

May 13 Wet day. 3 Fresh children admitted. The lower classes read very badly and the books they have at present are much too difficult for them.   **16** First Class improve in Writing & Dictation.

May 20 Admitted 2 fresh children. Weather very wet caused the younger children to be kept from School.   **23** Third Class begin to have some idea how to spell a few simple words.

May 27 New books for the lower classes.[54]   **30** Made the first class into 2 Divisions the Second division require their Arithmetic to be well looked into.

June 3 Second Class do not know their Multiplication tables properly, have put them back to learn them thoroughly.   **6** First Class work more freely without the 2nd Division. Revd E. Moore visited today & heard first Class read.

June 10 Second Class do their work much better since they have thoroughly learned their tables. Third Class improve in Arithmetic & Spelling. Three wet days this week obliged to lend some of the girls the School cloaks to cover them. **13** Fine morning better attendance of younger children. Third Class read much better from Jarrolds 2nd Standard than from Stevens & Hole's 1st Standard which are too difficult.[55] Introduced Haywoods Arithmetical Cards for First & Second Classes.

June 17 Hay making commenced several children gone to work or staying at home while their parents are in the hay field. 1st & 2nd Class do their work pretty well from Haywoods Arithmetical cards made 3rd Class into two divisions. Admitted two fresh scholars.   **20** The Measles are in the village several children at home ill with them. 3rd Class do their home lessons much better & their books are kept cleaner.

June 24 The Measles continue to spread nearly 20 at home with them. Revd E. Moore visited this morning & heard 2nd Class read.   **28** Visit from Revd E. Moore & Mr Fanning school a/c made up for the month & first Qr.

July 1 Victims to the Measles increase largely 3rd Class in Infant room only 2 Children left. First class only three.   **4** Lessons as per Time table nothing to record.

July 8 Measles still on the increase total number of children in Infant room 12. Registers not marked for this week.   **11** Revd E. Moore & Revd —— visited the school remarked upon the small number of children present. A few First Class boys at work in the Hay-field.

---

[54] An entry in the school accounts for 23 May shows £1 8s. 9½d. as spent on books etc. from the National Society.

[55] The books referred to are Jarrold & Sons, *New Code Reading Books*, first published in 1872, and said to be adapted 'to the requirements of the New Code 1871'; and E. T. Stevens and Charles Hole, *The Grade Lesson Books*, for which see above, p. 19, n. 27.

July 15 First & second class improve in their dictation 3rd Class know their multiplication tables much better. The Infant children seem ignorant of their language & do not understand commonplace words.

July 22 A return of children to school lately absent from Measles, a large number still absent. Admitted three fresh scholars. **25** Heavy thunderstorm lasted five hours, only 3 children at School by 10 o'clock, not marked the registers for this day. Revd E. Moore visited this morning & heard 2nd class read.

July 29 Haywoods Arithmetical Cards make a decided improvement in the first Class Arithmetic. Visit from Mr Forbes & the Chairman of the Reading School Board. **Aug. 1** Harvest has commenced. Revd E. Moore visited & heard 1st Class read. Visit from A. C. Forbes Esqr. **2** School broke up for Harvest holidays a month.

Sept. 2 Commenced school with improved attendence [*sic*] younger children seem to have forgotten what little they knew. **5** First class did their Tables (Weights & Measures) without a mistake. Third class dictation very imperfect. 2nd Class. Read much better.

Sept. 9 Admitted several fresh children in Infant room. 24 absent on the register. Harvest not completed. **12** First Class girls are now in Second Class, not able to work arithmetic in first class. Girls improve in their needlework. Third class improve in their arithmetic & seem to know the Multiplication tables.

Sept. 16 Truck load of Coals brought in for the use of School a much greater quantity than ordered. School well filled only two children absent in upper room. **19** Taught children 3 new School songs they are now acquainted with nine.

Sept. 23 Ordered by the managers to have the coals weighed, employed a man for the purpose, & found 1 Ton 15 cwt less than the quantity charged for.[56] **26** First and second classes improve in their Arithmetic and Dictation. Revd E. Moore visited & heard first class read.

Sept. 30 First class girls took their first lesson in Cutting out from measurement as required by Examination schedule. Third class improve in their reading and writing.

Oct. 7 Infant room now average 40 children they learn slowly but seem to improve in intelligence. **10** Great pains has [*sic*] been taken in both schools in improving the tone of the children's reading; but the lower classes still have a peculiar drawl which is very unpleasant.

---

[56] Four tons of coal were purchased at 29*s*. a ton (£5 16*s*. in all) from Edward T. Ashley, a Whitchurch coal merchant (School Accounts).

Oct. 17 Great improvement in the Arithmetic since the introduction of Haywood's Cards.

Oct. 21 Taught the children 2 fresh school songs they are now acquainted with eleven. **25** Very wet afternoon, girls not able to finish their needle-work owing to the darkness.

Oct. 28 Committee meeting held this morning. Revd E. Moore & A. Forbes Esquire present. They noticed an improvement in the reading of the upper classes. **31** Very wet afternoon and dark at 3.30 it was with difficulty the school work was carried on after that time.

Nov. 4 Examined all classes in their arithmetic & find a decided improvement. Revd E. Moore & Mr Forbes visited & heard first Class read. **5** Examined all classes in their dictation average number of corrections about 4 or 5.

Nov. 11 Third class know their Multiplication tables correctly. **14** First & second classes in Infant room make great progress in their lessons.

Nov. 18 Very wet weather several children absent from that cause. **22** Taught first & second division first class Metric Tables.

Nov. 25 Very wet afternoon lent 11 Girls from the hill[57] the School cloaks. **27** School cloaks all returned & well dried.

Dec. 2 Wet morning very few children at school from the hill. 1st Class did their Dictation very well. **5** A much better attendance weather finer 2nd Class do their arithmetic with more satisfaction.

Dec. 9 Mr Bryant [*sic*] repaired the roof of house & school where the water had made its way through & also the broken windows. Girls improve in their needlework. **12** A. C. Forbes Esqr heard 3rd Class read & remarked upon their improvement. The whole school sing the School songs very creditably.

Dec. 16 Dark wet days unable to do our work properly towards 4 O clock. **19** Examined all classes in their Arithmetic. First Class improve in their dictation. **20** Closed the School today for the Xmas holidays. Received the Government Schedules for the Examination on Jany 20 73.

Dec. 30 Commenced duties again this morning short attendances Xmas not concluded. **Jan. 1** Revd E. Moore & A. C. Forbes Esqr visited and purpose giving the Children a treat after the examination, cannot find any record of previous examinations.

---

[57] The 'hill' related to that part of the parish known as Upper Whitchurch. It occupied 'the middle part of a wide table land, the sides of which [sloped] steeply down to the river' (Baker, p. 1).

1873

Jan. 6 Greater number of children at school than usual drawn by the prospect of a treat.

Jan. 13 A. C. Forbes Esqr visited & proposes a present for each child presented for examination. **15** Girls finished their cutting out, and needlework specimens. **17** 1st Class (Infants) had a reading lesson instead of drawing as per Timetable because there were not enough slate pencils.

Jan. 20 Memorandum left by H.M. Inspector on his examination of this school.

Sewing & cutting out: It is wasteful to occupy more than 5 or 6 (or in a cutting out class 6 or 7) hours weekly at most, for any one girl upon this department. To shew unwashed samples in calico for every girl of 250 attendances exhibiting about a foot in length of every kind of stitch learned by her, & containing specimens of patching, darning, button-holes and marking in the case of girls in the upper Standards. Cutting out & placing to be taught and specimens shewn either in paper or in stuff in Standards IV–VI.

Reading Books: Not less than 2 or 3 different complete sets of Reading-books must be provided for every standard. Besides the mere mechanical power of reading aloud intelligently I expect throughout all the standards an intelligent acquaintance with a certain amount of useful matter treated of in the Reading Books the portions to be chosen by the Teacher. I wish also to see Memory & Modulation cultivated by making each child in these standards learn one or two of the easy poetry pieces by heart.

Mental Arithmetic: To be taught in every standard aiming in Standards III–VI to practise the children in the intelligent application of Arithmetic to ordinary practical questions & problems.

Music: 12 Songs to be learned in correct time & tune. In Infant School 6 Songs will suffice.

H.M. Inspector visited today 31 Scholars presented in Upper Room and 24 Infants none absent. **23** Mr Forbes & Family with Miss Fannings [*sic*] came to assist in giving the School children a Tea with Cake Oranges Sweets &c. &c. none absent. Miss Fanning presented books to the children as prizes for good attendance, good needlework, & cleanliness. A Magic Lantern performance was given after Tea to amuse the children. All passed off satisfactorily.

Jan. 27 Put the classes to work in the new standards admitted the big boys from the Infant room. **31** Revd E. Moore visited this morning & heard 1st Class read.

Feb. 3 Deep snow only 3 children in Infant room a much better number in Upper room than expected only 15 Absent. **5** No Register taken for Infant room this week. Gave the girls of the poorer class of labourers a cloak each by order of the Rector.

Feb. 10 A full number of children in both rooms the snow nearly all gone. Commenced Vulgar Fractions in First Class. Mixed chalk with the coals & find the rooms beautifully warmed by it.

Feb. 17

17a[58] [Report on] Whitchurch Parochial School Oxford

Mixed School: I am very pleased with the careful work done by the Master, and with the intelligence cultivated by him in all Departments.

Infant School: The Infants attainments are but fair. The Mistress will readily be able to raise their intelligence and results, by cultivating a far quieter tone of voice and a far more methodical style of Class management.

Such slates should never be seen in a National School.

The ninth Supplementary Rule must be literally observed in the Mixed School.

A duplicate set of Books should be provided for the use of the Mixed School.

Pictures are wanted for the Infants.

Thomas Litchfield   Certificated Teacher 3rd Class

Sarah Nash Litchfield   Certificated Teacher 2d Class

Another deep snow — only 5 children presented themselves gave holiday for that day.   **18** Snow continues to fall only one scholar present another days holiday given.   **19** Snow nearly all gone opened school with a fair number.

Feb. 24 Infant registers not marked for last week owing to bad weather scarcely any in the infant room presented themselves.   **27** A fair average of children in both rooms First & second class improve in their Arithmetic.

Mar. 3 Infant room thinned by bad weather 1st Class Infant room improve in Reading 2nd Class Upper room commenced Pence & farthings tables & First class Tables of Weights & Measures.

Mar. 10 Obliged to punish several boys out of Infant room for bad conduct yesterday.   **13** A. C. Forbes Esqr & Mrs Forbes visited & heard the children sing. Learned also from Mr Forbes who it was visited last week (a Gentleman called & asked many questions respecting school & management &c. &c. and gave no name) —— Wildrake Esqr of Purleigh Hall.[59]

Mar. 17 Visited the Parents of children on the hill & several fresh names are added to the admission book in consequence. Above 40 children present in Infant room.   **20** 3 class boys begin to know their multiplication tables. First & Second class improve in their Arithmetic. John Holmes commenced Algebra today and did six examples very correctly.

---

[58] Article 17(a) of the Code stated that: 'Before any grant is made to a school the Education Department must be satisfied that — (a) The school is conducted as a public elementary school (Article 6); and no child is refused admission to the school on other than reasonable grounds'.

[59] Probably Frederick Wilder, J.P., of Purley Hall, about two miles from Whitchurch.

Mar. 24 A bright mild morning a full school on consequence (both rooms), Charles Tayler to write Playing in Church 1000 times for his bad conduct there yesterday. Reading in all Classes very good especially First Class.

Apr. 1 Good attendance in both rooms gave 2nd class their first lesson in Compound Addition. 1st Division 1st Class improve in their Arithmetic. 3rd Class do not read as I should like them.   **4** A. C. Forbes visited this morning & wished a Balance sheet of school fund to be made out so that Contributors might see how their money was expended.

Apr. 8 Gave 2nd Division 1st Class Compound Weights & measures. Addition & Subtraction do not seem to understand much about it although they know the tables well.   **10** Mrs Forbes sent in some needlework to be done by the elder girls.

Apr. 15 Examined all the scholars in their Arithmetic. I think William & Alfred Cross will never learn to read they work very hard but do not seem to improve.   **17** Have given the 3rd Class an extra lesson in reading fancy I find a slight improvement.   **21** Have made out the Balance sheet for School Building fund & taken it to the printers Mr Forbes suggested that a sheet showing the whole matter be pasted in this Log Book.[60]

[Apr. 22–June 30: missing]

July 3 Examined 1st class Infants they work Subtraction of Thousands fairly, but do not always take their numbers down correctly.   **10** 2nd & 3rd Classes did their multiplication & pence tables very well. Gave the 3rd Class boys a table to learn at home & repeat next morning.

July 14 Revd Molyneux called & heard first class read.[61]   **16** Two strangers looked in this afternoon & heard children sing their school songs.

July 21 Harvest has commenced several children from the hill absent in consequence.   **24** Examined all classes in their work this week to test the loss during the holidays.

July 28 Several children absent, the harvest has become general, purpose closing the school this week for a month.   **Aug. 1** School closes today for a month re-open Sep. 1.

[60] No balance sheet appears in the log book, but two complete pages have been torn out at this point, so that all the entries for late April, May and June are missing.
[61] Reginald Edward Molyneux of Exeter College, Oxford, was curate of Whitchurch from 1873 to 1880 with a stipend of £120 per annum. He came from a curacy at Waltham St Lawrence and became vicar of Christ Church, Virginia Water, 1883. (See Diocesan Book of Bishop Mackarness, Bodl. MS. Oxf. Dioc. Pp.d. 761.) Between 1880 and 1883 he continued to live in Whitchurch, and appears there in *Kelly's Dir. Oxon.* (1883). In 1881–2 he acted as curate of the neighbouring parish of Mapledurham.

Sept. 1 Re-opened School this morning. Harvest not nearly completed. A Wet morning. Fair number of Scholars in upper room only a very few in Infant room. **3** Taken the Infant room first class into upper room to work with the 3rd Class.

Sept. 8 Full school nearly all the absentees returned. Examined First & Second Classes & find they have gone back considerably. **11** Revd Molyneux called & heard first class read.

Sept. 15 Find the children improved since last weeks drill. **18** Revd Molyneux visited this afternoon & heard children sing their school songs.

Sept. 22 Nearly all returned from the harvest work. Commenced working for Inspectors visit in January next. **25** Find the First Class want brushing up in their long division simple & Compound.

Sept. 29 2nd Class commenced reading a 4th Standard Book find it rather too difficult at present. **Oct. 1** Find the children from Infant room backward in their arithmetic & Multiplication Tables. Make them learn one at home each evening. **3** Children from Infant room improve in their tables. Examined all the classes in Arithmetic.

Oct. 8 Received a Notice from the Diocesan Inspector of Schools that he will visit this School for Inspection on Friday Oct 24 next. **9** Made the above Notice public by reading it to the children also the Act of Parliament relating thereto.[62]

Oct. 13 Commenced working all the Standards in their work for the next Annual inspection Standard 3 do not do their Arithmetic (Compound Subtraction) to my satisfaction. Gave 1st & 2nd Standards an examination in Dictation. **17** Several children from the hill gone home to dinner & not returned in time for School.

Oct. 20 Gave 1st 2nd 3rd Standards a rub in mental Arithmetic. **24** Very cold frosty morning obliged to have fires in both rooms several children absent in consequence. Gave 1st Class a good drill in Mental Arithmetic. The Inspector for the Diocese of Oxford came this afternoon (prepared for him in the morning) and inspected the Schools was much pleased with the children said they answered very nicely; left at 4 O clock. The Revd Molyneux was present during part of the examination.

Oct. 27 Sharp Cold weather continues several of the children in Infant room absent in consequence. **30** Received the following report from the Revd E. Moore to enter in this Log Book:

---

[62] This referred to the provision of the 1870 Elementary Education Act that no child was to be compelled to attend 'any religious observance or any instruction in religious subjects in the school or elsewhere'. Rich, *The Education Act 1870*, p. 96.

Whitchurch Oct 24

Infants: The little ones answered nicely & intelligently in Religious Knowledge.

Mixed: The State of Religious Knowledge is good & there is a nice tone about the School. Arithmetic is very good & writing good. Singing also Satisfactory.

EDWARD BARBER General Inspector of Schools for the Diocese of Oxford

Nov. 3 A mild morning a greater number of children present than last week. **6** First Class did not please me in their Arithmetic today. Dictation in 2nd Class good.

Nov. 10 3rd Class improve in their Arithmetic they seem to know their Multiplication table correctly as far as 8 times.   **13** Revd Molyneux visited to day & heard first Class read.

Nov. 17 Fresh supply of Copy Books came to day have been short for some time.   **19** The upper school girls commence needlework time at one o'clock because it is too dark between 3 and 4 to see to do it neatly.   **20** The subject of the Object lesson in Infant room today was 'Cloves' some of the ch. gave very intelligent answers.

Nov. 24 Revd Molyneux visited today & heard 2nd Class read.   **27** A. C. Forbes Esqr visited today & heard a dictation lesson to 2nd Class. Sent a note to Mrs Bartlett for the school pence due for the childrens schooling.[63] Sent an enquiry card to Mrs Cook to know why Kate was absent last week.

Dec. 1 Full School in upper room only 2 Absent.   **4** Girls improve in their needlework.

Dec. 8 Revd Molyneux called & heard first & 3rd Class read.   **11** Very dark at 3½ gave the whole School Mental Arithmetic & drill to make up the time.

Dec. 15 Mild open weather much better attendance in Infant room than last week owing to the severe weather.   **18** Revd Molyneux called. First & third class did their Arithmetic very well & the Second Class Dictation was also good.

Dec. 24 Closed the Schools to day for Xmas holidays reopen on Monday, January 5, 1874.

1874

Jan. 5 Reopened the School to day fair attendance of children. A. C. Forbes Esqr & W. Fanning Esqr called & proposed next Saturday at 11 a.m. to Audit School a/c for the year 1873.   **9** Arranged all classes & gave them a good drill in their work for Wednesday next the Annual Inspection.

[63] This may have been Emma Bartlett, the wife of a journeyman blacksmith. The family had two children of school age — a boy aged about 7, and a girl aged 5 (1871 Census).

Jan. 12 Full school in upper room one boy only absent. Revd Molyneux called & heard the First Class [read] their lesson as per Time-Table. **14** H.M. Inspector & his assistant visited the school this day.[64] Two Girls, Martha Allwright and Emily Wells were disqualified & shut out from the examination on account of *Talking* or as H.M. Inspector said "not that he heard their voices but he saw their lips move." Louisa Cook was also disqualified for looking upon her neighbour's slate which slate was clean & without any writing upon it whatever. The examination was otherwise very satisfactory. Gave the children a half holiday.

Jan. 19 Propose giving the School children their Annual Treat of Tea & Cake. Full school in consequence. **23** Collected from the Inhabitants (principal) £5.5 to defray the expences of the above named Treat, which was given this day. A full holiday given. A Magic Lantern was afterwards given which delighted the children very much.

Jan. 26 Admitted several fresh children from off the hill. **29** The Whooping Cough seems to be making itself heard the children in the Infant room seem to have it very badly was obliged to stop in our work in consequence. Several children have stayed away on account of its violence.

Feb. 2 The Whooping Cough is spreading very much it is quite distressing to hear the little ones. **7** Received the report from the Educational office this morning.

H.M.s. Inspectors Report for 1873[65]
Mixed School: The general results are decidedly satisfactory. The only points calling for criticism are the rather moderate Reading of the first Standard, and the too common habit of talking with neighbours over the work.

Infant School: The Infant's [*sic*] School work has decidedly advanced this year; and is now generally very fair in results.

S. Wells and H. Bushnell having been returned last year as over six, were disqualified by age for further presentation under Article 19(B)1.[66]

Sarah N. Litchfield   Certificated Teacher 2nd Class
Thomas Litchfield   Cert. Teacher 3rd Class

[64] Inspector's assistants were appointed from 1863 as a result of the introduction of the Revised Code with its examination requirements. The assistants were recruited from the ranks of certificated elementary teachers and were strictly confined to routine examination work, under the overall jurisdiction of the inspector. By 1871 there were 28 Inspector's assistants working with the 73 full Inspectors, whose own background and training were very different from those of the assistants. See Hurt, *Education in Evolution*, p. 44 for a discussion of the post of Inspector's assistant.

[65] The Government grant received in 1874 amounted to £57 1s. (in respect of the previous year's academic work), of which Mr Litchfield was paid half — £20 10s. 6d. In 1873 the grant had amounted to only £36 18s. and Mr Litchfield had been paid one-third of this (School Accounts).

[66] Article 19(B)1 limited the age of infants to those 'above four and under seven'.

Feb. 12 Gave the 3rd Standard a good drill in long division they seem to have forgotten them owing to the preparation for inspection. The whole of the classes working in their fresh Standards do their work very fairly.

Feb. 16 Several children at home owing to the Whooping Cough. 3rd Class did their reading in Jarrolds 2nd Standard reader very well for the first time. **19** A. C. Forbes Esqr called & inspected the Report, Registers, &c. and paid the deficiency due to School a/c left after the Treat — 2/8½.

Feb. 23 Whooping cough still prevails. 1st & Third class did their work remarkably well this morning. **26** Revd Molyneux came this morning and stayed half an hour.

Mar. 2 Several children absent to day owing to bad weather and Whooping Cough. 2nd Class did their work in Arithmetic very fairly must give them an extra drill in Multiplication (compound) with the fractional part. **6** A. C. Forbes Esqr called and inspected the registers, and heard the 2nd Class read. Whooping Cough still prevails among the younger children.

Mar. 12 Heavy fall of snow this morning sent home what few children came no registers taken this day.

Mar. 16 First class have done their work to day very indifferently, very cold morning. Several children still absent owing to the cold and Whooping Cough.

Mar. 23 Whooping Cough getting better several children returned again to School. 3rd Class commenced writing their dictation on paper, very fairly done for a commencement. **26** First and third Class did their arithmetic very well. Revd R. Molyneux called & heard first class read.

Mar. 30 Alfred Cross was expelled from the School today for disobedience. Sent for his Father who refused to listen to reason & the matter must be referred to the School Managers.[67] **Apr. 2** Close the School this day for a weeks [sic] holiday being Easter week.

Apr. 13 Reopened School this morning several fresh children admitted, 9 in number. Some Children in Infant room work badly owing to their being absent & fresh children admitted. **16** The Managers have decided that an apology be made by Alfred Cross publicly befor[e] the whole School & that Mr F. Cross the Father is not to come again to the school to interrupt its working.

Apr. 20 Alfred Cross readmitted into the school weather very hot & the children seem idle and sleepy over their work. **23** Second Class did their dictation very fairly this morning. Sums also fairly done.

[67] Alfred Cross was the second son of Frederic Cross, the Whitchurch tailor, who employed three men (1871 Census). At this time, in 1874, Alfred was about eleven — an age when many country boys felt that they were ready for work and were impatient at the restraints of school.

Apr. 27 Gave the 3rd Class a good rub with their Arithmetic (short division) have given each one in that class to learn at home & repeat next morning a table multiplication and division. **30** Find the learning the Tables at home a good thing the arithmetic being done much better.

May 4 Full school several fresh children admitted   3rd Class have forgotten their subtraction sums.

May 11 First class have new books to read in Lauries 6th Book; they read in them very fairly.

May 18 2nd Class are working through Haywoods Arithmetical cards Standard 3 some of the questions are quaint but otherwise they are very good.

May 25 Whit Monday no school this week.

June 1 Several fresh children admitted in the Infant room another Teacher is necessary the Mistress has over an average of 60 per day. Several boys from the Upper room are gone to strip rods at Harts Lock.[68]

June 8 3rd Class have had a good drill in subtraction & can now do very well. Have commenced pence tables with them. 2nd & 1st Class are working their Arithmetic higher than the required standard.

June 15 A. C. Forbes Esqr called but stayed only a few minutes. He inspected the Registers & then left. Mentioned to him that another Teacher is required for the Infant room he said he would talk to the other Managers respecting it.

June 22 Nearly all the boys in Upper room have returned from Rod Stripping which has filled the schools. The Mistress had over 70 children present this morning. The Revd R. Molyneux called. A. C. Forbes called this morning respecting another Teacher for the Infant room.

June 29 Revd R. Molyneux called. Girls had their needlework after 4 O clock for 1 hour the Mistress having so many children could not attend to them during school hours. A. C. Forbes has written to H.M. Inspector respecting another Teacher. **July 2** Have given the 2nd & 3rd Standard their Arithmetic one Standard higher. First class read Lauries 6th Book remarkably well except Thomas Tayler.

---

[68] The rods were used in the basket making trade. See K. S. Woods, *The Rural Industries Round Oxford* (Oxford, 1921), p. 116 for a mention of osier beds in Berkshire and Oxfordshire. Richard Jefferies, *Hodge and His Masters* (London, 1966 ed.), ii, 42, describes the rod stripping process. The rods were first cut 'about Good Friday — that is, just before the leaf appears'. They were stacked upright in long trenches of water until the leaves began to appear. The rods were then carried to the 'brakes', which somewhat resembled very blunt scissors permanently fixed open at a certain angle. As a rod was pulled through the brake, the iron edges of the implement tore off the bark and left a white stick behind.

July 6 Full School over 70 children present in the Infant room. The Mistress obliged to take the needlework after 4 O'clock. **9** A. C. Forbes Esqr called & brought a letter from H.M. Inspector respecting a Pupil Teacher. The first class (Infants) are very dull it is hard work to move them in Reading and Arithmetic, with two or three exceptions. The whole class are extremely *thick headed.* **10** A. C. Forbes Esqr called again & it is decided to ask Martha Allwright to be the Pupil Teacher. Called upon Martha Allwright's Father last night & he was quite willing for Martha to become the Pupil Teacher & Martha herself is quite delighted with the idea.[69] She is to come on Monday next.

July 13 Martha Allwright commenced her duties as Pupil Teacher this morning. 3rd Class children read Laurie's 4th Book very fairly. They as a class do their work to my satisfaction.

July 20 Several boys from Upper room have gone into the Harvest field to help their parents. Owing to the hot weather the harvest has come on very quickly. A very hot day neither the Children nor Teachers were able to do their work satisfactorily. **22** A. C. Forbes Esqr called and inspected the registers & decided that the Harvest holidays commence at once, the Harvest being fully commenced & the children drawn off to help their parents in the fields. School closes today reopen August 24th.

Aug. 24 School closes for another week owing to the workmen not having completed the repairs.

Aug. 31 School reopened this morning some of the Agricultural boys still in the harvest field, a fuller school than was expected. **Sept. 3** Find the children have gone back in their Arithmetic during the holidays.

Sept. 7 Full School this morning. Revd E. Moore called to [see] the repairs done to school room, was pleased with the general working of the school, he also remarked how clean & respectable the girls were. **9** Revd R. Molyneux called & heard 2nd Class read. The whole of the classes have again picked up what they seem to have forgotten in their Arithmetic. Have commenced Geography with the 2nd Class.

Sept. 14 First and Third class did their work remarkably well today. **16** 2nd Class have had a good drilling in long division have given each a seperate [*sic*] sum & make them do their work standing it being easier to correct the work than when in the desks.

Sept. 21 Have worked Arithmetic the same as above with the 3rd Class and find a decided progress they have not such opportunities for copying as when the

---

[69] Martha Allwright was aged about thirteen and was the youngest child of Francis Allwright, a wood sawyer (1871 Census).

slates are lying upon the desks.   **23** 2nd & 3rd Class did their Arithmetic also their dictation very well today. 1st Class Geography was also very good.

Sept. 28 Full School to day over one hundred present Mary Anne Hutt returned after being absent 25 weeks. First & second class did their tables (Weights & Measures) very well today. 3rd Class improve in their tables. **Oct. 1** Wet day several children absent in consequence.

Oct. 5 Full School this morning 2nd Class did their Dictation to my satisfaction. 3rd Class after much sharp drilling seem now to understand the rule of simple division & the 1st Standard that of simple subtraction.   **8** A Truck load of Coals are at the Railway Station for School Detfield has agreed to cart them in first load came about 1 P.M. did not complete their job before 5 P.M.[70]

Oct. 12 I like the Arithmetic in the square class better than in the desks the 1st & 2nd Standards are making decided progress by it.   **15** Charles Ashby shows great tact [*sic*] for a boy of his age in Arithmetic he did the whole of the questions in Moffatt's cards No 17 and 24 Standard 6th without a single mistake & never applied to me for any information.

Oct. 22 Cold & wet this morning had a fire in the Infant room several of the little children came in quite wet, quite a laundry looking room.

Oct. 26 Full school this morning fine & pleasant. The Revd R. Molyneux purposes opening an evening class during the winter the lamps &c. for the purpose were in the way of the ordinary school work consequently I removed them.   **29** First Class did their work remarkably well this morning. School room so dark was unable to see the children's faces distinctly at 4 O clock.

Nov. 2 Have the children in school half an hour earlier leave at 3.45 P.M. am unable to see to do our work properly at 4 P.M. especially the girls at their needlework.   **5** The Diocesan Inspector visited the school this morning and examined the Upper room. The Infant room went on with their work as usual. A proper notice was not fixed in the Infant room and for that reason was not Inspected. I believe he was well satisfied with his examination.

Nov. 9 A. C. Forbes Esqr called & examined the registers. He said it would be necessary for me to appear at Bradfield on Tuesday 17th Inst to appeal against the Assessment Committee respecting the School premises which are assessed at £25.   **12** The girls have begun, and are making tolerable progress in their Examination needlework.

Nov. 16 Admitted two fresh scholars. First Class dictation was remarkably good. Revd R. Molyneux called & heard 2nd Class read 3rd Class did their arithmetic with great care and attention only 7 sums wrong out of a class of 18

---

[70] On 18 November a bill for £8 9s. 4d. was paid for coals to Mr Brancker (School Accounts).

with 6 sums each. The lads belonging to the night school have splashed ink upon the wall which looks very bad.

Nov. 23 2nd Class in their Arithmetic were not at all Satisfactory. 1st & 3rd Class dictation remarkably good.

Nov. 30 The weather has been cold and afternoons dark was unable to do our work with satisfaction towards 4 o'clock gave the children Muscle drill to warm them & amuse them.

Dec. 7 Weather very cold several children absent First Class worked with a good will.

Dec. 14 Fall of snow some of the younger children are unable to come from off the hill in consequence. The Girls have worked very industriously to finish their needlework before Christmas.

Dec. 21 More snow and very deep a thin school in consequence 2nd & 3rd Class worked their Arithmetic with satisfaction. **24** Closed the school to day for Christmas holidays. Reopen the school on January 4, 1875.

1875

Jan. 4 Reopened school this morning the snow has nearly all disappeared. A fair number of Scholars. **5** A. C. Forbes Esqr & the Ladies gave the Sunday School children a Treat of Tea & Cake &c &c Also a Christmas Tree loaded with valuable and useful . . .

[Jan. 6–Mar. 14: missing]

Mar. 15 . . . plan has never been made a grating with one pipe in the chalk is all that can be found.

Mar. 22 Have commenced Grammar & History lessons with 1st & 2nd Classes. The other working of the school is very good. The workmen have commenced making a cesspool for the Girls & Infants side today.[71] **25** Closed the school this afternoon to allow of the workmen coming to remove the small gallery in Infant room.[72]

Mar. 29 Easter Week a Holiday.

Apr. 5 Reopened School this morning admitted four fresh children. The small gallery in Infant room is removed & the large gallery made 2 steps less which give more room in the body of the school to arrange the classes for reading &c. &c.

[71] This work was presumably carried out by men employed by Robert Briant, the Whitchurch plumber, who was paid a total of £32 4s. for bills covering 1873, 1874 and 1875 (ibid.).
[72] James Holder, carpenter, was paid £7 5s. 3d. for 'altering gallery', and there was also a payment of £4 1s. 6d. to Mr Morris, the architect (ibid.).

Apr. 12 Have ordered two new desks from Windsor to give more sitting accommodation in the Infant room.[73] George Langford & his sister Grace have returned to School after an absence of nearly 5 months. General working of the school very fair. Miss Hills has entered on her duties as an Assistant mistress, was strange to her work last week but has done fairly well this week, & is a great help in the Mixed room the average being over 60 each day.[74]

Apr. 19 Revd E. Moore called to see the alterations made in the Infant room & also the drains.

Apr. 26 Miss Hills does not at present seem to understand School work. First and Third classes did their work remarkably well. 2nd and 4th Classes were rather thinly represented owing to the weather.

May 3 Several of the elder boys and girls are gone to the rod stripping. 2nd Class are backward in their Arithmetic especially long division.

May 10 A. C. Forbes Esqr called respecting the boys and Girls employed at the rod stripping I gave him a list of all that are absent.

May 17 Whitsun week no school.

May 24 Miss Hills (the assistant Mistress) has improved a little but she is far from satisfactory, her manners are too austere.

May 31 2nd Class have had a good drilling in long division & now they seem to understand it better 3rd Class improve in the arithmetic & are a far more intelligent class of children than the 2nd. **June 4** Miss Hills who now superintends the needlework manages fairly, but is somewhat deficient in method.

June 11 Several fresh children admitted the total number on the registers being 149. Weather stormy several of the younger children absent in consequence.

June 18 Stormy weather continues the numbers have fluctuated throughout the week. Gave Geography lesson to the 2nd & 3 classes. The older boys have obtained leave of absence to attend the hay harvest.

June 25 Bad weather still prevails numbers short in consequence. Have commenced 5th Standard work with 4th Standard children. Miss Hills gave a criticism lesson on Arithmetic, the result as follows   Order Fair Discipline and Method deficient. The outline of the lesson was not made sufficiently clear. A fuller explanation respecting the value and order of the numbers is required, not

---

[73] The new desks cost £6 1s. (ibid.).
[74] Elizabeth Hills remained only to July; on 5 July she was paid £5 4s 11d. as her salary up to that date (ibid.).

a mere mechanical repetition after the Teacher. The order and discipline of a class is of great importance as unless attention is secured the object of the entire lesson is wasted. Method (in eliciting by questions the knowledge already possessed by the children of the subject) is not fully nor [sic] fairly obtained.

July 2 Revd R. Molyneux called this week twice. The 4th Standard children are doing 5th Standard work very fairly.

July 9 Miss Hills received her money from the Revd E. Moore with a hint to send in her resignation at the month's end as she did not seem likely to suit. Came the following day as usual, but has not been since.

July 16 A. C. Forbes Esqr informed me that Miss Hills had written to him to ask why they wished her to resign? He told me that as she had absented herself without permission no notice would be taken of her communication.

July 23 Hay harvest is over several Boys who have been employed have returned to School; numbers in the Infant room have been very irregular owing to the heavy rains.

July 30 School closes to day for a Month. Harvest Holidays.

Sept. 6 School reopened this morning, the harvest not finished several children absent in consequence.   **10** Find the children have gone back during the holidays they are not so well up in their work as before them.

Sept. 17 Several absent ones have come in, the harvest being now over. Commenced needlework for the inspection. Sent for 'Standard Needlework Book' as a guide in cutting out &c.

Sept. 24 School very full, no Assistant Mistress can be found in the neighbourhood Monitors not sufficient help for the work.

Oct. 1 Drafted several children from the Infant to the upper room, work very heavy for one teacher.

Oct. 8 Weather very wet several children absent in consequence. The first Class have finished their Geography lessons (as dictation) & will now each week learn a piece & repeat by rote.

Oct. 15 Find the home lessons in Geography improve the childrens minds & they have a more correct knowledge of the places they read of by hearing their parents talk of them.

Oct. 22 Heavy rains caused several children from off the hill to be absent. 3rd & 2nd Class dictation this week has been decidedly better The Arithmetic also is better. Received notices from the Diocesan Inspector that he will visit these Schools on Friday Novr 5, which notices I have put up in the school.

Oct. 29 Was compelled to go to London on business holiday was given in consequence. First & 3rd Classes have done their work this week very creditably 2nd Class improve in their writing heavy rains have caused several Infants from the hill to be absent. The Managers have decided to have a new Time Table for the Upper room have written for one to come by post.

Nov. 5 New Time Table arrived on Wednesday forwarded the same to the Managers for H.M. Inspector's signature. Received the New Time Table signed by H.M. Inspector on Thursday. The Diocesan Inspector called to day (Friday) & examined both rooms & expressed himself satisfied with the ready answers of the children to his questions. Out of 81 sums given to 2 & 3rd Class only 3 were wrong half holiday given this afternoon.

Nov. 12 On Monday the New Time Table was used for the first time. Revd E. Molyneux examined the Time Table & approved of it.

Nov. 19 Third Class unusually large nearly 30 children in it. Another Teacher is wanted to take this part of the work. First & 2nd Class do their work remarkably well.

Nov. 26 Have assembled the children at 1.30 P.M. owing to the darkness at 4 O clock, am unable to see the childrens [*sic*] faces at that time.

Dec. 3 Find the half hour earlier a decided advantage for the Girls at Needlework. Full school. Heavy work for one Teacher. Weather cold. Attendance in Infant Room good. Preparing for Inspection. School songs only fairly rendered the stronger voices have gone up into the other room.

Dec. 10 Deep Snow several children from off the hill absent in consequence. A. C. Forbes Esqr called and inspected the Registers.

Dec. 17 Gave 1st and 2nd Class an examination test the work on the whole was satisfactory. Weather dark and dull.

Dec. 23 School closed to day for the Christmas holidays. School to re-open on January 3.

1876

Jan. 3 School opened to day fair attendance weather dark and dull.

Jan. 8 Wrote to the employers of children who have boys at work & completed the required number of attendances to send the same boys to School to prepare for H.M. Inspector's visit on Jany 26th. Gave each class in the school an examination test, work on the whole fair.

Jan. 15 Very full school this week over 60 present in upper room. Examined each class seperately [*sic*] in their work for the examination, results better than last week.

Jan. 22 Examined each class again this week & find the test papers good for the children, as it accustoms them to work for the day of inspection. Very full school, weather mild. The girls have completed their needlework. Two or three absentees have had to work every afternoon for the past week to finish theirs in time.

Jan. 29 H.M. Inspector visited the Schools on Wednesday & expressed himself satisfied with the general working of the school. It being the Annual inspection half holiday given on that day.

Feb. 4 Arranged the classes for their new standards 1st Class did their work remarkably well 2nd & 3rd Classes fairly. A. C. Forbes Esqr called respecting an Assistant Mistress. Miss Higgs has been appointed will commence her duties on Monday next.[75]

Feb. 11 Miss Higgs the Assistant mistress came on Monday. She appears to understand her work thoroughly. She manages the needlework nicely and keeps the girls in order.

Feb. 18 The classes generally improve in their fresh standard work. Sent H.M. Inspector a list of Recitation pieces for approval, also a scheme for needlework as a special subject.

Feb. 25 The first class have commenced learning their recitation pieces. The Government report has been received, but is still in the hands of the Managers.

Mar. 2 Received the report of H.M. Inspector from the Managers this evening:

17a Mixed School[76] The general school progress for the year is very satisfactory; and the children are very orderly and interested in their work. The needlework too (the ages of the children being carefully remembered) gives me entire satisfaction.

Infants' School: This Infants' School has decidedly improved this year, and is in very fair practical working order.

The average attendance in the Infants' School has, notwithstanding last years warning, been allowed to exceed by two the limit prescribed by Article 17(c), and my Lords have felt great doubts in consequence whether they are justified in

---

[75] Miss E. Higgs remained at the school for over a year; according to a receipt for 3 Apr. 1877, she was paid at the rate of £40 per annum when she left in the summer of that year.
[76] '17a' in margin.

paying the grant.[77] They hope it will be clearly understood that the above Article will have to be strictly enforced in future.

Thomas Litchfield   Cert. Teacher 3rd Class
Sarah Nash Litchfield   Certificated Teacher 2d Class

The work done by the classes in their fresh standards is fairly satisfactory.

Mar. 10 Weather wet and cold several children absent in consequence. A. C. Forbes Esqr called & examined the registers.

Mar. 17 Third class children have done well in their Arithmetic this week. 4th Class are dull with theirs, but know their Multiplication tables better, each one having a table to say every morning as a home lesson.

Mar. 24 1st and second classes did fairly well in their Arithmetic & only fair in dictation. The home lessons in Geography & Poetry brighten their memory.

Mar. 31 First class have now learned 100 lines of poetry & repeat it round the class one line each from memory.

Apr. 7 A. C. Forbes Esqr called to day & inspected the registers. First class Arithmetic (Proportion Simple) was fairly done other lessons better than last week. 4th Class did their Arithmetic very fairly.

Apr. 14 Admitted 2 fresh children. The Scarlet fever having broken out upon the hill several children are absent in consequence. Two more families have it very badly.

Apr. 21 Easter week no school.

Apr. 28 Scarlet Fever still raging upon the hill. A. C. Forbes Esqr called & remarked upon the small number present, owing to the rod stripping having commenced, & the scarlet fever being in several houses. Revd W. Richardson of Leicestershire visited with A. C. Forbes Esqr.

May 4 Several children absent owing to the rod stripping & Scarlet Fever.

May 11 Numbers have not improved much this week, work in school fairly done.

May 18 General working of the school fairly satisfactory, nothing of importance to record.

May 25 Received from H.M. Inspector notice of approval of the needlework

---

[77] Article 17(c) laid down that the school premises were to be 'healthy, well lighted, drained, and ventilated, properly furnished, supplied with suitable offices'; under the 1871 version of the Code each child must also have at least 8 square feet of area.

Scheme and Recitation pieces, which were desired to be clearly entered in the School Log-book.

Scheme for Needlework

1. The *time*. Each class 3 hours per week.

2. The *Teachers*. The Infant's [*sic*] and Assist. Mistresses.

3. The *Classification*. I. Standard I Class IV Sewing, felling and hemming. Children to fold hems themselves.

II. Standard II Class III Sewing, hemming, marking on canvass, [*sic*] stitching, and patch. Ch. to fold hems and seams themselves.

III. Standard III. Class II To run and fell hem and sew, mark on stuff, patch, gathering, coarse darning and knitting. Ch. fold hems and seams.

IV. Standards IV & V — Class I Same as before with finer darning, herring-boning, button-holes and to hem and whip frills, also knitting.

V. Standard IV. To cut out garments on paper. Standard V. To cut out garments in calico and make up the same.

VI. Ch. to fix all but the most difficult parts of the work.

Pieces for recitation as approved are as follows.

The Village Blacksmith — Longfellow
John Gilpin's ride to Ware — Cowper
The Charge of the Light Brigade — Tennyson

Rod stripping still prevents many from attending. Nothing further to remark for the week.

June 2 Many children absent rod stripping not yet finished. First class did well in their Arithmetic. Third class have commenced Long division. A. C. Forbes Esqr visited & examined the registers.

June 9 Whitsun week no school.

June 16 Several fresh cases of Scarlet Fever this week several children absent in consequence; rod stripping not yet finished numbers have been small the whole week. The 1st & 2d Class girls commenced knitting, as the time for needlework is short, they have it for a home lesson.

June 23 General working of the classes very satisfactory.

June 30 Fresh case of Scarlet Fever reported. Arithmetic of First Class remarkably good.

July 7 Rod Stripping is finished several boys returned to School who have been so employed.

July 14 Weather severly [*sic*] Hot Teachers & children have not much ener[g]y for their work. Scarlet Fever still raging. Work in third and fourth classes fair. The Rod Stripping children are much behind those who have attended regularly.

July 21 Weather still very hot several boys are absent owing to the haymaking. Full school in Infant room. The girls in the upper classes have discontinued knitting for the present, their damp hands have made the needles too rusty for use. Other kinds of needlework progress slowly this hot weather.

July 28 Hot weather still continues, nothing has occured [*sic*] during the week worth recording.

Aug. 4 Hot weather still continu[e]s, School closed yesterday for the Harvest holidays re-open again on Sepr 4th.

Sept. 4 Reopened the School this morning, numbers thin. Harvest not yet finished.   **8** Several children returned on Tuesday, full school the rest of the week. Work rather dull, the holidays have made the children rather rusty. Hope to have a better record next week.

Sept. 15 Much better attendance this week all the classes have done their work very satisfactorily.

Sept. 22 Admitted several fresh children   the general working of the school is much improved.   A. C. Forbes Esqr called and inspected the registers.

Sept. 29 A. C. Forbes Esqr called to say he had ordered a Truck load of Coals for the use of the Schools. Very full school several children presented themselves who have been absent several months.

Oct. 6 Have commenced the afternoon work half an hour earlier for the winter season, many of the children have a long way to go home & at the usual time it is dark before they leave the school, very ful[l] school. Girls in 1st & 2d classes have recommenced knitting as a home lesson. Some have begun their specimen work for inspection.

Oct. 13 Very full school this week admitted two fresh children. The general work of the school has been fairly satisfactory.

Oct. 20 3rd Class have been careless in their arithmetic have kept several after school hours to work after the others were gone home. Work in 1st & 2nd Classes, creditable. Girls in Standard V have cut out an apron with bib to make up for inspection. The others are progressing fairly.

Oct. 27 Nothing of any importance worth recording.

Nov. 3 Full school, admitted several fresh children weather cold and frosty, no grate or stove in Infant room to warm the place, constructed a temporary one from the old stove which answers the purpose very well. The 1st & 2nd Class girls are now doing their knitting nicely. It is a home lesson still as there is no time for it in School hours.   **7** The Infant's [*sic*] mistress has gone to visit the Schools of St Stephens [*sic*] Reading to see their method.

Nov. 10 Weather bad several children absent in consequence; general working of the school fairly satisfactory.

Nov. 17 All classes have done their work this week with satisfaction. Wet weather continues attendance in Infant room short in consequence.

Nov. 24 Received a notice that Diocesan Inspector wishes to visit the Infant room on Tuesday December 12th which notice has been publicly posted in the Infant School-room. General working of the school very fair.

Dec. 1 Wet weather still continues many children from the Infant room absent. Several girls in Standards I, II & III have completed their needlework specimens.

Dec. 8 Geography in standards III, IV, V very satisfactory. Nothing of Importance to note this week.

Dec. 12 Diocesan Inspector expected this morning but did not come. **13** Diocesan Inspector visited this morning, examined the Infant room was much pleased with the ready and intelligent answers of the children, heard the children sing in upper room after 12 O clock. Half holiday given in consequence.

Dec. 22 General working of the school satisfactory. All the girls, (but those who have been absent from needlework) have finished their specimens. School closes to day for the Christmas holidays; reopen Jany 1 — 1877.

1877
Jan. 5 Received notice that H.M. Inspector will visit these schools Feby 1st.

Jan. 12 Gave the upper standards an extra drill in their Geography. Received an order by Post that H.M. Inspector has changed the date of Inspection to Jany 24th instead of Feby 1st.

Jan. 19 Examined all standards in their work as a test before the Annual Inspection which takes place next Wednesday.

Jan. 24 H.M. Inspector visited the Schools this morning. Holiday in the afternoon.

Feb. 2 Commenced the Standard work for the year   fair for a beginning.

Feb. 9 Standard 5th seem staggered with the fresh work especially in the Arithmetic.

Feb. 16 Standard 5th get on better this week the other standards generally fair.

Feb. 19 Received H.M. Inspectors report.

Report

This is a fairly good rural school. The Standard work generally very fair, and Sewing good and advanced for the ages of the girls. Geography is fair, but History is of worth.

My Lords cannot regard the conditions of Article 19(B) 1,c[78] as being satisfied since it appears that seven or eight children over seven years old taught in the Infant School, have had their attendances counted on Form IX as in the Mixed School, and that the Infant's Mistress leaves her Infants to the Assistant every afternoon and acts as sempstress in the mixed school.

Feb. 26 General working of the Standards fairly satisfactory. **Mar. 2** Two fresh registers ordered as requested by H.M.I to classify the standards.

Mar. 9 Admitted several fresh children in the Infant room. The general working of the school very satisfactory.

Mar. 16 Miss Higgs the assistant mistress has tendered her resignation, and accepted by the Managers.

Mar. 23 Standards 3rd 4th 5th have improved in their Grammar lessons, which are given as home lessons.

Mar. 30 School closes to day for the Easter Holidays reopens on Monday April 9th. General working of the standards fairly satisfactory.

Apr. 10 A whole day's holiday was given to celebrate the wedding of Miss Beacher of the Rectory. Cake, Tea, and Oranges were given to the whole school at 3 o'clock P.M.   **13** School work during the week has been fairly satisfactory.

Apr. 20 1st Class improve in their Grammar lessons. Dictation & Arithmetic in lower Classes slovenly done.

Apr. 27 Application has been made to admit several boys from the Goring Heath School. The lower classes have done their work this week very creditably.

May 4 Admitted 6 Boys from the Goring Heath School, 5 of them are not sufficiently up in their work, although over 7 years of age to be in the upper room.[79] They are therefore classed with the Infants for the present.

[78] There was no such provision in the Code, and Article 19(B)1, a, was probably meant. This allowed the payment of 8s. per child for the infants, provided they were 'taught as a *class* . . . suitably to their age . . .' See, for example, the Code for 1877.

[79] Goring Heath was a small village about two miles distant from Whitchurch. Its endowed school owed its existence to the charity of Henry Allnutt (d. 1724). In 1877 a new school was built to cater for 75 boys, with a house for the headmaster, while the old school premises

May 11 The Assistant Mistress has superintended the needlework since the Inspection. Additional bags have been made and every thing seems to be satisfactory. The boys from Goring Heath have with the exception of three been put in the lowest class. The others can do 1st class work very well.

May 18 Admitted two other boys from Goring Heath School. They also for the present are put in the Infant room. Several boys and Girls have gone to work Rod Stripping. Have informed the foreman that the children have not made sufficient number of times nor passed the proper standard to have a certificate for work.[80]

May 25 Whitsun Holidays   school closes for the week.

June 1 Miss Higgs resigns her post as Assistant Mistress to day. Miss Elliott from High Cross Herts. has been appointed her successor, and will commence her duties on Monday next.[81]

June 8 Miss Elliott seems to be very well qualified to fill the post as Assistant Mistress. General working of the school satisfactory.

June 15 The following Recitation pieces have been (this week) accepted by H.M. Inspector & ordered to [be] entered here in this Log Book

Lucy Gray	(by Wordsworth)	56 lines
The Jackdaw	do. Cowper	36 lines
Actions not words	do. Cowper	28 do.
The Battle of Blenheim	do. Southey	66 do.

June 22 First and third classes have done remarkably well in their Arithmetic this week, other classes fairly.

June 29 The School Attendance committee have supplied a book of notices to be sent to parents who neglect to send their children to school.[82] I have sent out

[80] Under the 1876 Education Act, children aged between ten and twelve, who had not passed their 'labour certificate' — usually the fourth Standard — were to make at least 250 attendances before they were allowed to work. Those from twelve to fourteen were required to make at least 150 attendances per annum before commencing work.

[81] Miss Rosa Elliott was paid at the rate of £40 per annum.

[82] School attendance committees (for which see Introduction, p. xxxiv) were established under the 1876 Education Act to cover those areas which were without a school board. Whitchurch was under the jurisdiction of the Bradfield School Attendance Committee. Parents who failed to send their children to school could be fined, but it was not until July and October 1878 that the Bradfield Committee began to prosecute offenders from Whitchurch. See below, p. 64 (entries for 5 and 19 July 1878) and also p. 65, n. 88 (entry for 10 Oct. 1878).

were converted into a girls' school. Two years later an infants' school was established. (G. E. B. Rogers, *History of the Goring Heath Charities* (privately published, 1928), p. 19; *Kelly's Dir. Oxon.* (1895), p. 99).

this week 12 of them to the parents whose children are absent and working at the rod-stripping.

July 6 Miss Elliott has gone to Hockerell [*sic*] college for examination.[83] no Needlework can be done this week in consequence.

July 13 Several children have come back to school from the rod-stripping the notices aforesaid have frightened the parents; some however are still at work and defy the authorities to do their worst.

July 20 The Grammar of Standard II on examination is unsatisfactory there is a want of intelligent discrimination between one part of speech and another. The first hour for needlework on Wednesday afternoon will for the present be devoted by this Standard to Grammar.

July 27 F. Willan Esq. called on Monday and examined the accounts. The general working of the school is satisfactory.

Aug. 3 The school closes to day for the Harvest holidays to reassemble on Septr 3d.

Sept. 3 Another weeks's holiday is given as the majority of the children are at work in the fields. The continued rains having delayed the Harvest.

Sept. 10 Reopened School this week many children absent owing to the harvest work not being completed.

Sept. 17 Received the following circular from A. C. Forbes Esqr sent to him by H.M. Inspector

1st *Always* mark Registers at exact time appointed however small the numbers.

2nd *Never* leave a *blank* whether for presence or absence.

3rd *Never* make a *knife* erasure.

4th *Always* enter in *ink* at the time of calling Registers in each Register the number present.

5th *Always* cancel in ink the mark for any child who may leave before the 2 hours are up altering the ink totals accordingly.

6th *Always* note on an attendance slate hung on the wall the number present *finding this number* by *yourself counting* heads.

7th *Always* compare the totals shewn by Registers with this slate total.

8th Copy this Memd. in Log Book.

C. D. DU PORT HMI per T.W.P.

Reading Sepr /77.

---

[83] Hockerill College was a Church of England teacher training college for women at Bishops Stortford, Herts.

Sept. 24 The greater number of the children have returned to school although the harvest work is not yet completed. General working of the School fairly satisfactory.

Oct. 1 The School Attendance committee have furnished us with forms to send to Parents whose children are absent. **5** Have sent out the above notices to the parents whose children are absent.

Oct. 12 Several children who have been absent are again present owing no doubt to the notices having been sent.

Oct. 19 Received two notices respecting the Diocesan Inspector's visit fixed for November 5th which notices have been duly posted in the Schools.

Oct. 26 General working of the School satisfactory.

Nov. 2 Have given notice to the children that the afternoon meeting of the School for winter months will commence at 1-30 instead of 2 o'clock. **5** The Diocesan Inspector visited the schools to day & was much pleased with the work done by the children. Four prizes have been awarded to the most intelligent children, two for each room.

Nov. 9 The girls are progressing with their needlework in a fairly satisfactory manner.

Nov. 16 General working of the school satisfactory. A full school, the Warnings furnished by the School Attendance Committee have had a decided effect upon the Parents.

Nov. 23 Miss Elliott Assistant Mistress has tendered her resignation, her term here will cease on Friday December 21st. She obtained a Scholarship in July & has been admitted into Hockrerl [*sic*] College.

Nov. 30 The afternoons are very dark & the children have some difficulty with their work especially the needlework.

Dec. 7 A. C. Forbes Esqr visited the Schools this week, was much pleased with the order and discipline. General working of the Schools during the week satisfactory.

Dec. 14 Nothing of importance worth recording.

Dec. 21 School closes this week for the Xmas holidays, reopen again on Monday Decr 31. Miss Elliott resigns her situation as Assistant Mistress to day. The general working of the school during the week fairly satisfactory. Miss Adah Prestoe has been appointed as successor to Miss Rosa Elliott.

Dec. 30 Xmas Holidays extend to the 30th. **31** School reopens this morning. Miss Adah Prestoe commences her duties as Assistant Mistress. **Jan. 4** Most of the girls have finished their needlework for the Inspection. A few who attend badly are still working at theirs.

1878

Jan. 11 Miss Prestoe seems well qualified to fill the office of Assistant Mistress Fair attendance several children absent from Colds.

Jan. 18 Have made enquiries respecting the *Child's Book* but at present have received no answer; it is understood that no child can now be admitted without one.[84]

Jan. 25 The Managers of the School met on the 19th to Audit the Accounts, & inspect the Registers for the past year. The School Attendance officer called this week, & took the names of all children who had not made 75 attendances during the past quarter.

Jan. 30 H.M. Inspector visited the school for the Annual Inspection & expressed himself satisfied with the general working of the whole School.

Feb. 7 Commenced working the classes in their fresh standards, the work on the whole fairly good.

Feb. 14 Admitted several fresh children but not without the Government School Book.

Feb. 22 Drafted 13 children from the Infant to the upper room this week, have 145 on the registers being 3 more than the School will accomodate [*sic*].

Feb. 25 Received the Report of H.M. Inspectors visit.

Whitchurch Parl. School Oxford
I am highly satisfied with this School in all points.[85] The Children are being thoroughly well grounded and their intelligence and interest are being well drawn out. The discipline is good. The Infants are making on the whole pretty good progress.

---

[84] Article 19, B(6) of the 1877 Code stated that under Section 24 of the Education Act 1876, regulations had been made that a 'child's school book' must be 'deposited with the teacher, in proof of age, *by every child admitted to a school after the 1st January 1878*'. For a specimen reproduction of the book (or Form No. 150 of the Education Department) see document 15 in *Education Act 1870*, issued by the Department of Education and Science in 1970. The book contained details of the child's date of birth, annual attendances and academic progress; it was phased out in 1882.
[85] '17a' in margin.

A. Prestoe is recognized as qualified under Article 32(c) — 13[86]
Thomas Litchfield   Master
Sarah N. Litchfield   Mistress
Ada Prestoe   Assistant
The following school songs were sung at the last annual Inspection   I walked and I walked. The Little wrens. Oh stay your hand. An April Song. The Seasons. Spring Time. My Father was a Farmer.

Mar. 4 General working of the school in the fresh standards fairly satisfactory. Three boys who have been employed contrary to the Act of 1876 have been forced into the school & to attend regularly so that they may receive a certificate to go to work. **8** First class standard 5th do their arithmetic remarkably well.

Mar. 15 Have received several certificates of Births from the Registrar & have entered the same in the childrens [sic] School Books.

Mar. 22 Nothing worthy of recording this week.

Mar. 29 A. C. Forbes Esqr has taken the post of Correspondent & Manager to the schools vacated by F. Willan Esqr.

Apr. 5 The Standards have worked well this week. The Geography being very well done.

Apr. 12 The Infants have lessons in needlework in their own room superintended by a monitor under the direction of Miss Prestoe the assistant mistress.

Apr. 19 Several boys have gone to work rod-stripping have made the School Attendance committe[e] acquainted with the matter. School closes to[day] for the Easter Holidays reopen on Monday April 29th.

Apr. 29 School reopened this morning   general working of the School satisfactory.

May 6 A. C. Forbes Esqr called & examined the registers respecting George Kent having a certificate to go to work having passed his 3rd Standard & attended over 250 times in the years 1876 and 1877.

May 13 School children received their prizes, nothing worth recording.

---

[86] Article 32(c) related to the employment of an Assistant Mistress, and Article 13 to the fact that if an Assistant Mistress withdrew during the course of the school year she could be replaced by another Assistant. Normally such Assistants would be ex-pupil teachers, who had 'completed their engagement with credit', but in 1875 a new 'supplementary' category was introduced, especially for Infants, which was without any formal training requirements. See Sellman, p. 83.

May 20 A. C. Forbes Esqr called respecting the employment of children (Rod Stripping) general working of the school satisfactory. **24** Sent a special notice to the Bradfield School Attendance committee respecting the children being employed Rod Stripping over 20 children being absent & at work some of them under 7 years of age.

May 31 The Geography and Grammar in Standards 3, 4 and 5 have been remarkably good other work satisfactory.

June 7 Nothing worth recording during the week School closes to day for the Whitsun week, reopen again on Monday June 17th. School managers meeting tomorrow at 10 A.M.

June 21 School Attendance Officer called respecting children who had not attended proper number of times during the last quarter 3 were ordered to attend & two have complied. Compulsion will be enforced upon the other. General working of the school Fair.

June 28 Nothing worth recording.

July 5 Attendance officer called to say that a Summons is to be taken out against Lewenden for not sending his son Charles regularly to School.[87] The girls in the upper school have now practised all the different stitches required in their Standards except herringboning. School managers meeting tomorrow.

July 12 Nothing worth recording.

July 19 Yesterday the Master was required to attend the Magistrates meeting at Henley to prove the Registers for the prosecution of Thomas Lewenden, for neglecting to send his son Charles Lewenden to School. The Bench fined him 5/– but afterwards forgave him, he having promised to send his son Charles regularly to school.

July 26 School work as usual the harvest has commenced in several places.

Aug. 2 The harvest has become general. School closes this day for a month, re-open on September 2 1878.

Sept. 2 Harvest not finished, another week being granted the children, to help the ingathering.

Sept. 9 Harvest nearly finished, several children still absent. **11** A. C. Forbes Esqr gave the whole of the children a treat. All over 6 years of age were taken by train to Reading, to visit the circus. The whole passed off without the

[87] Charles Lewenden, aged about twelve, was the third son of Thomas Lewenden, a garden labourer (1871 Census).

slightest hitch. The younger ones were entertained by Mrs Forbes in the grounds belonging to the house. **13** The Attendance Officer called respecting the absent children, notices having been sent to eleven different families.

Sept. 20 Full School this week. Harvest work finished, admitted 3 fresh children. General working of the school satisfactory. Mrs Busk of Coombe wishes to give two prizes to Standards IV and V for best needlework. The work to be done on finer calico with fine red cotton. *Shape* part of shirt sleeve. As the time for needlework is limited it is proposed to make the same specimens part of the work submitted to H.M. Inspector.

Sept. 24 Received a reply from H.M. Inspector, accepting the two pieces for recitation (viz.) The Brook 52 lines, by Tennyson also Amphion 80 lines by Tennyson. A. C. Forbes Esqr called and inspected the Registers. **27** The Attendance officer called & examined the Registers respecting the Attendance of ten children whose parents have received a summons to appear at Henley next Thursday.[88]

Oct. 4 Nothing worth recording. School work satisfactory.

Oct. 8 The Revd E. Barber called to day to examine the school in Religious Knowledge. The following is the report

Whitchurch

Infant Department. The little ones are carefully taught & answered nicely in Religious Subjects.

Mixed. Religious Knowledge generally is Satisfactory & the children in each class as a whole answered very fairly. Writing is good & Singing very good.

Emma Burgess (Prize)   Annie Brown (Commended)

EDWARD BARBER General Inspector of Schools for the Diocese of Oxford

11 A half holiday was given on Tuesday last after the Inspection as recorded above, general working of the School Satisfactory.

Oct. 18 Owing to the evenings being too dark to carry on School work the School opens on Monday next at 1-30 instead of 2 P.M. Nothing worth recording.

Oct. 25 The Attendance officer called again to inspect the Registers, the Parents of several Children have received notices respecting the irregular attendance of their children The dictation & Arithmetic of the upper standards is good. The Geography on the whole fairly done this week.

---

[88] On 10 Oct. 1878, four parents from Whitchurch were charged with neglecting to send their children to school. In each case an Order was made by the Henley bench, requiring them to send the children to Whitchurch school. However, three of the offenders — Joseph Bartlett, a journeyman blacksmith, James Wallis, a bricklayer's labourer, and Thomas Tyrrell (or Tyrell), an agricultural labourer — continued to transgress and again appeared before the Henley bench in March 1879 (Henley Petty Sessions Minute Book, Bodl. MS. D.D. Henley A.XVI. 10).

Nov. 1 The Standard needlework for inspection is progressing satisfactorily. Some girls have finished their knitting.

Nov. 8 Nothing worth recording.

Nov. 15 The standards have done their work fairly satisfactory [*sic*].

Nov. 22 The School Attendance officer called respecting the children who have not made the proper number of times the last quarter (viz.) 50.

Nov. 29 Received notices respecting H.M. Inspectors visit on Friday Jany 17th at 9.30 A.M.

Dec. 6 Attendance officer called again respecting those children who have not made the required number of times.

Dec. 6 General working of the school fairly good. Geography in 4th Standard very good. Grammar fair. The other standards fair.

Dec. 13 Received notice altering the date of H.M. Inspector's visit (viz.) Wednesday Jany 15th at 1.20 P.M. for Infants & Standard work. The 17th to remain as first noticed for the remainder of the Examination.

Dec. 20 The girls of the various Standards are working hard to finish their needlework specimens. A few have completed theirs.

Dec. 27 Xmas week School closed.

1879
Jan. 4 A. C. Forbes Esqr called & inspected the registers. Received a Post Card from the publishers of Jarrold's Registers stating that they are out of Registers ordered for the New Year, will forward them by post as soon as they are ready. Have made a temporary register for the remainder of the week ending January 4th 79 — & on to the end of the quarter, March 25/79 if needed.

Jan. 11 The Managers of this school met this week to examine and Audit the accounts, a balance in hand of £7.7.7 was voted to the purchase of a new stove, for the infant room, the present one not being large enough to warm the room properly. Several children absent owing to the severe weather & sickness.

Jan. 18 H.M. Inspector visited the school on Wednesday afternoon last & seemed much pleased with all he saw, Mr Pearce H.M. Inspectors assistant visited on Friday morning & completed the work of examination   the work passed off remarkably well. Gave the children a half holiday.

Jan. 25 Commenced working the classes in their new Standard work, work fairly done for the first time.

Feb. 1 The children on the whole are making fair progress in their new Standard work.

Feb. 7 Miss Prestoe the Assistant mistress was unable to attend the school yesterday owing to a severe cold wet weather has prevented many of the children from Attending.

Feb. 14 Miss Prestoe is still unable to do her work here, is now confined to her bed. Received H.M. Inspector's report this morning which is here entered

Whitchurch Parochial School, Oxford
The Senior school gives me thorough satisfaction all round. In the Infants room there are signs of pains, and there has been some very fair progress, but there is not enough precision or thoroughness about the work, with closer and more accurate class work there would be many less cases of old but ignorant children.
Thomas Litchfield   Ct. Master
Sarah N. Litchfield   Ct. Mistress
Adah Prestoe   Assistant Mistress

ALEXANDER C. FORBES   Manager

Feb. 21 General working of the school satisfactory.

Feb. 28 Attendance officer called respecting children not having made proper number of Attendances.

Mar. 7 Nothing worth recording.

Mar. 14 Attendance officer called respecting the non attendance of children, he having requested by the sanction of the managers that I attend the Bench at Henley went Thursday to prove the registers.[89]

Mar. 25 Have tendered my resignation jointly with my wife to the managers of this school that our duties as School-master & School mistress terminate 3 months from this date (viz.) June 24 — 1878 [*sic*].[90]

THOMAS LITCHFIELD

Mar. 28 A days holiday was given on Thursday last owing to my having to attend at Henley to prove the school registers respecting Tyrells and Wallis's children. Wallis was fined 1s. each child and another order was made upon Tyrell.[91]

[89] Joseph Bartlett and Thomas Tyrell (or Tyrrell) were charged on 13 Mar. 1879 with failing to send their children to school. In each instance the case was allowed 'to stand over', with the parents promising to send their children to school in future (ibid.). See below, p. 73, n. 94, and p. 77, n. 97.
[90] The posts were advertised in *The Schoolmaster* on 5 Apr. 1879, at a joint salary of £100 and 'half the Grant', plus 'House and firing'. The 'Last Grant' was put at £99. An Assistant Teacher and a Monitor were also to be employed.
[91] James Wallis was fined 1s. for each of his three children by the Henley bench and was 'allowed a week to pay' (Bodl. MS. D.D. Henley A.xvi, 10, entry for 27 Mar. 1879).

Apr. 4 General working of the school satisfactory.

Apr. 11 Nothing worth recording.

Apr. 18 Easter week (holiday).

Apr. 25 Several children have gone to the rod-stripping, the Attendance officer called respecting them.

May 2 Notice has been given to the Parents and children that proceedings will be taken (without further warning) if they continue to go to the rod stripping.

May 9 The whole of the children who were absent at the rod-stripping have returned to school. General working of the School satisfactory.

May 16 A great number of children especially the Infants are absent, being ill with Measles.

May 23 The Measles continue to spread nearly 50 children being absent in consequence.

May 30 Many children have returned to school who had been absent with Measles.

June 6 General working of the school very satisfactory. The Attendance officer called, no complaints.

June 13 All children have returned to school who had been absent through Measles. Very full school. Standard work throughout the school satisfactory.

June 20 We the undersigned certificated Teachers terminate our duties as Master and Mistress of this Whitchurch School today June 24th 1879.
          THOMAS LITCHFIELD   Master   SARAH NASH LITCHFIELD   Mistress

Mr & Mrs Winchester commenced duties as Master & Mistress of this School.

July 7 I find very many of the children have been placed in their wrong Standard. 9 names, which ought to have been on the 1st Std Register, were entered as under 7 years of age on the Register of the Infants. I examined the various classes & found every subject except Reading in a very unsatisfactory state. Many scholars absent. A. C. Forbes Esq. visited the school. **10** School Attendance officer called. A. C. Forbes Esq. visited to arrange about the purchase of material for Needlework. At present there is nothing for the children to begin with. During the past 6 mths it appears the Girls have done 'Knitting' socks only.

July 16 Recd some school material from Moffat Paige & Co. **17** A. C. Forbes Esqre visited the school. **18** Recd material for Needlework on the 9th inst. The children have, therefore, commenced their examination work in that subject. Several scholars have absented themselves, without leave, during part of the past week. Many children have progressed favourably in the various subjects. The average for the week = 129. No. on Books = 153. Being unable to work the classes in accordance with the Present Time Table I have drawn up a new one, and am working accordingly. If I find this arrangement works satisfactorily, I shall forward the Time-Table to H.M.I. for approval.

July 20 [*sic*] The Revd Molyneux visited the school. Recd some school material from Moffatt & Co. **23** The attendance officer called and took the names of several boys, who have gone to haymaking. One or two of the boys returned in the afternoon. **24** More children have been employed at haymaking. **25** The attendance was very bad indeed in the afternoon, 20 boys only were present in one class out of 37 on Books. I have again examined the various standards during the past week and still find them far from satisfactory. Arithmetic is very weak. The Revd Molyneux & A. C. Forbes Esq. visited, the former in the morning and the latter in the afternoon. The average for the week = 128.3. No. on Books = 152.

July 28 Very many children absent with the 'mumps'. The Assistant Mistress was absent throughout the day. **30** The attendance was very bad, only 98 out of 152 being present. I gave an extra Geography lesson to the Secd and Thd Standards, as they are very backward in that subject. **Aug. 1** The average this week is only 112. No. on Bks 152.

Aug. 4 Bank Holiday. School was closed for the day. **5** Very fair attendance, several children still absent with mumps. **7** The Revd — Molyneux visited and heard the 1st Class [say] their catechism. Put up New Time Tables which had been 'Approved' by H.M.I. and commenced working accordingly. Examination of 1st Std showed that the children in that standard had improved, but were still very backwd. **8** Attendance very low; several boys gone haymaking. Average attendance for past week only 114. No. on Books = 153.

Aug. 11 Punished 5 boys for playing the 'Truant' on Friday afternoon. 5 more girls away with mumps. The attendance still only fair. **14** A very great number of children absent with the mumps. Only 96 present in the morning. Punished John Cross & Ernest Grist for fighting in school yard. The attendance officer called on the 13th inst. There were several cases of bad attendance. **15** The Revd — Molyneux took the 4th to 6th Stds in Scripture this morning. The attendance was very bad, only 86 were present in the morning — and 83 in the afternoon: over 50 absent with 'mumps'. Those children, who have attended regularly, have improved very much during the past 5 weeks. Many are now able to do their standard work. Very fair maps are executed by the 4th 5th and 6th Stds. The 1st Std (45 strong) have greatly improved but they are at present very backward.

Aug. 19 Gave an extra Geography lesson to the 1st Class from 3.30 to 4 p.m. **20** The attendance during the past 3 days has been very low indeed, owing to the prevalence of 'Mumps'. Today only 58 presented themselves and I thought it advisable to close school for the usual Holiday term — to re-open on Septr 22nd.

Sept. 15 Re-opened School, very low attendance. The Harvest not yet over. **19** The average for the past week =58 only. The Misses Forbes visited in the morning.

Sept. 22 I issued warnings to those parents who insist upon keeping their children at gleaning. **23** About 50 more scholars presented themselves this morning; several are still gleaning. **26** The average for the week = 98.

Sept. 29 Revd — Molyneux gave a Scripture lesson to first class. Very fair school, although many are still absent. **Oct. 1** The Attendance Officer called for a list of irregular children. About 30 were found who had not made 50 times out of 83 during the past quarter. I punished several boys for rude behaviour in the playground. **3** Revd — Molyneux called in the morning. I gave an extended Geography lesson to the 1st Class in the afternoon.

Oct. 6 Revd — Molyneux gave a scripture lesson to the upper standards. I examined the 1st Standard in the three R's, and found a very great improvement had taken place during the past month. **8** Finding the Stds 4 to 6 backward in Geography, I have decided to give an extra lesson in the subject on Thursdays from 11 to 11.30 a.m. **9** Examined Stds II and III in Arithmetic, Results satisfactory on the whole. **10** Average for past week = 115.5.

Oct. 13 Very full school. In the morning 137 and in the afternoon 135 were present. Rev. — Molyneux gave a scripture lesson to the upper Standards. Several scholars returned after an absence of several weeks. **15** Still a good attendance. Work throughout the day satisfactory. **17** Examined the Infants in Scripture. Results satisfactory. Rev. — Molyneux visited. The attendance throughout the past week has been very satisfactory; the average being 130.9: and the No. on books 147. I examined the 4th & 6th Stds in Geography and found a great improvement had taken place since the last examn a month ago especially in the 6th Std.

Oct. 20 Very full school. 140 present. Began fires. Revd — Molyneux gave a scripture lesson to the 1st Class. **21** Admitted Emily, Mary, and Eliza Winch. **22** Wet day, only 102 present. **23** A. C. Forbes Esqre visited. Very good attendance. **24** The average for the week =130.9, and the total on registers 147. Examined the Second Standard in arithmetic, satisfactory results.

Oct. 27 A. C. Forbes Esq. visited. Attendance very good. **28** Mr Bunce, attendance officer called.[92] **31** The average for past week — 129.2. A. C.

---

[92] William R. Bunce, like other attendance officers employed by school attendance committees, combined his educational work with employment as a relieving officer. In the Reading Petty Sessional Minute Book for 1879–81, for example, he is shown taking action

PLATE 1.   Whitchurch School, 11 February 1904

(This shows the side of the chalk-pit at the rear, and the general unattractiveness of the site and building. From a print held by Oxfordshire C.C. Education Department)

PLATE 2. Interior of Whitchurch School, 8 June 1907

(This shows the Infants' School, with a corner of the Mixed School beyond. From a print held by Oxfordshire C.C. Education Department)

Forbes brought forms from the Education Department. Took Julia Law's name off the Books; she having returned to London. Charlotte Hine has also gone to Reading to stay some weeks, she is expected to return about Xmas.

Nov. 3 Revd R. Molyneux visited. Full school. **5** A. C. Forbes Esq. paid a visit. Still a very good attendance. Recd notice that the Diocesan Examination would take place on the 20th instt. **7** Revd R. Molyneux visited and took the 1st Class in Scripture. The average for the past week = 132.3 being the highest the school has attained since the beginning of the year.

Nov. 10 Revd R. Molyneux gave a scripture lesson to the 1st Class. A good attendance. I examined the 2nd and 3rd Standards in the three 'R's. Results very satisfactory. **12** The attendance officer called respecting several children whose parents had warning a month since. **14** The average for the week = 131.2. Took A. Holloway's name off the books, he having gone to work.

Nov. 20 The school was examined in Religious Knowledge by the Diocesan Inspector — the Revd Thos Williams. Half-holiday in the afternoon. **21** Several children absent. A heavy fall of snow in the afternoon. Average for the week = 129.8.

Nov. 27 Gave an extra Grammar lesson to the upper Standards from 3 to 3.30 p.m. **28** Several children have been absent the whole of the past week with severe colds. Average for the week = 129. Recd notice that H.M. Inspector proposes visiting this school on Jany 14th 1880, at 9.15 a.m.

Dec. 1 Several scholars absent owing to the bad state of the weather. Only 119 present. Revd R. Molyneux visited and gave a scripture lesson to 1st Class. **2** Very fair attendance. Examined the 2nd and 3rd Standards in the three R's. Results very satisfactory. Owing to a 'Penny Reading' taking place in the evening, the afternoon school commenced at 1 p.m. and closed at 3.10. The Registers were marked accordingly, viz. 1–1.10. **5** Revd R. Molyneux visited. Attendance rather low, especially in the afternoon. Average for the week = 122.5.

Dec. 12 The attendance during the past week has been very low owing to the children having severe colds.

Dec. 19 Closed for the Xmas Vacation, to re-open on the 29th inst.

Dec. 29 Re-opened with a very fair attendance. **Jan. 2** A. C. Forbes Esq. visited the school. Several children have been absent during the past week with colds. Average for the week = 117.5.

---

against offenders under the poor law regulations. (Minute Book at Berks. County Record Office, Reading, PS/R.)

1880

Jan. 5 Alice, and Ada Newman returned to school after being absent 5 wks with severe colds.   **7** The attendance Officer called respecting those children who have made less than 75 attendances during the past Quarter.   **9** The attendance, especially in the Infants' room has only been fair during the past wk. Recd 4 Tons of coal for use in school. Revd R. Molyneux called in the Afternoon. A meeting of the School managers is to be held on the 10th inst. to Audit the accounts for 1879.

Jan. 14 The school was visited by H.M. Inspector. School was closed for the remainder of the week. Recd the Diocesan Report on the 13th inst —

The Religious Knowledge seems very well cared for, the answering being remarkably intelligent and accurate. The First Division wrote out a parable with exact accuracy, only two faults of spelling being observed in the whole division. The Second Division wrote the Catechism statement of our duty to God with almost equal exactness. Writing very neat and good. An intelligent acquaintance with the geography presented called my attention as very unusual in the schools of my district. Reading very fair throughout — in many cases very good.

Emma Burgess   prize   Annie Brown   prize

THOMAS WILLIAMS   Diocesan Inspector

Jan. 23 The school has been closed during the past week.

Jan. 26 The school reopened with a fair attendance. Commenced the new work for the ensuing year.   **27** Recd the Duplicate Examn Schedule and arranged children in the new standards.   **30** Many have been absent during the past week with severe colds. Consequently the average is very low, especially in the Infants' class.

Feb. 3 Weather very foggy; many children absent. A fall of chalk has occurred at the back of the school, and as it is considered very dangerous for the children I have forbidden the girls entering by the usual gate until the thaw has been fully established.   **4** The attendance greatly improved.   **7** Revd R. Molyneux gave a scripture lesson to the 1st Class. I gave an extra Grammar lesson from 11.30–12 to the 4th standard. The classes are all making very fair progress in their new standard work.

Feb. 13 The work throughout the week very satisfactory. Admitted Selina Lewendon on the 9th inst. The Attendance officer called on Wednesday. Several names were given him, of children in the parish over 5 years of age, who do not attend any school. Attendance has been very fair, the average being 126 out of 142 on the books.

Feb. 16 Recd H.M. Inspector's Report —

The year's changes considered, the general results are good. But there is a good deal of imperfect work done in the first Standard, and the Grammar of the third Standard as well as the Analysis generally, are imperfect. Geography is good,

Needlework fair. The Infants, although too many six year old children are in the Second class, are very fairly instructed and handled. Discipline is thoroughly good all through the school.

E. Clark is recognised as qualified under Article 32(c)3.[93]
Herbert W. Winchester   Certd Teacher 2nd Class
Henrietta Winchester   Certd Teacher 2nd Class
Ellen Clark   Assistant Teacher.

ALEXANDER C. FORBES   Manager

20 Admitted Selina Lewendon & Ellen Knight on the 17th inst. Many scholars have been absent during part of the past week owing to the very wet weather. The classes are making very fair progress in their new work. Revd R. Molyneux gave a scripture lesson to the first class.

Feb. 23 Received information that James Lewendon and Rosalind Trinder had left school; the former has gone to work & the latter is about to leave the neighbourhood.   **25** A. C. Forbes Esq. visited, and proposed getting prizes for those who have passed the recent examination.   **26** The attendance during the past week has been very fair in the upper depart and very good in the Infants'.

Mar. 3 A. C. Forbes Esq. called and heard the children sing.   **4** A. C. Forbes Esq. and Revd — Slatter, the new Rector, visited in the afternoon. **5** The attendance has been very good throughout the week, the average being 131.4, and the No. on Registers 144. The work is progressing very satisfactorily. Several of the First Stand children, however, are very backward, and they will require hard drilling during the ensuing year to prepare them for the Examination.

Mar. 10 A. C. Forbes Esq. accompanied by Mrs and Miss Forbes came at 12 o'clock to distribute prizes to those scholars who passed the Examination in January. Annie Cross had a reward of 5/– for making the most attendances last year. The Attendance Officer called and took the names of 4 children who have been irregular during the past few weeks.   **12** The Average for the week is 135.4, being the highest the school has ever attained.

Mar. 15 Admitted 3 new scholars.   **17** The attendance Officer called and examined the registers respecting the attendances of 12 children. He informed me he had recd instruction to take proceedings against the parents of these children.[94]   **19** Revd R. Molyneux called. The Attendance has again been very satisfactory. Average for the week = 139.7.

[93] Miss Ellen Clark was recognized as a 'supplementary', a position officially introduced in 1875 to replace the monitor. She was thus without formal training. See Sellman, p. 83.

[94] On 27 Mar. several of the parents were charged before Reading petty sessional court. They included Joseph Bartlett and Thomas Tyrell, who had earlier been charged before the Henley petty sessions: Bartlett was required to pay a fine of 5s. for each of the two children involved in his case 'or distress to issue' — in default, 7 days' imprisonment. Tyrell was fined 2s. 6d. per child 'or distress to issue — in default 7 days'. He was allowed a fortnight to pay. Richard Hine and James Wallis were also fined 2s. 6d. per child. (Minute Book at Berks. R.O. PS/R).

Mar. 25 School closed for a week's holiday.

April 5 Re-opened with a good attendance. **7** A. C. Forbes Esq. visited in the morning. Mr Bunce also called for the quarterly return of attendances. **9** The average for the past week = 137.8. Admitted James Kent on the 5th inst.

Apr. 11 Ditto. Elizth Barrett. **12** Very wet day. Many children away. **13** Another wet day. A. C. Forbes Esq. visited.

Apr. 19 Full school. Took Josiah Taylor's name off the registers. A. C. Forbes Esq. called in the morning. **20** Began working according to the New Time Table. **22** Six girls were taken out of school at 11.30 a.m. by Miss Sykes[95] who was going to accompany them to Reading, in order to see the Circus. Their attendances were therefore cancelled. **23** The Average for the past week = 134.

Apr. 26 Admitted Annie Lewendon. Revd R. Molyneux gave a scripture lesson to First class. **30** Mrs Scrivens and a Friend visited in the afternoon and heard the children sing.[96] Average for the week 130. Recd information that the Father of Ellen Hazell had been summoned to appear before the Reading Bench on Saty to answer a charge for neglecting to send his child regularly to school.

May 2 Admitted three new scholars. **4** Attendance Officer called. Revd Mr Slatter visited and examined Std 3 in Geography. **7** The work of the week has been very satisfactory. The classes are making great progress in the various subjects. Average for the week = 136.9.

May 14 Good attendance throughout the week. The average, 142, is the highest the school has ever attained. I examined the 1st 2nd and 3rd Stds on the 11th inst. and found they had made satisfactory progress since last inspection.

May 17 Whit-Monday — school closed for the day. **18** Another holiday given owing to a small number of scholars presenting themselves. **21** Attendance has been good the past three days.

May 24 Admitted two new scholars. Full school. **26** A. C. Forbes Esq. called. **28** Average for the week = 143 being the highest the school has ever attained.

June 2 Attendance Officer called — no defaulters. Recd notice that Rosa Trinder had left the parish. Her name has, therefore, been cancelled. **4** Examined Std 2 in Grammar — results satisfactory. This week the children have attended remarkably well. The average is 146 and the total on registers 155.

---

[95] Of Rose Cottage, Whitchurch.
[96] Mrs Scrivens [sic] was probably the wife of John Bagot Scriven of Whitchurch (*Kelly's Dir. Oxon.* (1883), under Whitchurch).

June 9 A. C. Forbes Esq. and a Friend called and heard the children sing. The Assistant Mistress was absent on the 8th inst, being too ill to attend to her duties. **11** Eliza Fabry informed me she had left school. The average for the past week is 143.

June 18 Many scholars have been absent during the past week with severe colds.

June 21 Rev. — Slatter gave a Scripture Lesson to 1st Class. **25** A. C. Forbes Esq. visited. Many Infants are still absent with Whooping Cough. Average 134.

June 29 The school was closed in the afternoon, as the teachers all went to the Sunday School Centenary at Henley. There was a Meeting of the School Managers on the 26th inst. **July 2** Many children have been absent throughout the past week with whooping cough. The average is only 124. On books 157.

July 5 Whooping-cough continues to spread. The number of Infants attending is very low. **9** Average for past week = 125.

July 14 Wet day. Many absent in consequence. **15** Another wet day. Attendance small. **16** Whooping Cough still prevailing, in consequence of which many Infants are still absent. An average of 121 only for the week.

July 19 Attendance very much improved although several are still absent with whooping-cough. Revd J. Slatter visited in the morning. **21** Attendance Officer called. Admitted two scholars on the 19th inst. **23** The children have attended much better during the past week. The average being 135.6.

July 29 The school was closed in the afternoon owing to the Annual Flower show taking place. **30** Another 'halfholiday' given in the afternoon; the children being entertained with a 'Treat' provided by the Revd R. E. Molyneux, the late Curate of Whitchurch. Many were absent today and yesterday in the morning. A. C. Forbes Esq. visited. Eliza Dicker's name has been taken off the books, she having left school.

Aug. 6 Harvest having commenced, the school closes today for the summer vacation. To reopen on Septr 4.

Sept. 4 Re-opened with a very small attendance; the harvest not yet finished.

Sept. 6 The numbers have increased considerably — still they are very low. Only 110 present out of 157 on books. **10** Took Wm, Albert, Chas & Thos Holloway, Florence Goodall, Alice Stubbings, Edward and Edith Jeacocke off Admission Register. The Revd J. Slatter visited in the afternoon and asked the 1st Class a few questions in geography. Mrs Slatter also inspected the needlework of Standards I–III. The average for the week is only 106.2. Some of the children have gone back considerably during the month's holiday.

Sept. 13 Full school. All the boys, who have been at work in the fields, have returned.   **15** Attendance Officer called and took the names of several who have been irregular during the last few weeks.   **17** A. C. Forbes Esq. called and heard the children sing some songs. All the standards are making very satisfactory progress in their work. Admitted Julia Ridge on the 13th inst. Average for the week =134. No. on books 150.

Sept. 20 Revd J. Slatter visited — and gave a scripture lesson to the first class. **21** Recd a Circular Letter from the Clerk of the School Attendance Committee, authorizing me to fill in the first page of the 'Child's School Book' from information given by the parent of the child. Attendances throughout the week, very fair.   **22** Attendance Officer called.

Sept. 28 The lower class girls had sewing in the afternoon, as a holiday was expected on the Friday.   **Oct. 1** No school in the afternoon, Sunday-school children had a treat. I gave an extra Reading lesson to Std I from 11 to 11.25 a.m. Recd a certificate that Sarah Weller was too ill to attend school. Average for the week = 132. Mrs Slatter visited on the 30th ult.

Oct. 3 Revd J. Slatter gave a scripture lesson to the first class.   **6** Wet day. Poor attendance. Gave a dictation lesson to Std II instead of Geography. A. C. Forbes Esq. called in the afternoon.   **8** Jemima, Charlotte and Sarah Hine have been absent, with bad heads, for over a fortnight. Sarah Weller is also absent with diarrhoea. Owing to Tuesday and Wednesday being wet, the average for the week is only 128.5. I have examined all the standards during the past week. The results were very satisfactory, with the exception of Grammar in standard 3, and the general work of a few children in Std 1.

Oct. 12 Revd J. Slatter called, and gave a lesson to the 2nd Class.   **14** Punished George Shaw for using bad language in the playground. The attendance has been good during the past week, the weather having been very fine. Began fires on the 12th inst. James Smith has been absent, with a severe cold, since the 11th inst.

Oct. 18 Wet day. Many children absent.   **22** Another wet day, several away in consequence. On the 25th inst. the afternoon meeting will commence at 1.30 instead of 2, owing to its getting dark before some of the children can get home.

Oct. 26 The weather being very wet, very many scholars were absent throughout the day.   **27** I wrote to the attendance officer on the 22nd inst. respecting several boys who have been very irregular, but have received no reply. The children appear to stay away from school whenever they can get an excuse for so doing, and no notice seems to be taken of the fact, although I am repeatedly complaining to the Officer.   **29** A. C. Forbes Esq. called and brought the Examination Schedule &c. for next Inspection. The Diocesan

Examination is to be held on Monday, Novr 8th. The average for the week is very low, especially that of the Infants, owing to the two or three wet days. The children do their standard work and also the class subjects very well indeed — with the exception of 6 first Std boys, whom it will [be] impossible to prepare for the work by the Examination.

Nov. 1 Commenced the afternoon meetings at 1.45 instead of 1.30 as many scholars cannot get here by the latter time on Wednesday and Thursday owing to Church Practice occurring on those days. Admitted Sarah & Eliza Spanswick. **2** Ditto. Fanny, Emily, William, and Minnie Tomlin. **5** Attendance has been very good during the past week. Average 145. Punished Joseph Hine and James Wallis for playing truant on the previous afternoon.

Nov. 8 Diocesan Inspector visited, and examined the school. **9** Admitted Mary Spanswick. Full school. **12** Average for the week = 146. No. on Bks 159. The attendance Officer called on the 10th inst.

Nov. 17 The attendance Officer called to examine the registers as to the attendances of Wm & Mary Tyrell, Charlotte & Elizabeth Barrett, & Alice Newman, whose parents are to be proceeded against.[97] The School Attendance Committee have agreed to leave our Bye Laws unchanged. Recd. the Diocesan Inspector's Report:—

Whitchurch School   Inspected Novr 8th 1880
The Scripture answering was very ready and intelligent, showing good and full acquaintance with the periods presented.
The upper Standards (IV, V, VI) wrote out the Parable of the Good Samaritan in beautiful style and without one single error either of omission or of false spelling. The two next standards were equally perfect in the 'Duty towards God'.
Knowledge of text of Catechism very good.
THOMAS WILLIAMS   Dioc. Inspector
First prize   William Grist   Secd do. Fredk Pocock

19 The attendance has been very fair throughout the week, but not so good as last week. Fanny, Emily, and Albert Tomlin have been to Reading for examination, so have been unable to attend school during the past few days. Joseph Hine, and Ch. Barrett have also been absent with illness. I have examined the various classes this week; the results were very satisfactory, especially in arithmetic and reading. Julia Alice Weller was admitted on the 15th inst. There are now 160 on the Admission Book.

Nov. 24 Miss Barrett took her son John out of school without my permission. I shall, therefore, refuse to admit him again until the case has been brought before the Managers of the school, for consideration. The child had been kept in for

---

[97] The recalcitrant Thomas Tyrell had not only been fined 2s. 6d. for the non-attendance of two children on 27 Mar. 1880, but also a further 5s. for one child on 17 Apr. 1880. On 27 Nov. 1880 he was again fined 5s. for each of his two children and was allowed 14 days to pay (Reading Petty Sessional Minute Book at Berks C.R.O.).

misbehaviour. It was 5 minutes past the usual time for dismissal when he was taken away. **26** Very wet morning, consequently many of the little ones were absent. Very good attendance throughout the past week, average 146. **27** Pupil Teacher's Examination at Reading. Edith Grist sat as a candidate for Pupil Teachership. Notice of the above Examn was received on the 21st inst.

Nov. 30 The 1st Class will have a Grammar lesson on Tuesdays, from 2.30 to 3.15 p.m. instead of writing, until the Examination. **Dec. 2** Revd J. Slatter and another gentleman visited in the afternoon. **3** Took Chas Barrett, Emma Robinson, Chas Haylock and Thos Haylock off books. Work throughout the week very satisfactory. Average 148, the highest during the year. Sent an order to Natl Socy for school material &c.

Dec. 9 Ernest, Kate, Selina, & Annie Lewendon were sent home, as the doctor thinks the last mentioned child has the measles. **10** Attendance during the past week very fair. Average 141. No. on Bks 156. Recd Books &c. from Natl Society's Depo[t].

Dec. 17 The attendance during the week has been very poor, owing to the prevalence of severe colds among the smaller children. Average for the week only 129. Revd J. Slatter came in the afternoon and gave prizes to those who passed well at the Diocesan Examination last November. Work throughout the past few days very satisfactory, with the exception of the spelling of Standard 2, several children in that class being rather weak in the subject at present. The Lewendons have returned to school, it having proved that measles were not prevalent in the family.

Dec. 24 Closed school for the Christmas vacation. To reopen on Jany 3rd 1881. Registers were marked 9.20 to 9.30, and children dismissed at 11.40. Recd notice that H.M. Inspector's visit will take place on Jany 13 1881 at 9.15 a.m.

1881

Jan. 3 Re-opened school with a very fair attendance. Three scholars were absent with 'chicken-pox'. Revd J. & Mrs & Miss Slatter called & distributed articles of clothing to some of the children. **5** A. C. Forbes Esq. visited in the afternoon. **7** Average for past week = 142. No. on Bks 157.

Jan. 13 H.M. Inspector visited. The examination passed off very satisfactorily. A. C. Forbes Esq. & Revd J. Slatter were present. Holiday given for the remainder of the week.

Jan. 17 Cold weather — many absent. Arranged children in their new Standards. **18** Heavy fall of snow. No school in the afternoon. **21** No school has been held since the morning of the 18th inst. in consequence of a great snowstorm — which prevented the children from leaving home.[98]

[98] In the nearby parish of Mapledurham the bailiff on the Blount family's estate noted on 19 January 1881: 'Snow penetrated all barns, stables, &c. doing great mischief the wind

Jan. 28 Very poor attendance throughout the week, owing to the bad state of the roads. Average only 96.5. No. on Bks 157. Took Edwd Edith & Lilian Jeacocke, Ethel Briant, & Minnie Tomlin off books. They attend a private school in the village.

Jan. 31 Began working according to a New Time-Table, which was approved by H.M. Inspector on the 26th inst. More time will, in future, be given to the Needlework. Nelson's Geographical Readers for Standards 2 and 3 recd. Those for the higher standards have not yet been published. Specimens have been promised as soon as issued. **Feb. 1** Wet day — very poor attendance. **2** No school. Only 50 children presented themselves at 9.30 — so they were dismissed before the time fixed for marking the registers. **3** Another wet day — many children absent. **4** Average for the week = only 122. No. on Bks 152. Progress in the new year's work is very slowly made, owing to the irregularity of some of the children — which causes a repetition of a great portion of the work. A great fall of chalk has occurred at the back of the premises so that the girls are obliged to enter by the Master's private gate.

Feb. 11 Owing to bad weather the attendance has been very poor throughout the week. Received H.M. Inspector's Report:—

The Needlework only excepted, which is, as a rule quite below par, the School results are thoroughly good. The Discipline is excellent. It is only fair to observe that Needlework could hardly be much better at so very small an expenditure of time weekly. The first Standard Needlework was, however, good.
Mrs Winchester will shortly receive her Certificate.[99]
Herbert W. Winchester   2nd Class Cert.
Henrietta Winchester   2nd Class Cert.
Ellen Clark   Assistant Teacher
Edith Grist   Pupil Teacher 1st Year

ALEXANDER C. FORBES   Manager

Feb. 18 The Attendance has greatly improved during the past week. Average 128. A. C. Forbes Esq. & Revd J. Slatter visited on the 14th inst. The names of Ernest Lewendon & Eva Lewis have been taken off the books. Edith Grist has been made Pupil Teacher, the engagement to be calculated from Jany 1st 1881 and to last 4 years. Two children absent with severe colds.

---

[99] According to the Code: 'Candidates for certificates, after successfully passing their examination, must, as teachers continuously engaged in the same schools, obtain two favourable reports from an inspector, with an interval of one year between them. . . . If the second . . . report is favourable a certificate is issued' (See, for example, Article 51 of the New Code, 1871).

---

bitter cold yesterday and of such immense force as to do great damage to thatch both on ricks and cottages. The roads completely blocked. Baker's cart to be left in the snow — unable to get along — never such a deep snow known about here by the oldest inhabitant' (Wages Book, Bodl. MS. D.D. Blount, c. 175).

Feb. 21 Revd J. Slatter visited and gave a Scripture lesson to the first class. The Attendance officer has not called for nearly a month.   **25** Took Fredk and Albert Day's name off the Books. They have gone to Goring Heath School. Admitted Robt and Thomas Wallis on 21st inst. Although nearly 10 years old Robert only just knows his letters. Thomas is more ignorant still. The Attendance during the past week has only been very fair. Average 130 out of 152 on Books. Satisfactory progress is being made, by the different standards, in the new work. The Geographical Readers for Standards 4, 5 and 6, have not yet been received. We are, therefore, working geography in the same manner as in past years.

Mar. 1 Revd J. Slatter visited and gave a scripture lesson to the 1st Class. **3** The Attendance officer called and took the names of several boys who have been irregular during the past few weeks.   **4** Annie Martin's name has been taken off the books. She has passed Std 5. Wet day, consequently many children absent.

Mar. 7 Revd J. Slatter visited.   **9** Rev. J. Slatter and A. C. Forbes Esq. visited.   **11** Rev. J. and Mrs Slatter called in the afternoon. Attendance throughout the week only fair — might have been much better.

Mar. 18 Satisfactory progress has been made during the week. Several children absent; no reason given.

Mar. 21 Revd J. Slatter visited and gave a Scripture lesson to the 1st Class. **25** Admitted 3 new children on the 21st inst. I sent lists of irregular scholars to the Attendance Officer last week, and he brought them under the notice of the Local Authority, who did not consider any of the cases very bad, although some had only made 63 Attendances out of 96 openings — so that no further notice has been taken. Several children continue to absent themselves without any reason being given. One boy has been at work 4 days out of the past 5.

Apr. 1 Revd J. Slatter visited. Good attendance throughout the week. Recd a memm from Nelson & Sons to the effect that the 4th Standard Royal Geographical Readers will not be issued for, at least, 10 days. The lower classes are not making so much progress as could be wished, in Geography. The upper standards are doing very well.

Apr. 6 Revd J. Slatter and A. C. Forbes Esq. visited.   **8** The attendance during the week has been much better than it has been for some time past. The average is the highest recorded since the Examination. Kate Lewendon's name has been taken off the books.

Apr. 14 School closed for Easter Holidays. To re-open on the 24th inst.

Apr. 24 Admitted three infants. Very good attendance — 148 present. Mrs Forbes visited and assisted with the needlework of the upper standards. Took the names of Clara and Annie Goodall off books. Thos Ridge returned to school after an absence of several weeks. **29** Revd J. Slatter, and A. C. Forbes Esq. visited in the morning. Miss Forbes came in the afternoon and assisted with the needlework of the lower standards. Average for the week = 147.

May 5 Attendance very good throughout the week. Average 146. No. on Books 155. Revd J. Slatter visited on the 2nd 4th & 6th inst. The Royal Geographical Readers have been recd from Nelson & Sons. The Upper Standards appear to appreciate their use much more than Stds II & III do. Owing to the greater regularity of the children, the work of the classes is progressing much more satisfactorily.

May 13 Revd J. Slatter has visited twice during the week. The Attendance Officer called on the 11th inst. to enquire about the boy Thomas Ridge, who has recently been at work. Re-admitted Elizth Detfield on the 9th inst. Miss Clark, the Assistant Mistress, has sent in her resignation. She will be at liberty on August 12th.[100] The children have attended very well indeed throughout the week. Average 146.8.

May 18 A. C. Forbes Esq. & a friend visited in the morning. **19** Revd J. Slatter visited. The 2nd and 3rd Standards will have Arithmetic instead of a Reading lesson from 9.50 to 10.35 on Thursday mornings for a few weeks — as those standards are rather backwards in their Arithc. **20** Revd J. Slatter visited in the morning. Owing to the weather being unsettled the attendance has not been so good as last week.

May 23 Admitted Thomas Whiting & Constance Andus. Revd J. Slatter called. Miss Forbes assisted with the Needlework in the afternoon. **27** Several boys absent — no reason given. Average for the week = 144. On books 157.

May 30 Revd J. Slatter visited. **31** Miss A. Forbes assisted with the needlework of the Infants, in the morning. **June 3** Several children absent in the afternoon no excuse. Average for the week = 143. School closed till the following Wednesday owing to a 'fair' being held on Monday and Tuesday in Whitweek.

June 8 Re-opened school — rather thin attendance. **9** Numbers slightly improved — several still absent. **10** Revd J. Slatter visited.

June 17 Took George Wells & Thos Ridge off books. Good attendance throughout the week. Revd J. Slatter called in the morning, and heard the Scripture Lesson of the 2nd Class.

---

[100] The post was advertised in *The Schoolmaster* on 18 June 1881. It called for 'an Ex-Pupil Teacher as Assistant MISTRESS . . . To take Standards II and III, and assist with needlework'. The salary was £32 a year and a furnished room.

June 23 The II & III will do their usual lesson according to the Time-Table, on Thursday mg for the future. Admitted Ada and Gertrude Turner on the 21st inst. Ellen Hine absent with the 'Mumps'.   **24** Miss Ellen Watkins, of East Moseley, called respecting the post of Assistant Mistress. She appeared to be a person likely to give satisfaction. The attendance has not been so satisfactory as usual during the past week. Average only 138. No. on Books 153.

June 27 Miss Watkins has been appointed to succeed Miss Clarke, after the harvest vacation. Recd notice that the school will be visited by the Diocesan Inspector on Wednesday July 13th.   **July 1** Sent a list of irregular children to the Attendance Officer. Numbers low throughout the week.

July 4 Sent George Hazell home for disobedience. He refused to do any work, although I punished him several times. He is encouraged to be disobedient by his parents. On Wednesday last I punished him for the same offence, and consequently he was kept at home on the two following days.   **6** Very wet day — Attendance bad.   **7** Improved numbers. No notice has been taken of the list of irregular children — although one girl only comes 3 days in each week, and has only made 77 attendances out of a possible 123.

July 11 Re-admitted Albert Wells.   **13** The School was visited by Revd E. Barber, General Diocesan Inspector. Holiday in the afternoon.   **15** Average for the week 144.

July 17 Admitted Mary, Eliza & Walter Turner. Took Annie Detfield off books.   **19** Attendance Officer called respecting the number of times made by Eliza Spanswick.   **22** Recd the Diocesan Inspector's Report:—

The general condition of Religious Knowledge is quite satisfactory. The answering in the lower room was fair, and the children had learnt by heart Holy Scripture &c. In the other Divisions the answering was very even and good, & the Repetition excellent; whilst the Writing & spelling were admirable. Private Prayers should be taught.

Commended — Annie Cross (Prize)	Wm Grist (had Prize)
Elizth Ashby	Wm Burgess
Fanny Tomlin	Fred. Pocock (had Prize)

EDWARD BARBER   General Inspector of Schools for the Diocese of Oxford

July 27 The Attendance officer called — and informed me that the father of Eliza Spanswick was fined 2/6 on Saturday — at Reading.   **28** Revd J. Slatter visited and threatened to punish boys whom he found throwing stones at his apples.   **29** Several children absent in the afternoon — no reason being given.

Aug. 1 Bank Holiday. The school was closed for the day, owing to a Temperance Fête, to which a great many of the children go.   **5** Revd J. Slatter came in the afternoon and distributed the Prizes to those who passed the last Government Examination, after which the School closed for the Harvest Holidays — to re-open on Monday Sept. 4th. Miss Clarke, the Assistant Mistress resigns today.

Sept. 5 Re-opened School with a very fair attendance. Harvest not yet finished. Miss Watkins entered upon her duties as Assistant Mistress. She seems likely to suit in every respect. **9** Village Flower Show. Half-holiday given in the afternoon. Average for the week =137. No. on Bks 163. A. C. Forbes visited on the 7th inst.

Sept. 16 Revd J. Slatter visited in the afternoon and promised the children a treat on the 21st inst. Average for the week = 146.

Sept. 19 Albert Newman has the *Scarlet Fever*. The Sanitary Inspector has advised that the Brookers (who live next door to the Newmans) are also kept away from School until further notice. **21** Half-holiday in the afternoon — School treat. **22** Stds 2 and 3 will have Arithc instead of Reading, on Thursday morning, for a few weeks, as they are weaker in Arithc than in Reading. **23** Wet morning. Many children absent, only 133 present. Average for the week = 143. The Infants' Mistress has been absent from School during the past three weeks, and Monitors have been employed in the Infant Room. No more cases of Scarlet Fever have been reported; Albert Newman is making satisfactory progress towards recovery. William Sargent, Harry Robinson, Walter Turner and Nellie Beveridge have left the School. Their names have, therefore, been taken off the books. The Attendance Officer called on the 21st inst., respecting the attendances of several children, whose names had been recently sent to the School Attendance Committee.

Sept. 26 Revd J. Slatter visited and gave a Scripture lesson to the 1st Class. **29** Revd J. Slatter visited. **30** Revd J. Slatter visited and gave a lesson in Scripture to Standards II and III. Good attendance throughout the week.

Oct. 7 The Newmans & Brookers still absent in consequence of the "Scarlet Fever". The Spanswicks have left the parish. Revd. J. Slatter visited on the 4th and 5th inst. and gave Scripture Lessons. Attendance very fair.

Oct. 12 Attendance Officer called. **14** Many children absent. Only 89 present in the upper room. Very windy day. Part of the wall at the side of the Infants' Room was blown down. Fortunately no children were near at the time.

Oct. 19 The School Attendance Officer called and gave notice that the Bradfield School Attendance Committee had decided to take proceedings against the parents of those children who were absent three times during a fortnight, in the future. **21** Took Fredk Wayman's name off the books. The men have been busy repairing the wall of the Infants' Room, during the past week. Average for the past week rather lower than usual; only 131.6. No. on Books 154. No additional cases of Scarlet Fever have been reported. The Newmans & Brookers will return to school on Monday next. They have been absent five weeks.

Oct. 24 The Brookers have come back to school, but the Newmans have been given an additional week. **25** Several children, belonging to the Church choir, were absent in the Afternoon. Examined Standard I in Reading, Writing and Arithmetic. Results very satisfactory. Arithc is the weaker [sic] subject. **28** The singing lesson was omitted, and other subjects substituted, in the various classes. Kate Chapman & Jessie Andus have been taken off the books. Elizth Bushnell and Thomas Franklin have been absent since the 24th inst. with severe colds. Average for the week = 133.9.

Nov. 2 Mrs Brooker's baby has the measles; the other children are, therefore, absent from school. The Newmans have not returned to school yet. The 2nd and 3rd Standards will have writing in dictation books instead of Copy-books, on Wednesday afternoons for a few weeks. Examined Standards II & III in the three R's on the first inst., and found them very satisfactory, with the exception of spelling in Std II. **4** The Revd J. Slatter called. Commenced opening school on the 31st ult. — at 1.45 p.m. instead of 2, owing to the distance some of the little ones have to go after school has closed. In consequence of the damp state of the weather during the last day or two, the average is much lower than usual.

Nov. 7 Ada & Emily Newman came back to school, after an absence of several weeks. Albert Newman is still too ill to attend. **9** The Attendance Officer called for a list of irregular scholars. **11** Thos Franklin has been absent for a fortnight with a severe cold. The Brookers have not returned to school. Attendance for the week very fair. Av. 132.

Nov. 16 The Attendance Officer called, and said the School Attendance Committee had decided to summon the parents of Edward Shaw, Mary Winch, and Thomas Franklin. Examined Standard I in Arithmetic & Writing. Results, with the exception of the work done by 6 boys and 1 girl, very satisfactory. **17** The Brookers returned to school on the 13th inst. Charlotte Whiting still absent with Rheumatic Fever. Received notice that the Pupil Teacher's Scripture Examination would be held, on Saturday Decr 3rd, at St Mary's Schools, Reading. **18** Average for past week = 138. Emily Tomlin has been absent during the week with a severe cold: Minnie Tomlin has also been away three days. Examined Standards 4, 5 & 6 in Geography and Grammar. The results were satisfactory on the whole, with the exception of a few boys in Standard 4, whose work in Grammar was only fairly done.

Nov. 21 Albert Newman returned to School after an absence of 9 weeks. Edward and Charles Reeves have the 'Itch' and are, therefore, away from School. Wet morning. Several children away in consequence. **25** The Revd J. Slatter visited and gave a short Scripture lesson to standards 4 to 6. Recd Notice from H.M. Inspector, on the 20th inst. that the Annual Inspection would be held on Wednesday Jany 11th 1882 at 9.15 a.m.; also that the Examination of Pupil Teachers would take place on Saty the 26th inst. at St Giles' Nat. School, Reading, at 9.30 a.m. Fanny Tomlin has been absent all the week, with a bad cold. The weather during the past week has been very unsettled; therefore the average has been considerably lower than that of last week. **26** Took the Pupil Teacher to the Examination at Reading.

Nov. 28 Revd J. Slatter visited. **30** Wet morning; many children away. Edward & Chas Reeves still absent with 'Itch'. **Dec. 2** Ada Rossiter, and John Cook have had bad colds, and so have stayed away all the week. **3** Pupil Teachers' Examination in Religious Knowledge at St Mary's School, Reading.

Dec. 6 Took other lessons in the various standards instead of Singing from 11.25 to 12. **9** Average for the week =137.8. Took James Lane's name off Books. Revd J. Slatter called and reproved some of the boys for throwing mud at people's doors on their way home from school. Punished Alice Lewendon for impudence, & she was kept at home in the afternoon.

Dec. 16 The Assistant Mistress has been absent at the Certificate Examination all the past week. Revd J. Slatter called on the 15th inst. The Attendance Officer visited on the 14th. Alice Lewendon has not returned to school. I have today sent a list of 8 irregular children, to Bradfield S.A. Committee.

Dec. 19 Mrs Winchester being too ill to attend school during the ensuing week, Monitors will be employed in the Infants' Room. Most of the girls having finished the Needlework for Examination, they will do other lessons instead of Needlework for a fortnight. Rev. J. Slatter visited and gave a Catechism Lesson to the 1st Class. **22** Several children absent in the afternoon. **23** Closed school for Christmas Holiday. To re-open January 2nd 1882.

1882

Jan. 2 Re-opened School with a very good attendance. **3** Revd J. Slatter called. A Meeting of the School Managers is to be held on Saturday, the 7th inst. to audit the yearly accounts. Edward Jeacocke still too unwell to come to school. Edward & Charles Reeves have returned after an absence of 6 weeks. Received the result of the Pupil Teacher's Scripture Examination — she has gained a First class.[101] **6** A. C. Forbes Esq. visited. The attendance has been very good during the week, the average being 141.7. No. on Bks 149. **7** Meeting of The School Managers, to Audit the Accounts for the year.

Jan. 11 School visited by H.M. Inspector — & his Assistant. Revd J. Slatter, & A. C. Forbes Esq. called. Half holiday given in the Afternoon. **12** Re-arranged the classes, and commenced the new work. Average for the week = 144. Fanny Tomlin, & Eliz. Ashby taken off Admission Book.

Jan. 15 Fanny Tomlin has been appointed Monitress, to assist with the Infants.[102] **17** Recd the Duplicate Examination Schedules from H.M.

---

[101] In March 1881, the incumbent, the Rev. J. Slatter, had informed the Bishop of Oxford that he would examine the 'Pupil Teacher . . . weekly in Religious Kn. at the Rectory' (Clergy Visitation Returns for 1881, Bodl. MS. Oxf. Dioc. Pp. c. 347).

[102] Fanny Tomlin was possibly a daughter of George Tomlin, Mr W. Fanning's farm bailiff, who appears in *Kelly's Dir. Oxon.* (1883).

Inspector. Many of the scholars absent with Bronchitis. **20** Took Ada Rossiter and Alice Lewendon off the books. Admitted James Gutteridge & Bertram Inglis on the 16th inst. The majority of the children seem interested in their new work. Average for the week only 131. No. on Books 151.

Jan. 23 For the future the school will be opened in the afternoon at 2, instead of 1.45. I find the New Time-Table works satisfactorily. **24** Revd J. Slatter visited in the morning. **27** Revd J. Slatter, & A. C. Forbes Esq. called, and proposed giving the children a Treat & Magic Lantern some time the following week. Many are still away with Bronchitis, and the average for the week has only reached 124 out of 148 on Books. Mrs Winchester has been absent throughout the past week, owing to the illness of the baby. The children appear to be making very fair progress in the new work: but, owing to so many absentees, there is not so much progress as I should like. A great deal of the work will have to be repeated when the children, now absent, return to School.

Jan. 30 Full school. All children returned who had been absent with Bronchitis. **Feb. 3** The attendance has been very good indeed all the week. Average 145 out of 148 on Books. Half-holiday given in the Afternoon. The children had a Treat at 4 and a Magic Lantern at 5 p.m. They thoroughly enjoyed both. Recd some books, on Specific Subjects, for 4 — Standard 6, from National Society. I have decided to take Literature, Physical Geography, & Mathematics for the boys, and Literature, Phy. Geog. & Domestic Economy for the girls who have passed Standard 6.[103]

Feb. 6 Revd John Slatter visited and questioned the 1st Class in Scripture. **10** Revd J. Slatter called. Satisfactory progress throughout the week. The Attendance has been fairly good. Av. 141.

Feb. 13 Received H.M. Inspector's Report:—

Whitchurch (Reading) Parochial School (Oxford)
The Order is very good indeed. The general results, too, are good. But Needlework, though somewhat improved, remains certainly below par.
E. L. M. Grist has passed well.
Herbert W. Winchester   Certd Teacher 2nd Class
Henrietta Winchester   Certd Teacher 2nd Class

---

[103] 'Specific subjects' attracted a grant of 4s. for each scholar passing in a relevant subject and prior to the Code of 1882 it had been possible for scholars who had 'previously passed in Standard VI' to be presented for examination in *three* specific subjects, in place of the normal limit of two. But under the 1882 Code (Article 109(g) (ii)) no scholar was to be presented for examination 'in more than two specific subjects'. Under Article 109(g)(iv) of the same Code no scholar could be presented 'for examination in any specific subject who is not also presented for examination in elementary subjects in Standard V, VI or VII'. In 1882 Standard VII was also introduced, requiring the student to 'read passage from Shakespeare or Milton etc,. or from a History of England: write theme or letter: work sums in averages, percentages, discount, or stocks' (Sellman, p. 115).

PLATE 3. Staff and pupils, Whitchurch School, 1896?

(Herbert Winchester is on the right, and the lady on the left may be his daughter Lilian; only some of their pupils are shown. From a print held by Mrs L. E. Simmonds, Whitchurch)

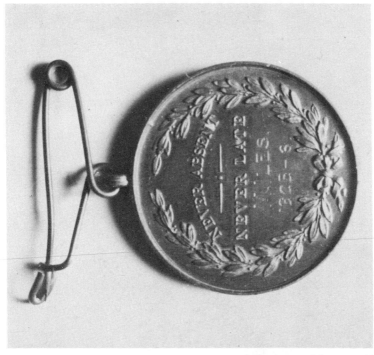

PLATE 4.   Attendance Medal issued by Oxfordshire Education Committee
(From the original held by Mrs Margaret Watson of Reading, to whom it was awarded in 1906)

Ellen Watkins   Assistant Teacher
Edith L. M. Grist   Pupil Teacher 2nd Year

ALEXANDER C. FORBES   Manager

17 A. C. Forbes Esq. visited. Good attendance throughout the week. Revd J. Slatter and Revd & Mrs Henham of Streatley, called on the 16th inst. Took Ethel & Bessie Briant and Kate Smith off books. Admitted E. Yates on the 13th Inst. Kate Lewendon absent with a severe cold all the week.

Feb. 21 Admitted Louisa Yates. Took Amos Lewendon off books.   **24** Rev. J. Slatter visited, and took the 3rd Class in Scripture. Attendance very good throughout the week. Average 144. No. on Books = 150. Recd. Notice, from Rev. E. Barber, that the Examination for Pupil Teacher's Exhibition would be held at St Mary's School, Reading, at 9.30 a.m. on Saturday, March 11th 1882.

Mar. 3 Attendance has been good. Revd Canon Slatter visited. Satisfactory progress has been made.

Mar. 10 A. C. Forbes Esq. called on the 9th inst. Very good attendance throughout the week.   **11** Pupil Teachers' Exhibition Examination at St Mary's School, Reading.

Mar. 13 In order that the Girls may have clean hands for Needlework, that subject will, in future, begin at 2.10 instead of 2.45. The 1st Lesson, as per time-table, will therefore, be taken from 3.40 to 4.15, and the other Lessons arranged accordingly.   **17** Revd J. Slatter visited, and gave a Scripture Lesson to the 2nd Class. Good attendance during the week. Alice Stubbings, and Ellen Hazell have been absent with severe colds. William Ridge & Ebenr Bartlett have been taken off books. Julia Ridge & Eliz. Taylor admitted on the 13th.

Mar. 20 Admitted two new children, in the Infants' Room. Received information from the Education Dept that Ellen Watkins, Assistant Mistress, had been placed in the Second Division of the Class List of Candidates for Certificates.[104]   **24** Revd Canon Slatter visited and took the First Class in Scripture. Recd the Prizes from National Society's Depos. Attendance very good indeed.

Mar. 28 A. C. Forbes Esq. visited.   **31** Satisfactory progress. Good attendance. Average 144. No. on Books 151.

---

[104] Practising teachers in elementary schools who were over 21 years of age and had either 'completed an engagement as pupil-teacher satisfactorily'; or 'obtained a favourable report from an inspector upon the school in which they [were] still employed' were allowed to take the certificate examinations held at the 'several training schools under inspection' each December; see for example Article 47 of the New Code of 1871. As the Cross Commission showed, by the mid-1880s these 'untrained' certificated teachers comprised over half of all certificated female teachers and around one-third of the certificated males (*Final Report of the Royal Commission on the Elementary Education Acts (England and Wales)*, P.P. 1888, xxxv, p. 81).

Apr. 6 Closed School for Easter Holidays.

Apr. 17 Re-opened School. Fair attendance. Several children ill. Admitted 4 new scholars. **21** Revd J. Slatter visited. Took E. Newman's name off books. Average for the week = 141.5. No. on Books 155.

Apr. 28 Wet morning. Several scholars absent. Revd J. Slatter visited, and gave a Scripture Lesson to the Upper Standards. Joseph Hine has been ill during the past fortnight — and unable to attend School. Satisfactory progress in all Standards. Average for the week lower than usual. Admitted John Gutteridge on the 24th inst.

May 2 Revd J. Slatter visited. Fair attendance. Examined Std II in Arithc & Dictation — results not very satisfactory as a rule. **3** No School was held in the Afternoon, as a great number of the children were required to sing at the Church — at a Confirmation Service. **5** Rev. J. Slatter called — and gave a Scripture lesson.

May 11 George & Ellen Hazell were sent home on Monday for obstinacy. They had been told by their parents to refuse to hold out their hands for punishment, consequently, I could do nothing with them. The case has been laid before the School Managers for consideration. Ellen Brooker was admitted on the 8th inst. The children have attended very well during the week. **12** Several boys absent at Rod stripping. Have sent messages to their parents. The Attendance Officer has not called for over a month. I sent several names, or irregular children, to Bradfield on Saturday last, but have heard nothing since.

May 17 The Attendance Officer called. **19** Rev. J. Slatter gave a scripture lesson to Std 3. Several boys absent. Attendance during the week very fair.

May 25 The School was not opened today. **26** The attendance has not been so good as usual, during the last few days. Several boys go to rod stripping one or two half days in the week. School closed for Whitsun Holiday. To re-open on June 5th.

June 4 Re-opened School after Whitsun vacation. **6** Miss Watkins, Assistant Mistress, sent in her resignation. **10** Satisfactory progress has been made during the week:— Average 141.3. No. on Books 156. George & Ellen Hazell, & Joseph Hine returned to the School on the 6th inst. The Attendance Officer visited on the 8th inst., when there were no bad cases of irregular attendance to report. Esther Ridge, John Higley and Ada Lewendon absent with colds &c.

June 16 Punished Richd Lewendon, Edward Wallis & Alfred Wayman for Playing truant. Esther Ridge, John Higley & Alice Stubbings absent all the week through illness. Average for the week = 141.3. No. on Books 156.

June 23 Revd — Tom[p]kins, the new Curate, visited on the 19th & 22nd inst. and gave scripture lessons.[105] Revd J. Slatter visited this morning and gave a Scripture lesson to Std 3. Recd notice that the Diocesan Inspection had been postponed till Novr, our usual month. Esther Ridge, John Higley, Ellen Hazell, & Henry Head, have been absent with colds &c. all the week.

June 26 Revd — Tompkins visited.   **28** Rev. J. Slatter visited, and gave a Scripture lesson to upper standards. I sent George Hazell home for refusing to hold out his hand. The case has been reported to the School Managers. **30** Revd J. Slatter visited — and took the scripture of Standard 3. Miss S. J. Brown, from St Peter's National School, Devizes, called respecting the post of Assistant Mistress — she was appointed by the Managers — to enter upon duties on Septr 6. 1882. Attendance throughout the week very satisfactory — except in Stds 5 & 6. Esther Ridge still absent.

July 7 Rev. — Tompkins visited on the 3rd, 4th & 6th inst. Revd. J. Slatter visited on the 5th inst. and gave a Scripture Lesson. In future the Lesson from 11.30 — 12 on Friday morning will be an open one, instead of Singing as per Time Table. Arthur Lyford's name has been taken off the books. Esther Ridge, Mary Tyrell & Alice Lewendon absent, through illness, all the week. The work of all standards is progressing satisfactorily, with the exception of Std 2. in spelling.

July 14 The school was not opened yesterday afternoon. Many children absent, especially those of the upper Standards. Esther Ridge & Fanny Lewendon returned to school on Monday. George Hazell, Joseph Hine & Ellen Hine have left school; their names have been taken off the Books.

July 21 Revd J. Slatter visited once, and Revd — Tompkins twice, during the past week. Attendance throughout the week, good. Mary Tyrell is still too ill to attend.

July 26 Admitted Minnie Clatworthy & Sophia Turner.   **28** Rev. J. Slatter visited. Average for the week = 138.3. No. on Books 153. Sent a list of irregular children to Bradfield.

Aug. 1 Several boys absent, at work. Notices sent to the parents.   **2** Boys who were at work returned to school. Attendance only fair.   **4** Rev. J. Slatter visited. Average for the week 134.7. No. on Books, 153. Selina Lewendon ill all the week.

Aug. 8 Attendance very low — only 103 present. Many boys and girls, some only 6 years old, being engaged in the fields at harvest work.   **9** Still a very low attendance.   **11** Closed school for Harvest Holidays — one month — To re-open on Sept. 11th. Miss Watkins, the Assistant Mistress, resigns on Septr 8th. Registers marked 9.15–9.25. Children dismissed at 11.30.

---

[105] Herbert Chilton Tompkins, of New College, Oxford, was curate at Whitchurch from June 1882 until he became rector of Leckhampstead in his native Bucks. in 1883.

Sept. 11 Re-opened school, Attendance very fair. Several boys still absent, Harvest not quite finished. Miss Brown entered upon her duties as Assistant Mistress. **15** Selina Lewendon & Wm Wayman absent through illness all the week.

Sept. 18 All the boys absent at work last week, returned to school today. Full school. **20** Revd Canon Slatter visited, and gave a Scripture Lesson to Std 3. **21** Four boys and one girl went to Reading fair. Attendance rather lower than usual. Admitted Christopher Gray. **22** Satisfactory progress has been made in the various subjects — although some of the children are still backward in spelling. Rev. Canon Slatter visited.

Sept. 29 Selina Lewendon, Chas Wells and Ellen Yates have been too ill to attend school during the past week. Revd J. Slatter visited today. The attendance has not been so satisfactory as usual. Some children frequently absent themselves, and give no reason. Took Christ. Gray's name off books. Admitted Chas & Kate Chapman on the 25th inst.

Oct. 2 Re-admitted Alice Weller. Received a message to the effect that Chas Wells and Arthur Lewendon were ordered by the Doctor not to attend school for another week. **4** Received a note from the Attendance Officer asking for a list of defaulters. Eight names were returned. Revd J. Slatter visited, and gave a Scripture Lesson to Standard II. **6** Examined Standard I — satisfactory results — Punished 4 boys for playing truant. Attendance throughout the week very fair.

Oct. 8 A. C. Forbes Esqre called — cautioned the boys about throwing stones, &c. **9** Examined Standards 2 and 3 in all subjects — and found Grammar in both standards and reading in Std 2 rather unsatisfactory. **10** Examined Standards IV–VI — results, with the exception of Grammar in Std 4, very satisfactory. **13** Many children absent, only 130 out of 150, present in the afternoon. Revd J. Slatter visited, and fixed the 30th inst. for Examination in Religious Knowledge. Received notice that Arthur Lewendon had gone to work. He was 13 on the 9th inst. William and Emily Pocock have left the parish.

Oct. 16 Very wet day. Only 69 present. Arthur Lewendon returned to school. Selina Lewendon still absent through illness. **18** Attendance Officer called and took names of some irregular boys & girls. Commenced afternoon meetings at 1.45 instead of 2 o'clock — Registers marked 1.45–1.55. **20** Took Wm & Emily Pocock, and Elizabeth Detfield off Admission Book. Average for the week =121.3. No. on Books 148.

Oct. 24 Heavy rain throughout the day. No school was held. **25** Attendance good, only 4 absent. **27** Another wet day. Many absent in Standard II. Punished Arthur Cook yesterday for impertinence; he was kept away this morning. Esther & Julia Ridge, and Louisa Bushnell, are unable to get to school, owing to the rise of the river.

Oct. 30 School visited by Diocesan Inspector. **31** For the future, the sewing lessons for Infant girls will be held on Wednesday afternoon and Friday Morning instead of Wednesday Morning and Friday afternoon. **Nov. 3** A. C. Forbes Esq. called and brought the Government Forms. Agnes Lewis, Fred Shaw, and Charles Reeves absent all the week through illness. Several boys absent in the afternoon, no reason given. Sent a list of irregular children to the Bradfield S.A. Committee. Examined Standard I in Arithmetic and dictation; there was only one failure in each subject.

Nov. 6 Miss Brown, the Assistant Mistress, was absent during the afternoon. **10** Revd Canon Slatter called and brought the Report of the Diocesan Inspector:—

Whitchurch School, 1882
The Children seem intelligent and have been carefully instructed in Holy Scripture and the Church Catechism.
The writing is good, and attention has evidently been paid to spelling.
The Infant School is also in a satisfactory state.
Prize — William Burgess
C. G. WODEHOUSE   (Diocesan Inspector of Schools)

Nov. 13 Admitted Bertha A. Lyford from Goring Heath Schools. Attendance Officer called. **16** Heavy fall of snow. Only 60 children presented themselves. **17** Several children have been too ill to attend school during the week. Examined Standards III in Arithc — results very satisfactory, although the children are not so ready in working problems as I should like. During the week I have also examined the Second Standard, in all subjects, with very fair results, except in a few cases.

Nov. 20 Some of the girls having finished their needlework for the examination, they will do their other lessons instead of needlework for a few weeks. **22** Standard 3 girls had an extra lesson in needlework. Revd Canon Slatter visited. Recd Notice that H.M. Inspector would visit these schools on Jany 29 1883. The Pupil Teachers' Exam — to be held at St Giles' Boys School, Reading on Saty 25th inst. A. C. Forbes Esq. called. **24** Julia Ridge, Charlotte Detfield, & Fredk Smith have been absent, through illness, all the week. Charles Detfield & Charles Yates have been taken off books. Examined the first class in all subjects — results very satisfactory. **25** Pupil Teachers' Examination at St Giles' Sch. Reading.

Nov. 27 Full School — Bertha Lyford absent with a sore-throat. **28** A. C. Forbes Esq. & Mrs Forbes called in the afternoon. It has been arranged with H.M. Inspector that our Examination will be held on Jany 15. at 9.15 a.m. instead of Jan. 19th as previously notified. **Dec. 1** Satisfactory attendance throughout the week. Most of the girls have finished their sewing. **2** Pupil Teachers' Scripture Examination at St Giles Boys' School, Reading.

Dec. 5 Attended without notice to check the Registers 103 B & G 36 Infts. [J. SLATTER]. Revd J. Slatter visited. Recd Notice from H.M. Inspector that he had finally fixed Jany 10th 1883 at 9.15 a.m. for our Examination. **8** Heavy fall of snow. Poor attendance in consequence, 62 absent in the morning, and 67 in the Afternoon. Charles Reeves has been away, with a severe Cold, for several days.

Dec. 15 Amy & Henry Wells, & Edward Jeacocke away all the week through illness. Sophia Turner, & Fanny Knight absent, being unable to attend for want of shoes. Many children have stayed away several days during the past month. Two lists have been forwarded to the Bradfield School Attendance Committee but no notice has been taken of them. The Girls have been forbidden to enter their playground by the usual way, for fear of accidents from falling chalk. Examined the first class in all subjects, with very satisfactory results. Some of the children rather careless over the spelling of small, easy words. A blackboard has been fixed in School, on which the No. of Scholars absent each day will be recorded, so that visitors will be able to see at a glance how the children attend. During the past week the average No. of absentees = 18, or 12 per cent of the No. on Books.

Dec. 20 A. C. Forbes Esq. called. **21** Attendance Officer called, respecting the irregularity of Edward Wallis, whose parents are to be proceeded against. **22** The percentage of absentees during the past week = 14.5. Closed School for Christmas Holidays. To re-open of [*sic*] January 1st 1883.

1883

Jan. 1 Re-opened school — very fair attendance. **3** Attendance Officer called. Several children absent. **4** Emily & Minnie Tomlin, Harry Wells and Mary Turner absent through illness. Esther & Julia Ridge unable to attend, owing to the flood. A Meeting of the School Managers is to be held on Saturday — to Audit the accounts &c. **5** A. C. Forbes Esq. called — 24 children absent. The attendance during the past week has been worse than usual — Average only 130, out of 143 on the books. **6** The School Managers met to audit the accounts &c. for the past year. Recd notice that Edith Grist had gained a 'First Class' in the recent P.T's Scripture Examination.

Jan. 10 Examination. H.M. Inspector and his Assistant visited and examined the school. Rev. Canon Slatter called. Half-holiday in the afternoon. The following Recitation Pieces were submitted to H.M. Inspector, and approved —

Std I	The Clucking Hen.
Std II	The waves on the seashore.
	Which loved best.
Std III	We are seven (Wordsworth)
Std IV	The Village Blacksmith (Longfellow)
	The Black Prince (Smedley)
Std V.	Introduction to the Lay of the Last Minstrel (Scott)
Std VI & VI[I]	Selection from The Ancient Mariner (Coleridge)

H.M. Inspector also approved of the Grouping of Standards 4–7 for Geography. **11** Re-arranged the Classes; and commenced the new work. Good attendance.

12 Edward Wallis, and Herbert Ward absent with Bronchitis. Average for the week, 130.7. No. on Books 141. Punished Charles Barrett for playing truant.

Jan. 17 Punished 8 boys for playing truant the previous afternoon. Attendance Officer called to get the attendances of Alfred and William Wayman, and Julia and Herbert Ward, whose parents are to be summoned. Mrs Winchester will be absent from school during the ensuing month, and monitors will be appointed to take charge of the Infants. **19** Historical Readers for Standards III–VII, and Geographical Readers for Standards I & II have been received. The Geogl Readers for the other standards have not yet been published. Edward Wallis, Chas Wells, Ada Newman, Charles Reeves, Wm Cox, Frank Lewendon, & Minnie Tomlin absent with severe colds &c. Eliz. Bushnell, Amy Wells, & Eva Whiting have left school. Average for the week only 120.5.

Jan. 26 Visited without notice to check Register. No. correct 123. J. SLATTER. Mary Tyrell, Edward Jeacocke, Edwd Wallis, Sarah Knight, Frank & Louisa Fabry, Julia Ridge and Mary Stubbings absent with colds &c. The Attendance Officer called on the 24th inst. Sarah Ridge has left School. Emily Tomlin has succeeded her sister Fanny as Monitress in the Infants' Room. Margaret Gamble was admitted on the 22nd inst. The attendance during the past week has again been rather poor, the average being only 124. At present there is a very low number of children under 7 years of age attending school, the No. on the Infants' Book = 18 only.

Jan. 29 Weather very damp — consequently a poor attendance. Walter & Elizth Taylor absent with severe colds. **31** The Attendance Officer called to obtain information relative [to] the recent attendances made by the Wards and Waymans. Rev. H. Tompkins gave a scripture lesson to Standards 2 and 3. **Feb. 1** Rev. J. Slatter visited and brought the Govt Report on the school. Punished Albert Wells for idleness, after which he was very impudent, and got the poker, to strike me. Copy of Her Majesty's Inspector's Report.

Whitchurch (Reading) Parochial School (Oxford)

In many respects good Infants' instruction is being carried out, though I would like to see the babies kept for much less time over their A, B, C. The sewing, as a whole, seems fair. The Discipline of both rooms is good, and the general results in the "Standard" Classes are good.[106]

E. L. M. Grist has passed fairly, but should attend to Teaching.

Herbert W. Winchester   Certd Teacher 2nd Class.

Henrietta Winchester   Certd Teacher 2nd Class.

---

[106] Under the Code of 1882, Article 109(b), a *merit grant* was offered, 'amounting to 1s., 2s., or 3s., if the Inspector, allowing for the special circumstances of the case, reports the school to be fair, good, or excellent in respect of (1) the organization and discipline; (2) the intelligence employed in instruction; and (3) the general quality of the work, especially in the elementary subjects'. Parliamentary Papers, 1883, LIII. For infants, the merit grant was 2s., 4s. or 6s. There was also a *fixed grant* of 4s. 6d. per child for the older scholars, and of 7s. or 9s. each for infants.

Sarah Jane Brown   Assistant Teacher.
Edith L. M. Grist   Pupil Teacher Third Year.

ALEXANDER C. FORBES   Correspondent

Received a Prize for the Pupil Teacher for proficiency in Scripture, from Revd E. Barber, the Diocesan Inspector of Schools. **2** Wet day. Poor attendance, only 8, out of 18 present in Infants' Room. Recd 30 'Robinson Crusoe', from Moffatt's, for use in Standards 5–7, instead of ordinary reading books. Geographical Readers for Standards 3 to 7 have not yet been forwarded. The general progress made by the several Standards in their new work is, on the whole, satisfactory. The average for the past week = 120, No. on Books 137.

Feb. 9 Attendance during the week only fair. Took Fanny Lewendon's name off books. Re-admitted Charles Yates on the 6th inst. Sent a list of irregular scholars to Bradfield. Sarah Hine fell down & cut her eye, and was sent home by the doctor.

Feb. 12 Weather very wet and windy — consequently a very poor attendance. **16** Many children have been absent throughout the week, with severe colds & coughs — and the average attendance lower than it has been for several months. Average for the week 107.5. No. on Books 138.

Feb. 18 Admitted Mary Ann Winterbourne. Took Margaret Gamble off books. Mary Tyrell returned after an absence of 4 weeks. **20** Attendance officer called — and gave notice that the Bradfield School Attendance Committee had resolved not to take proceedings in cases where the child had passed the Fifth Standard in two subjects only. **23** Revd Canon Slatter visited, and gave a Scripture lesson to the First Class. Attendance has very much improved during the past week. Average 126.3. No. on books 136. The Carpenter brought a plan of the School and Playground for the use of Standard I. Satisfactory progress has been made during the past 6 weeks, except in cases where the scholars have been irregular. The Royal Geographical Readers for Standard 3 have been received.

Mar. 2 Revd Canon Slatter visited — and examined the Second and Third Classes in Scripture. Very fair attendance during the week. Received a certificate from the Mistress of Goring Heath School, to the effect that Bertha Lyford had passed Standard I in that School. Miss Forbes called in the afternoon. Walter Taylor absent with a severe cold.

Mar. 5 Re-admitted Charles Detfield. Charles Yates & Ellen Brooker returned to school after several weeks' absence. A great number of boys and girls went to a treat given at the chapel. Although the time fixed was 5 o'clock, they all went home to dinner & did not return. **7** Revd Canon Slatter examined the 2nd Class in Scripture. **9** The average for the past week = only 119, out of 137 on books. A list of irregular children has been forwarded to Bradfield School Attendance Committee. Received some Needlework material from Moffatt's. Punished Alfred Wayman for being impudent.

Mar. 16 Took Charles Detfield and Ellen Brooker off books. The average is again low. Many boys have been away getting wood. Sent another list of irregular scholars to Bradfield. No notice has been taken of the last list sent.

Mar. 21 Revd. J. Slatter examined 1st Class in Scripture. No notice has been taken of the list of irregular scholars sent last week. **22** Closed school for Easter Holidays — to re-open on April 2nd. Very poor attendance throughout the week.

Apr. 2 Re-opened school — only a fair attendance. Admitted Harry Smith — a boy 6 years old, who has never attended any school (although he has always resided in this parish), and does not know a letter. A. C. Forbes Esq. visited, and asked me to get the school prizes. **3** A concert was held in the evening. The school was opened at 1.30 instead of 2 in the afternoon. Registers marked 1.30–1.40. **6** Attendance throughout the week very bad — Average only 117. No. on Books 136. Sent another list of irregular scholars, to Bradfield School Attendance Committee.

Apr. 11 Rev. Canon Slatter visited. **12** Recd. School Prizes from Natl Society's Depôt. **13** No notice has been taken of the list of Irregular scholars. Many children absent. Only 29 present in the 1st Class out of 45 on Books. Recd a Doctor's Certificate for Fredk Shaw, who is suffering from a diseased brain.

Apr. 17 Funeral of Fred. Shaw. His death was caused through play going home by which his head was bumped against the wall and being of delicate constitution it produced inflammation. Counted number present in afternoon without notice 129. JOHN SLATTER. **18** Attendance Officer visited. Admitted 4 new Scholars on the 15th inst. **19** George Martin, and Eliz. Barrett absent through illness. Wet morning; consequently several away. A. C. Forbes Esq. and — Wilson Esq. (chairman of the Reading School Board) visited in the afternoon.[107]

Apr. 23 Re-admitted Charles Detfield. Received notice from the Mistress of Bright Waltham Schools that Mary Winterbourne had not passed any Standard while in that School. **25** Attendance Officer called, and said that the School Attendance Committee has resolved not to prosecute in any case where the child had passed Standard 4. The Standard fixed by the Bye-Laws for this parish is Standard 5. I have mentioned the matter to the School Managers. **27** Took Arthur Lewendon's name off books. Attendance has slightly improved during the past week — Average 130. No. on Books 144. Charlotte Hine absent all the week with a bad leg. Recd Gill's Standard 4 Whitehall Geographical Readers, and commenced using them, in Stds 4–7. The children are, on the whole, making very fair progress in their work. Miss Brown, the Assistant Mistress received notice, on the 14th inst. from the Managers, that her services would not be

---

[107] Joseph Henry Wilson (1821–1896), J.P., was chairman of the Reading School Board for twenty-five years, from the Board's inception until shortly before his death. He was a personal friend of Bishops Wilberforce and Mackarness (Obituary in *Reading Mercury*, 30 May 1896).

required after July 14. If accommodation can be provided, two transfer Pupil Teachers will be substituted for the Assistant.

Apr. 30 Admitted two new scholars in the Infants' Department. **May 4** Revd Canon Slatter, Mrs & Miss Slatter came and distributed the Prizes to those who had passed the Govt Examination. Albert Newman and Elizth Barrett away all the week with rheumatism. Took Thomas Barrett and Edward Shaw off registers. Attendance throughout the week very good. The Boys who have only passed in two subjects in Standard 5, are still at work, no notice being taken of them by the Local Authorities.

May 9 Revd Canon Slatter called. **10** Many scholars absent owing to the weather being very wet. Heavy fall of snow. **11** Several still away — although the weather was fine. Closed school for Whitsun Holidays — to last one week. Recd Moffatt's Geographical Readers for Std 3, which will be used instead of Nelson's. Satisfactory progress has been made during the past few weeks — some of the children are, however, still rather backward in Arithc. On the 9th inst John Cross had to be sent home for refusing to do a task after school, and afterwards not holding out his hand for punishment. His father brought him up the following morning, and promised to chastise him severely if he were sent home again for insubordination.

May 20 Re-opened school after Whitsuntide Holidays. Admitted Albert Sargeant. Received Medical Certificates for Alfred Hine & Eliza Turner — Frank Fabry, Ellen Yates & Charlotte Turner away through illness. **24** Revd H. C. Tompkins visited. Weather very sultry — almost unbearable at the end of the afternoon. Miss Brown, the Assistant Mistress, fainted. **25** Heavy thunderstorm, children unable to leave school till 4.45 p.m. Edward Jeacocke away from home all the week. Took Albert Bartlett, Joseph Dicken, George Higley & William Wallis off books. Average for the week 125. No. on books 139.

May 29 Admitted Alice Lawrence. **June 1** Eliza Turner, Elizth Taylor, Charlotte Turner, Charles Yates and Elizth Sharp Absent throughout the week, through illness. Alfred Hine returned to school on the 28th inst. Sent a list of irregular scholars to Bradfield. Examined the Arithmetic of all standards during the week. The results, with the exception of Standard II, were satisfactory. At present the 4th Standard, especially the boys find it difficult to read the geographical books which contain a good many hard words. The same difficulty is experienced in Standd 3.

June 4 Admitted Henry John Taylor, and Louisa Shaw, the latter, although 5 years of age last Septr has not attended School previously. This is the Third case this year, in which a child has attained the age of 5 years some time before attending school. Both of the other cases have been reported to the Local Authority but no notice has been taken. **6** Arthur Cook was kept at home in the afternoon because he was detained in school after 12 o'clock. Punished Charles Barrett for refusing to do his lessons. **7** Half-holiday given in the afternoon, as I was compelled to be absent, attending a person who had met with an accident. **8** Satisfactory attendances throughout the week. Took Fredk Pocock and Sarah Wallis off books.

June 13 Attendance officer called, and examined the Registers. **15** Satisfactory progress has been made during the past few weeks. Attendances during the week very fair — Fredk Bushnell away through illness. Mary Tyrell absent two days without any reason being given. Average for the week = 130. No. on Bks 140. Alice Wells has left school.

June 18 Miss Talbot called respecting the post of Assistant Mistress. **20** A. C. Forbes Esq. & — Gardiner Esq. visited. **22** A. C. Forbes Esq. called. Punished A. Tomlin & M. Tyrell for going home before the completion of their task. Mary Turner and Alice Knight absent all the week through illness.

June 25 Mary Turner and Alice Knight returned to school. **27** Miss Young, from Ashfold, called respecting the post of Assistant Mistress — and the Managers offered it to her, as she appeared likely to give satisfaction. **29** The attendance during the week has been fairly satisfactory.

July 2 Admitted George W. Barrett. Recd Medical Certe for Willm Cox, who was suffering from ulcerate[d] throat. **4** Revd J. Slatter gave a Scripture Lesson to Class I. Miss Young has been appointed Assistant Mistress in the Place of Miss Brown, who will leave on the 14th inst. **6** Sent a list of Irregular Scholars to the Bradfield S.A. Committee. Many of the older children were absent in the afternoon — only 92 being present. Average for the week = 127. No. on Bks 139. Cautioned the boys about throwing stones in the playground. Sent a New Time Table for Infant's Dept. to H.M. Inspector for approval.

July 9 Revd Canon Slatter called and promised the Sunday School a treat on the 12th inst. **10** Recd New Time Table from H.M.I. and commenced working according to the same in the Infants' Deptt. **12** A. C. Forbes Esq. called. Recd a letter, from Miss Young, to say that as she was not strictly a church woman, she declined the post of Assistant Mistress. **13** Miss Brown, the Assistant Mistress, left — her engagement having terminated. Took Wm Grist, Wm Burgess, John Cross and Edw Reeves off Books. Average for the week = 128. No. on books 139.

July 16 Recd Medical Certificates for George Martin and George Barrett — who were suffering from headache. Rev. Canon Slatter called. **17** Miss A. Attwood came to give temporary assistance for a few days. **18** Punished William Hine and Arthur Cook for playing truant. **20** Very fair attendance during the week. **21** Miss Worrell had an interview with the School Managers, respecting the post of Assistant Mistress.

July 25 The attendance Officer called and examined the registers. **26** A. C. Forbes Esq. visited. Recd Medical certificates for Julia Ward & Thos. Wallis. **27** The average for the past week is much lower than usual, owing to illness. Thos Wallis, Julia Ward, Emma Thorpe, and Charlotte Turner, have been absent all the week. Miss Ada Wrightson, of Ramsgate Holy Trinity Mixed School, has been appointed Assistant Mistress, to commence duties on the 30th inst. During the past few days I have examined, thoroughly, Standards I and II, and find their work, as a rule, especially in Arithmetic, not at all satisfactory. The work of Standard III has very much improved lately.

July 30 Admitted Gertrude, and Hetty Cullum, who have come to stay in the district for a few weeks. Rev. J. Slatter called. Miss Ada Wrightson entered upon her duties as Assistant Mistress. **Aug. 1** Attendance Officer called and examined the books. **2** Whitchurch Flower Show. Many scholars away in the morning. Holiday given in the afternoon. **3** Wet morning. Very many children absent. The average attendance for the week much lower than usual. The Arithc & Dictation of Standard II, still very unsatisfactory. Sent a list of irregular children, to Bradfield.

Aug. 8 Verified the Register this morning and found present 97 Boys & Girls in the Upper School 29 in the Infant Dept. All in good order. JOHN SLATTER. Attendance Officer called, and received a list of several children of school age, and not in attendance. **10** Took Gertrude & Hetty Cullum off books. Average for the past week only fair.

Aug. 15 Closed School for Harvest Holidays.

Sept. 17 Re-opened school with good attendance, Harvest quite finished. Re-admitted George Smith, & Admitted Emily Kirk. **19** Attendance Officer called. Several children of school age are not attending any School. **20** Punished Arthur Cook for playing truant on previous day. Examined Second Standard, results in Arithmetic & Dictation still very unsatisfactory. **21** Alice & Mary Stubbings having removed to Streatley, & Alice Knight and Edith Lewendon, having left, their names have been taken off the Books.

Sept. 28 A. C. Forbes Esq. called. Louisa Smith has been ill all the past week. Arthur Cook played truant on the 26th & 27 inst. Average for the week only fair. Some of the 1st Class not attending at all satisfactorily.

Oct. 1 Recd notice that Fanny Lewendon and Mary Ann Winterbourne had left school. Wet day. Many children away. **5** The weather has been very damp all the week, and the average attendance low, in consequence. Louisa Smith still too unwell to attend. Took Fanny Lewendon & Mary Winterbourne off books. Sent a list of irregular children to Bradfield.

Oct. 8 A. C. Forbes Esq. visited. **10** Attendance Officer called and asked several children what they did, when not at school. **12** The attendance during the past week has been very good; especially in the Infants' Department — where no children has [*sic*] been absent at all. On the 10th inst. Stds 5 & 6 had Map drawing instead of C'B's.[108]

[108] An abbreviation for Copy Books.

Oct. 17 The Attendance Officer visited, and reported that the S.A. Committee had resolved to summon the Parents of Bertha Lyford. **19** The Fifth Standard will practise Map drawing instead of writing in Copy Books for a few weeks. **20** Wet day. Many scholars absent in the afternoon. Louisa Smith and Edward Jeacocke absent through illness. Examined Standard 2 in Arithmetic; results fairly satisfactory.

Oct. 25 A. C. Forbes Esq. called. **27** Louisa Smith still absent — Alfred Wayman is, also, under medical men, and has been absent all the week. Attendance during the week only very fair. Most of the standards are making good progress in their work — but the Arithc of Std 2, though improving, is not very satisfactory. The school Managers have agreed to an arrangement by which Mrs Winchester will resign the post of Infants' Mistress after the Govt Inspection, when an Assistant will be employed instead.

Oct. 30 Miss M. McLennan has been appointed to the post of Assistant Infants' Mistress — to commence duties after the Govt Examination in January 1884. **Nov. 2** A. C. Forbes Esq. & Revd Canon Slatter visited. Recd Notice that the Diocesan Inspector for the district intended visiting these schools on the 20th inst. In consequence of the opening of a New Church in the parish on the 31st ult, a half holiday was given on that day.[109] Attendance during the past week very good.

Nov. 5 Louisa Smith returned to school after an absence of several weeks. Afternoon meetings commenced at 1.45 instead of 2 o'clock. Alfred Wayman has gone to the Reading Hospital to be treated for a bad leg. **8** Revd Canon Slatter visited, and examined Standards 2 & 3 in Catechism. **9** Recd a medical certificate for Harry Lawrence, who is suffering from Consumption. Frank Fabry has also been ill all the week, with an eruption on the head. Attendance throughout the week very fair. Recd Notice that the Pupil Teacher's Scripture Examination will be held at St Giles's School, Reading on Saturday Decr 1st.

Nov. 11 Admitted Charles Hazell, aged 6, and Thomas Hazell, aged 7 years — neither knowing his letters. **16** George Martin fell down in the playground on the 13th inst. and hurt himself so much that he is under medical care. Edward Wallis has been absent with croup all the week. Frank Fabry & Willm Newman still too ill to attend. Examined Standard 5 in Arithmetic — results not very satisfactory. The Arithc of Stand 2 has much improved during the past fortnight.

Nov. 20 School examined by the Diocesan Inspector. Half-holiday given in the afternoon. **21** A. C. Forbes Esq. visited. Recd notice that H.M. Inspector intended examining the schools on January 9th 1884, at 9.15 a.m. also that the Pupil Teachers Examn would be held at St Giles' School Reading on the 24th inst.

---

[109] This was the Church of St John the Baptist at Whitchurch Hill, which was consecrated by Bishop Mackarness in 1883. The land for the Church was donated by Mr C. L. Gardiner and the total cost of the building and furnishings was about £1,891. See Baker, p. 34.

Nov. 28 Attendance Officer called.   **30** Revd Canon Slatter visited, and brought a report from the Diocn Inspector.

Whitchurch C.E. Schools. 1883
The children have been very well instructed in Religious Truths, and give intelligent and accurate answers.
The writing is good, and Spelling above the average.
The Infants were anxious to answer & passed very creditably.
Prize   Ernest Ashby
Commended   Frank Grist   George Smith   Albert Tomlin
                              C. G. WODEHOUSE   Diocesan Inspector

A. C. Forbes Esq. & Mrs Forbes visited in the afternoon, and brought the books &c. requisite for a Boot Club, which is to commence on Decr 3rd. Sophia Turner & B. Lyford absent through illness. Attendance during the week very fair.

Dec. 1 Pupil Teachers' Scripture Examination at St Giles' Boys' School, Reading.   **5** Visited the school to prove the Registers Present 97 & 28 Infts. = 125. J.S.   **8** Several children have been too ill to attend school during the past week. Omitting those the average has been very good, especially in the Senior Deptt where the average = 98 out of 100 on books. Alfred Wayman has come out of the Hospital but is still very ill. Examined Standards 5 and 6 in Map Drawing. A few of the maps were fairly done — the others not at all satisfactory.

Dec. 14 Emma Thorpe has been absent during the last fortnight, through illness. Took Alfred Wayman's name off books. He has been away, owing to a bad leg, for 8 weeks, and probably will not be able to come to school for some time. The attendance has improved this week, av. 125. Also took Henry Lawrence off books. The Doctor does not think he will ever again be strong enough to attend school — being in consumption.

Dec. 19 Visited to check the Register. Present 90 & 32 Infts. J.S.   **20** Mrs & Miss Forbes visited, and gave all the girls nice ullsters [sic].[110]   **21** A. C. Forbes Esq. called. Closed school for the Christmas Holidays — one week. To re-open on Decr 31st.

Dec. 31 Re-opened school — attendance very fair. Several children too ill to attend. Admitted Charles Hearn.   **Jan. 4** Average for the week only 120. No. on books 134. Bertha Lyford, who, by the order of the Doctor, has been kept at home to attend to her mother, who is very seriously ill, has not returned to school yet. The following children have been absent through illness during the past — week Mary Turner, Eliza Turner, Charles Barrett, James Wallis, Thomas Franklin, Henry Taylor.

1884
Jan. 6 Recd Notice that H.M. Inspector intended visiting these schools on Thursday the 17th inst. instead of next Wednesday. The School Managers met to

[110] Ulsters were long, loose overcoats, often worn with a belt.

audit accounts &c. All those who had been away through illness return to School. **10** Revd Canon Slatter called in the morning and reported the result of the P.T. Scripture Examn. **11** Several children went home to dinner and did not return to school in the afternoon. Edward Wallis, Charlotte Wells, Albert Newman, and Agnes Lewis absent through illness. Average for the week = 125, No. on books 134.

Jan. 14 The children absent through sickness during the previous week returned to school. **17** School visited by H.M. Inspector, for the Annual inspection. A. C. Forbes Esq., and Rev. J. Slatter visited. **18** Took Charlotte Lambourne's name off admission Bks. Arranged the children in their new Standards. Half holiday given in the afternoon. Mrs Winchester resigned the post of Infants' mistress. Average for the week 126. No. on Books 135.

Jan. 21 Miss M. McLennan entered upon her duties as Infants' Mistress. Commenced working according to the New Time Table. Began needlework in the Mixed school under the superintendence of the Assistant Mistress. **25** Charlotte Wells, James Wallis, Elizth Sharp, Alice Weller absent with severe colds & coughs. Attendance throughout the week only fair.

Jan. 27 Recd Duplicate Examination Schedule, from H.M.I. **28** Issued circulars to the effect that the School Managers had decided to raise the School fees from 1d. to 2d. & to return, at the end of the year, 1d. for each week of regular attendance. **30** The Attendance Officer visited, to examine the registers. **Feb. 1** Took Annie Lewendon's name off books. Several children absent in the afternoon. Average for the past week, 128. No. on books 134.

Feb. 4 About 20 children were sent home to get their school fees. Recd a medical certificate for Bertha Lyford, and also for Eva Hazell. **5** Admitted Joseph Hutt. All children sent home for pence returned to school. **8** A. C. Forbes Esq. visited. Attendance since the 4th inst. very good indeed.

Feb. 11 Admitted Ernest Simmonds. **15** Took John Cook's name off books. Recd Notice that Miss Wrightson had been recognised as an assistant in these schools. The Attendance throughout the week has been very good. Average 126.4. No. on Bks 135. Copy of H.M. Inspector's Report —

Whitchurch (Reading) Parochial School (Oxford)

The general results are certainly good. Needlework was fair. The fourth Standard Reading fell below par, and so did the Composition of the fifth Standard. The Geography was generally good, and the written Grammar exercises fairly good on the whole. Frequent oral exercises both on Grammar and Mental Arithmetic would do great good here. The singing was pleasing.

The general working and results among these Infants' Classes are good. The Needlework fair.

E. L. M. Grist has passed well.

Herbert W. Winchester   Certd Teacher 2nd Class.

Ada Wrightson   Assistant teacher.

Margaret J. McLennan   Assistant Teacher.
Edith L. M. Grist   Pupil Teacher 4th Year.

ALEXANDER C. FORBES   Manager

The following Recitation pieces for 1884, have been sanctioned by H.M. Inspector

Std I	The Boy and the Sheep	20 lines
,, II	Compassion (Aikin)	40 ,,
,, III	Lucy Gray (Wordsworth)	60 ,,
,, IV	The wreck of the Hesperus (Longfellow)	88 ,,
,, V, VI, VII Lay of the Last Minstrel (Scott)		
	Canto I: 100 & 150 ,,	

Feb. 18 Re-admitted Alfred Wayman, who had been away for several months with a bad leg.   **19** A. C. Forbes Esq. visited.   **20** Attendance Officer called for names of defaulters.   **22** The Attendance, since the school fees have been raised, has greatly improved. Satisfactory progress in the various subjects has been made during the past 5 weeks. Commenced learning recitation pieces.

Feb. 25 Admitted Ashton and Salisbury Brewer.   **29** Took Mary Tyrell, Agnes Lewis, and Char. Hine off the Books. Attendance throughout the week very good. The men came to take measurements for curtains to separate the classes in the Mixed School. Sent a list of defaulters to Bradfield S. A. Com.

Mar. 4 Attended to verify the Register found 101 in Larger Schlrm, 16 in Infants' Total 117. [J. SLATTER]   **6** A. C. Forbes Esq. visited in the afternoon. **7** Owing to illness, and damp weather, the average during the week has been lower than usual.

Mar. 12 Punished Edw. Wallis & Wm Hine for playing truant.   **14** Emma Thorpe, Eliz. Goodall and Bertha Lyford away through illness. Very fair attendance during the past week, av. 124. Good progress has been made in all standards during the past month.

Mar. 18 Admitted Elizabeth House. Had notice that Alice Lawrence had left school as her parents were leaving the parish.   **20** Revd Cluff, the new curate gave a scripture lesson to Standards IV to VII.[111] A. C. Forbes Esq. visited to see the new curtains, which prove very useful indeed as they prevent the children seeing what is going on in different parts of the room, so that their attention is fixed more on their own work.   **21** Fred Bushnell & Bertha Lyford still too ill to attend school. Average for the week = 124.3. No. on books 134.

Mar. 24 A. C. Forbes visited. Bertha Lyford returned to school. Lily Jeacocke ill. Made an alteration in the Infants' Time-Table, so that a little

---

[111] William Charles Cluff, the new curate, took a Fourth in Modern History from St John's College, Oxford, in June 1883, and remained at Whitchurch from Dec. 1883 to 1887, when he became curate at St Saviour's, Hoxton.

additional time might be given to needlework, as the boys will take that subject as well as the girls in the future.   **28** Good attendance throughout the week.

Apr. 1 A. C. Forbes Esq. visited in the morning. Charlotte Wells & Sarah Dicker away through illness. Punished Edwd Wallis, Jas Wallis & Chas Lewendon for playing truant.   **3** Revd Cluff gave a scripture lesson to Stds iv to vii. Punished John Barrett for great impertinence — & disobedience. Sent Herbert & Joseph Hutt home because they were in such a dirty state, that they were not fit to mix with the other boys.   **4** Owing to illness, the attendance during the past few days has only been very fair. The Attendance officer called on the 2nd inst for a list of irregular scholars. Took George Martin's name off books.

Apr. 7 Very wet day — only 100 present.   **8** Recd Medical certificate for Annie & Alice Lewendon.   **10** The attendance during the past week has been rather low, owing to sickness and damp weather. Had notice that Salisbury and Ashton Brewer would not attend school again as they were leaving the neighbourhood. Closed school for Easter holidays.

Apr. 25 Visited to verify, found the number present 98 and 21 Infts = 119. J.S. Attendance Officer visited on the 23rd inst. Henry Wells, W. Hutt, Louisa Sargent and Edward Wallis absent, through illness all the week. Sent Albert Wells home for disobedience and impudence. He has always given a great deal of trouble at school. Attendance during the week rather below the average.

Apr. 28 Henry Wells, Wm Hutt, Louisa Sargent, & Ellen Knight too ill to attend school.   **30** Attendance Officer visited.   **May 2** Six new children have been admitted during the week. Took H. Higley & Charlotte Wells off books. Average for the week only 121. No. on books 136.

May 8 Opened school at 1.45 for 2 — owing to a concert being held in the evening. Attendance Officer visited on the 7th inst. Revd W. C. Cluff gave a scripture lesson to 1st Class.   **9** Ellen Knight, Ernest Simmonds and W. Hutt absent through illness all the week. Attendance during the week only very fair.

May 13 Admitted William Turner. Edward Wallis and Robert Wallis left school, each being 13 years old.   **15** Revd W. C. Cluff gave a scripture lesson to the upper Standards.   **16** Took Edwd Wallis & Robt Wallis off books. Elizth House, Emma Thorpe, Wm Hutt, Florence Lewendon absent through illness. The average for the past week = 120.4 only. During the last few days all the standards have been examined, with very fair results.

May 19 Admitted Fredk Robinson & Harry Painter.   **22** Attendance Officer visited.   **22** Revd Canon Slatter called.   **23** Attendance during the week very fair. Ernest Simmonds, Fanny Lewendon, Elizth House & W. Hutt, away through illness.

May 26 Thomas Franklin returned to school — after an absence of some weeks. Transferred John Barrett, Chas Lewendon & Joseph Ridge from Std 3 to

Std 2 — as they appeared unable to master the work of the upper Std.   **28** The
Attendance officer called.   **29** Revd W. C. Cluff visited, and took the 1st Class
in scripture.   **30** Attendance throughout the week very fair. Sent a list of
irregular scholars to Bradfield. Closed School for the Whitsun Holidays.

June 3 Re-opened school. Very poor attendance in the morning — but improved slightly in the afternoon.   **4** Sent T. Franklin, Jas Wallis, Chas & John
Barrett home for their school money as they refused to bring it. They did not
return to school.   **5** Average for the week only 110 out of 137 on the books.

June 11 Revd W. C. Cluff called and read prayers in the morning.   **12** Took
Ernest Simmonds & Elizth House off the Books. Attendance during the week
only very fair. W. Hutt, F. Lewendon & Emma Thorpe ill.

June 18 Attendance Officer called, and took the attendances of Ellen & Sarah
Knight, and Julia & Herbert Ward, whose parents were to be proceeded against.
20 The attendance has been good during the past few days, considering the
number of absentees through sickness. Joseph Hutt, Fanny Lewendon, Louisa
Shaw, and Bertha Lyford still away. During the week I have examined the lower
standards, and with the exception of arithc in Stand. 3, the results were good.

June 24 Revd W. C. Cluff called. Punished Albert Tomlin for disobedience.
27 Poor attendance throughout the week, owing to sickness. Received medical
certificates for Louisa & Frank Fabry, Charlie Yates, Alice Lewendon, Bertha
Lyford & Herbert Ward.

July 1 Admitted A[u]gustus Ridge.   **2** Visited to verify, find 89 present in
large room & 34 Infts. Total 123. [JOHN SLATTER] Revd Canon Slatter visited.
4 Herbert Ward, Ch. Yates, & B. Lyford still absent. Average for the week only
122. No. on books 136.

July 7 Admitted Ernest Simmonds & Edith Ashby. H. Ward returned to
school.   **10** Very wet day. Many little ones absent.   **11** Took Arthur Streeter
off books. Average for the week = 123.5. No. on books 138. Bertha Lyford,
Elizth Bartlett, Harry Smith, Harry Taylor & Allen Wells ill.

July 14 Admitted William Smith. Took Chas Reeves off books.   **16** Attendance
Officer called. Several children absent.   **17** The School had a day's holiday
owing to a Meeting of the Band of Hope (to which a great number of the children
belong) being held in the neighbourhood.   **18** Recd a Med. Certificate for John
Tyrell. Several children away. Bertha Lyford, A. Hine, Chas Hearn, Thos
Whiting and Harry Taylor ill. Average for the week lower than usual.

July 21 Admitted Emma Wallis.   **22** Revd W. C. Cluff visited & read
prayers in the morning.   **25** Wet morning. Several Infants away. Attendance
for the week very fair.

July 29 Revd W. C. Cluff visited in the morning.   **Aug. 1** School closed for
Harvest Holidays. To re-open on Sept 8th.

Sept. 8 Re-opened School. Very fair attendance. Several children have left school, being 13 years old. **9** Rev. W. C. Cluff called. **12** Punished H. Ward, E. Ward & J. Hearn for stealing. Average for the week only 117. No. on books 137.

Sept. 15 Admitted Arthur Seaman. **19** Esther Ridge, Louisa Yates, Alfred Wayman, Mary Winterbourne & Charles Hearn having left school, their names have been removed from the books. Average 121. No. on books 132. Revd W. C. Cluff called and read prayers in the morning.

Sept. 22 Several boys and girls went to Reading. Recd the 'Britannia' Arithc Cards for Stds 4–7. They appear very suitable. The stories for composition in Standard 5 are especially good, and also the Essays for Std 6. **26** Recd Notice that the Examination for P.Ts would be held at the British Schl. Reading on Octr 25th. Fair attendance only during the week. Av. 118.

Sept. 29 Re-admitted Elizth House. **30** The Church choir went to Oxford, consequently several children were absent. **Oct. 3** Revd W. C. Cluff visited. Recd Notice of the Diocesan Examination, to be held on Monday the 20th inst. at 10 a.m. Average for the week — 119.9. No. on books 130.

Oct. 6 Punished Clarence Bartlett for disobedience & impertinence. Sarah Hine returned to school. **10** Emma Wallis, Wm Smith, Alice Lewendon, & Harry Taylor away through sickness. Fair attendance during the week.

Oct. 15 Punished A. Tomlin & F. Bushnell for great disobedience in my absence. The Attendance Officer visited. **17** Frank Fabry has been ill all the week, & Julia Ward for the last 3 days. Average for the week only 119. No. on books 128.

Oct. 20 The school was visited by the Diocesan Inspector. Holiday given in the afternoon. **24** Visited to verify numbers. Present 86 B & G & 34 Infants J.S. Rev. Canon Slatter visited, and brought the report of the Diocesan Inspector.

Diocesan Inspector's Report

The Religious Teaching continues to be carefully and systematically given and the order and discipline are good.

The Infants & Standard I answered brightly and well, and their repetition was distinct and accurate.

The two higher classes knew their Scripture Subjects well and repeated the catechism accurately, but its meaning requires to be more fully explained. The 1st Class should learn something of the Services of the Prayer Book. The written work was, on the whole, very satisfactory.

Dioc. Prize   Louie Bushnell

Commended   Ernest Ashby (Had prize)   A. Pocock   F. Grist

25 Pupil Teachers' Examination in Reading at the British Schools.

Oct. 31 Eliza Winch, W. Turner, Wm Smith, Sarah Wallis & Henry Head absent through illness. In consequence of sickness, the average (114) for the past week has been much lower than usual.

Nov. 3 Revd W. C. Cluff called. Recd Notice of the P.T's Scripture Examn to be held in St Mary's Schools Reading — Decr 6th at 10 a.m.   **7** Took Emma Wallis & Wm Smith off books. Chas Hazell absent all the week owing to an accident to his hand. Satisfactory progress in all standards has been made during the last few weeks. Average for the week = 117.5. No. on books 128.

Nov. 11 Admitted Edwin Chambers.   **14** Frank Grist has been absent all the week with a bad leg. Took Fredk Robinson off books. A. C. Forbes Esq. called in the afternoon. Average for the week = 117.

Nov. 18 F. Grist returned to school.   **20** Punished Arthur Cook and Albert Newman for playing truant on the previous day.   **21** Louisa Gutteridge absent through illness. Ellen Knight went home in the afternoon, with the head-ache. The attendance during the week has been good. The parents of two or three little ones under 5 years of age have sent word that they should not send their children during the winter months, which is very annoying, just as they were getting used to school habits. Average for the week = 119. No. on books 127.

Nov. 24 Admitted George & Frank Woodward — who had not attended school previously, and were, therefore, very backward.   **28** Punished Arthur Cook for playing truant. Emma Thorpe, John Barrett & Harry Bushnell absent all the week, through illness. Recd the Examination Schedules &c. from the Educn Department. Average for the week = 116.7. No. on Books 129. Sent of[f] list of irregular children to Bradfield.

Dec. 2 Recd notice from Mrs Goodall that Henry Wells had left the school, and gone to a private one in the village.   **5** Mrs Winch sent word that her daughter Eliza had gone away for the benefit of her health and would not be at school for a long time. Mary & Charlotte Turner, Emma Thorpe, Sarah Dicker, Herbert Ward, Harry Bushnell, Edith Ashby & John Gutteridge absent through nettle-rash, sore throats & severe colds. Owing to the prevalence of illness the average for the past few days has been very low indeed. Recd Needlework material from Moffatt & Paige.   **6** Diocesan Examination for Pupil Teachers, held at St Mary's Schools Reading.

Dec. 9 Took Henry Wells, who has gone to a private school in the neighbourhood, off books.   **12** Sarah Dicker, Edward Simmonds, Edwd Gutteridge, Harry Painter, Ada Newman, Thomas Lewis, Alice Weller & Edith Jeacocke, absent with nettle-rash & severe colds. Took Eliza Winch, who has gone away from the district off books. She will be a great loss to the 5th Standard. Average for the week only 114.7 No. on books 127.

Dec. 17 Attendance Officer called and took the attendances of Emma Thorpe.   **19** Alice Weller, Lilian Jeacocke, Edwd Gutteridge & Sarah Hine absent with nettle-rash — all the week. Average for the week = 115. No. on books = 126.

Dec. 24 Closed school at 12 o'clk till the 29th inst. Several children still absent with nettle rash.

Dec. 29 Re-opened school. No needlework lesson was given to the upper standards — the Asst Mistress not having returned. **Jan. 1** Began New Registers. Miss Forbes visited. Mrs Forbes, assisted by other ladies of the parish, have kindly made arrangements by which 17 of the poor children will be provided with a good dinner of soup &c. on Monday, Wedy & Friday each week throughout the winter months. **2** A. C. Forbes Esq. called. The average for the week = 110. No. on books 125. Edwd Jeacocke, Sarah Dicker, Chas Yates, Ellen Brooker, Edith Ashby, Rosa Weller, & Alice Bartlett absent through illness.

1885

Jan. 5 All the children, who had been ill during the previous week, returned to school. Recd a Medical certificate for William Cox. **6** Revd W. C. Cluff visited in the morning. **7** — Wilson Esq., A. C. Forbes Esq. & Mrs Forbes called in the afternoon. **9** Recd a medical certificate for Sarah Weller — who was suffering from sore throat. Miss Forbes visited, and proposed giving a treat to the children next week. Average for the week = 119. No. on books 125. The School Managers met to Audit Accounts &c.

Jan. 12 School examined by H.M. Inspector and his Assistant. Holiday given for the remainder of the week. Approved pieces for recitation, 1885.

Std I   Fred and the Cherry tree
,, II   Casabianca
,, III   The Collier's Child (Farmer)
,, IV & V   The Idle Shepherd Boys (Wordsworth)
,, VI & VII Horatius (Macaulay)

A. C. Forbes Esq. & Rev. Canon Slatter visited. **16** A treat was given to the children in the afternoon, and a Christmas tree in the evening.

Jan. 19 Re-opened School. Re-arranged the children in their different Standards, and commenced the new work. **20** Recd the Duplicate Examn Schedules from H.M.I. Edith Grist, the Pupil Teacher, left the school, and went to fill the post of Assistant Mistress, in the Maidenhead Natl Girls' Schools. Had Notice that Edith Grist had gained a First Class in Scripture; and Fanny Tomlin a 2nd Class. **23** George Woodward and Elizth Lewendon have been away, through illness, all the week. Took Ernest Ashby's name off books, as he had passed Standard 7 in all three subjects. Average for the week = 117. No. on books 124.

Jan. 30 The weather has been very wet all the week, and the attendance very low. Average only 111. Sarah Wallis, Rosa Weller, Harry Smith & Edith Brooker ill. Satisfactory progress has been made in the new work.

Feb. 5 A. C. Forbes visited in the morning and brought the Report of H.M. Inspector. Revd Canon Slatter called in the afternoon. Recd notice that Fanny

Tomlin had passed the examination for a three years' engagement as Pupil Teacher.   6 Ada Newman, Albert Tomlin, Fred Bushnell & George Woodward absent through illness all the week. Took Sarah Hine off books as she had left school, having passed the 5th Standard. Average for the week = 115.1. On Books 127. Report of H.M. Inspector of Schools:

Whitchurch (Reading) Parl Schools

Mixed School   This continues a good school. Here and there the quality of the Reading drops to fair, as does the quality of the Grammar work and of the Geography of Standard 3; but the general working and results are thoroughly good.

Infants' Class   I am pleased with the New Teacher's work here. The general Elementary progress has been good, and the little ones were happy and interested in their other lessons and occupations.

E. L. M. Grist has passed well. She should be informed that she is now qualified under Art. 50 but not under Article 52.[112] H.M. Inspector reports that her teaching capacity is not sufficient to warrant her recognition under Art. 52.

Herbert W. Winchester   Certd Teacher 2nd Class.
Ada Wrightson   Asst Teacher.
Fanny A. Tomlin   Pupil Teacher 2nd year.
Margaret McLennan   Asst Teacher.

ALEXANDER C. FORBES   Correspondent

Feb. 9 Fanny Tomlin has been appointed Pupil-Teacher, under a three years' engagement.   **13** A. C. Forbes Esq. visited. Recd Medical certificates for Mary Turner and Emma Thorpe. Louisa Bushnell and Sarah Dicker also away, ill. Average for the week = 115.

Feb. 17 Rev. Canon Slatter visited.   **20** The Attendance during the week has been very low, owing to sickness. Mary Turner, Emma Thorpe, Ellen Yates, Albert Newman and George Woodward ill all the week. Satisfactory progress has been made in the various subjects. Arthur Seaman has left the neighbourhood.

Feb. 24 Revd Canon Slatter called. Admitted Annie Higley.   **26** A. C. Forbes Esq. visited, and gave notice that the dinners to the poorer children would be continued for another month, but only twice a week instead of 3 times. **27** Ellen Yates, Louisa Smith, Alice Lewendon, Geo. Woodward, Louisa Sargent, Sarah Dicker, Louisa Gutteridge, ill.

---

[112] Article 50 of the 1885 Code of Regulations stated: 'Pupil teachers who have passed satisfactorily either the examination for the end of the last year of their engagement or that for admission to a training college may be recognised as assistant teachers in public elementary schools'. Article 52 laid down that pupil teachers who had passed satisfactorily the examination for the end of the last year of their engagement or had obtained a place 'in the first or second class for admission to a training college' could be recognized as 'provisionally certificated teachers in charge of small schools' if they were 'specially recommended' by the H.M.I. 'on the ground of their practical skill as teachers'. See the Code of Regulations for 1885 in P.P. 1884–5, lxi.

Mar. 2 Admitted William & Ernest Simmonds. Took Arthur Seaman off books.   **4** Arthur Cook played truant.   **6** Owing to illness the average during the week has again been low. Miss E. Stowe, of Olney Bd Schools, Bucks, has been appointed to succeed Miss McLennan as Assistant, on April 1st. Eight children have been absent with colds &c all the week. Average for the week = 110.8. No. on books 125. Had no returns for Feby, to make to the Bradfield School Atte Committee, owing to the regular attendance of all who were not compelled by sickness to be absent.

Mar. 12 Punished A. Cook for playing truant.   **13** During the week the attendance has again been low. Several girls absent with severe colds &c. The Woodwards have left the neighbourhood and will not attend school here again. Forwarded Balance Sheets to the Subscribers to the School. Satisfactory progress has been made.

Mar. 16 Admitted Edith Franklin.   **19** The Pupil Teacher was absent with a severe cold &c.   **20** Emma Thorpe, Mary Turner, Louisa Smith & Thos Hazell away, through illness, all the week. Took Minnie Tomlin & Julia Ward off books.

Mar. 23 Most of those who had been absent with colds &c, returned to school. Admitted Wm Smith & Emma Wallis.   **25** A. C. Forbes Esq. & Mrs Forbes visited. Took Kate Lewendon's name off.   **27** Sent Joseph Hutt home, as he was too dirty to mix with the other scholars. He came back in the afternoon, much cleaner. Average for the week = 115.7. No. on books 122.

Mar. 30 Admitted Thomas Smith.   **31** Miss M. J. McLennan resigned the post of Infants' Mistress.   **Apr. 2** Closed school for the usual Easter holiday — one week. Av. for the week = 115.

Apr. 13 Re-opened school. Admitted Mary Lewendon & re-admitted Minnie Tomlin & Chas Whiting.   **16** Miss Forbes called.   **17** Good attendance throughout the week — av. 120.

Apr. 20 Admitted Fred & Wm Robinson & Fred Woolford.   **24** Examined the lower standards and found the general progress had been good — especially that of Standard 3. Edith Brooker has been absent for a fortnight owing to the death of her father. Average for the week = 122. On books 129.

Apr. 27 Re-admitted A[u]gustus Ridge.   **May 1** Sarah Weller — Edith, Wm & Nellie Brooker have left the neighbourhood — and their names have been taken off the books. Good attendance during the week in the Senior Deptt — but only fair in the Infants' Deptt.

May 4 Admitted Lilian Grist and four Terrys.   **8** Took off the books Chas & Thos Hazell who had gone to Goring Heath School. Good Attendance throughout the week, av. 122. Elizth House still away with the ringworm & John Gutteridge with chicken pox.

May 11 Admitted Luke Lambourne — Julia Ridge absent with 'mumps'. **15** Examined Std 111 in Arithc — with good results. Good attendance during the week.

May 22 Very wet day. Many scholars absent. No school in the afternoon. During the week Clarence Bartlett & Thos Goodall have been transferred to a lower class, as it seemed impossible for them to make satisfactory progress in their proper work. Closed for Whitsuntide holidays — 2 days.

May 26 Several children away with chicken pox. **27** Eliz. House & Fanny Simmonds absent with measles. **29** Revd W. C. Cluff called in the morning and read prayers. Only 112 present out of 130 on books.

June 4 Sarah Knight was sent home — being too dirty about the head. **5** Took Fredk Bushnell's name off. Examined the 1st class Infants in the three R's — results fairly satisfactory. Began learning poetry in upper standards. Wm Cox, Wm Wayman & Annie Lewendon away with the measles, and several with the chicken pox & severe colds, therefore the average for the week = 118 only.

June 8 Admitted Wm Willis. Extremely wet day. 15 Infants absent. **9** All children who had been away with the measles returned to school. **12** A. C. Forbes Esq. visited in the morning. Sophia, Mary, & Wm Turner have been away for several days owing to severe colds &c.

June 15 Admitted 3 new scholars — in the Infants' Dept Making a total of 47 Infants. **18** Verified the Register. 80 Boys & Girls. 44 Infants. JOHN SLATTER. **19** A. C. Forbes visited. Sarah & Jas Wallis, Fanny Simmonds & Rosa Lewendon away with the measles. Took Chas Wells, name off as he had gone to work — having passed Std 5. Cautioned the boys against throwing stones over in Mr Forbes's gardens. Average for the week = 118. No. on books 137.

June 23 Sarah & Jas Wallis & Fanny Simonds returned to school. Recd notice that Ellen Ward had left school. **26** Thos Lewis has been absent, for a fortnight, with measles. During the past week the attendance has been rather better than usual. Louisa Bushnell was absent, yesterday & to-day, owing to the illness of her father. I have examined the 1st Class in the Infants' room today and found a little improvement has taken place in Arithc & Reading during the past month. Elizth Detfield's mother sent word today that the girl has gone to reside in Reading and probably will not attend this school again.

June 29 About 40 boy[s] & girls have gone to a Sunday school treat, consequently the attendance is very low. **July 1** The Attendance Officer called to day for a return of irregular scholars. **3** Punished Ida Hazell for stealing another girl's hat, and hiding it in the wood, intending, as soon as an opportunity should occur, taking it home. Emma Thorpe, Mary Dettfield, Mary Turner & John Lambourne are away through illness. The Average for the week is only 107.

July 9 Revd Canon Slatter visited and reproved some boys for quarrelling on their way home from school. He also threatened to expel Ida Hazell if she continued the habit of stealing &c.   **10** Several children have been too ill to attend school all the week. Called without notice to verify Register found 77 B & G 37 I. Total 114. JOHN SLATTER   Admitted Fredk & Amelia Green on the 9th inst. Took Elizth Detfield's name off the books. Examined the Infants, and found, with a few exceptions, a great improvement in the first class.

July 13 A. C. Forbes Esq. visited. All children, who had been absent, returned to school. **15** Revd Canon Slatter called.   **16** Most of the village children went to a Band of Hope Anniversary, and considering the thin attendance during the morning, I thought it advisable to give half holiday in the afternoon.

July 20 Sent Sarah Knight home, for she was too dirty about the head to sit near the other children.   **21** Lilian Grist Elizth Barrett & A[u]gustus Ridge absent with the measles. Admitted Arthur Hall.   **22** Several additional children absent — with the measles, which are spreading rapidly.   **23** Two more absent with measles.   **24** A. C. Forbes Esq. called, and arranged for the harvest holidays to commence at once, owing to the prevalence of measles — and to last 6 weeks if necessary instead of five.

Sept. 7 Re-opened School, with very fair attendance. Several children absent with sore throats.   **8** Revd W. C. Cluff called in the morning. Examined the Standards and found many of the children had forgotten a great deal.   **10** Revd W. C. Cluff gave a scripture lesson to the first class.   **11** Wet morning. Many Infants absent, only 20 out of 46 being present. Chas Lewendon, Fred. Woolford, John Higley, Emily Whiting and Sarah Wallis have been away all the week with sore-throat. Took Mary Detfield and Lilian Grist off books. Admitted 3 new scholars on the 7th inst. Average for the week = 110. No. on books 134.

Sept. 14 Fredk Woolford And Albert Newman away with bad fingers. Frank and Mary Grist have been advised to stay at home for a week on account of their sister having the measles. Alice Weller, also has the measles.   **17** Rev. W. C. Cluff gave a scripture lesson to the upper standards.   **18** The attendance has improved during the past week.

Sept. 21 By the doctor's orders, Harry, Fred, Wm & Louisa Smith have been advised not to attend school, owing to one of them having the sore throat. **23** The Attendance Officer called for a list of irregular scholars.   **25** The attendance, except on Monday (Reading Fair day) has been very good in the upper dept. & very fair in the Infants'.

Sept. 28 Cautioned the children against throwing stones at the walnut tree — several boys having been injured.   **29** Revd Canon Slatter visited, and brought notice that the Diocn Examn would occur on Decr. 5th.   **Oct. 1** Rev. W. C. Cluff gave a Scripture Lesson to the upper standards. Sophia Turner, Ida Hazell & B. Higley away, ill.   **2** The Govt Examn of Pupil Teachers has been fixed for Saturday Octr 31st at 9.30 a.m. to be held in the British Schools Reading. Attendance during the week has been better than usual — and the children have, since the measles epidemic stopped, made very satisfactory progress.

Oct. 8 Revd Canon Slatter, and another clergyman visited in the afternoon. The Diocesan Examination has been fixed for the 26th inst. **9** The average for the week = 112 only — owing to Measles, colds &c. Several Infants have been away all the week.

Oct. 12 William Newman away with Scarlet fever. **14** I recd instructions to send the four Terrys home for 6 weeks as they lived next door to the Newmans — for fear of spreading the scarlet fever. Revd W. C. Cluff called and brought notice of the Diocesan Examination — to take place on Wednesday the 28th inst. **16** Elizath Lewendon absent still with measles; and many other children with severe colds &c. Average for the week = 110 only. No. on books 131. During the week we have used one of Portway's Slow Combustion Heating Stoves and in consequence, the room has been beautifully warm. It will prove economical both in fuel & time. First used the Ebor word-building cards, on the 15th inst and found them of great use.

Oct. 22 Received information that Ida Hazell was dead. She had been suffering from Scarlet fever. **23** Very many scholars have been absent for several weeks, some with measles, others with colds. Average for the week = 106. No. on books 130.

Oct. 26 Sarah Dicker absent with scarlet fever. **28** Revd C. Wodehouse, Diocesan Inspector, examined the school, and expressed himself highly satisfied with the answering. The Attendance Officer called and said that most likely the school would have to be closed for 6 weeks, on account of the fever. Revds Canon Slatter & W. C. Cluff also visited. **30** Attendance has been very low throughout the week. **31** Pupil Teachers' Examination British Sch. Reading, Fanny Tomlin attended the same.

Nov. 2 Frank Elizth & Flor. Lewendon were coming back to school — but they were ordered by the doctor to remain at home some time longer as they resided near Sarah Dicker, who has the fever. Recd Medl Certificates for Chas Yates & Emily Kirk — who were suffering from coughs. **6** All the Higleys (4) were sent home owing to Annie Higley having the Measles. Average for the week = 100. No. on books 127. Took Ellen Yates, John Barrett and William Hine off books.

Nov. 9 All the Painters have been advised to stay at home on account of measles. **10** George Detfield absent with measles, and all the rest of the family kept at home in consequence. Only 92 scholars present. Revd W. C. Cluff called and brought the Diocesan Inspector's Report.

Diocesan Inspector's Report
The Children have been carefully instructed in Holy Scripture and the Church

Catechism, and give intelligent and accurate answers. The singing is very pleasing. Writing good.
The Infants acquitted themselves in a very creditable manner.
General tone excellent.
Diocesan prize   Mary Grist
Commended   Albert Pocock   Julia Simmonds

                  C. G. WODEHOUSE, Diocesan Inspector

No further information has been received respecting the closing of the school on account of fever. **13** Several additional cases of measles have been reported, also one or two cases of scarlet fever. The attendance throughout the week has been very low indeed — 23 children have not attended at all — and the average for the whole school is only 84, out of 127 on the books. All the scholars, who have been able to attend, have made very good progress, & are in a very satisfactory condition.

Nov. 16 All the Terry's [*sic*] and Newmans (with the exception of one), who had been absent for 5 wks on account of fever, returned to school.   **19** Mr Pearce, H.M. Inspector's Assistant, visited in the morning at 10.15 and stayed till noon. He expressed himself pleased with the working of the school. A. C. Forbes Esq. called in the afternoon.   **20** The attendance during the week has been again very low, especially so in the Infant's Room. Averages for the week

        Senior Dept   69.   No. on books   85.
        Infants' do   28.   do   43.

Nov. 23 Recd notice that Alice Weller had gone away for several months. **27** The attendance during the week had been worse even than last week, many fresh children having been absent with sore throats. We have been very much hindered in our work during the past 3 months, owing to irregular attendance in consequence of illness. As soon as one batch of scholars returns, other children are taken ill — and so no real progress can be made, only a repetition of the same work. Recd the Examn Schedules &c from the Edn Dept.

Dec. 1 Admitted George Davis, who ought to have attended school in Septr. **3** Had to sent the family of Bartletts home, as the younger sister was suffering from measles.   **4** Called to check the Register.   Present 62 children   35 Infts. Total 97. JOHN SLATTER   Again the attendance has been very low indeed. 25 children have been away all the week. Most of Standards I & II, who have been absent a long time, have come back, and now the other standards are suffering. Today only 41 were present out of 58 in Stds III–VI. The average = 97. No. on books = 128. Took Alice Weller's name off, as she has gone away for some months.

Dec. 8 Admitted Ernest Bacon. Thos Emily & Chas Whiting absent, owing to measles.   **11** Miss Stowe, the Infants' Mistress, has been ill all the week — and the infants have been taught by the Pupil Teacher. There has been a somewhat improved attendance during the past week — the average rising about 10 per cent. The girls have had a little extra needlework this week, as they will get none next week — owing to the Assistant Mistress having to attend the Certificate Examination. Wm Robinson's name has been taken off books — as he will not attend again till spring. Average for the week = 106. No. on Books 128.

Dec. 14 Miss Stowe still absent, through illness.   **16** Miss Stowe returned to school. Most of the scholars have come back — some after 9 weeks' absence. **18** The attendance has improved greatly during the past week — the average being 112.[113] Miss Wrightson has been away at the Certificate Examn all the week, and the girls have not had any needlework. The children who have been absènt so long owing to epidemics, are in rather a backward condition. Sarah Dicker has not yet returned. Sarah & Jas Wallis, & Elizth Sharp, absent, owing to measles in the family. This week the ladies have kindly commenced providing the poorer children with dinners three times a week.

Dec. 21 Called to verify the register — found 74 B & G & 34 I. Total 108. JOHN SLATTER   Sarah Dicker returned after an absence of 8 weeks.   **24** Closed at 12 o'clock for Christmas. To re-open on the 28th. Holidays to be given after the Examination. The attendance during the week has been fairly good. Louisa Bushnell ill all the week.

Dec. 28 Recd medical certificate for L. Bushnell. Elizth Sharpe returned — also Sarah Wallis. 6 scholars in the Mixed Dept & 4 Infants away.   **Jan. 1** The attendance during the week has been good in the Senr Dept — and very fair in the Infants' Dept. Louisa Bushnell is very ill — and it is very doubtful if she will recover sufficiently to attend school by the examn day. This is very unfortunate as she is the best child in her standard. Average for the week = 114. No. on books 124. The Managers will meet on the 9th inst. to audit the accounts &c.

1886
Jan. 6 Heavy fall of snow — only 40 children presented themselves and they were nearly all very wet, so that no registers were marked, and the children dismissed.   **7** Only 37 scholars in the Senr Departt and 6 Infants present. **8** Owing to the state of the roads, there were only 33 children present at the time the roll should have been called. No registers were, therefore, marked and the children were again dismissed for the day. The average attendance for the 3 days the school has been opened during the past week = 97. No. on Books 124.

Jan. 11 Government Examination. Although a very bad day — the ground being still covered with snow — all the Standard children, with the exception of Louisa Bushnell, who was ill, were present. A. C. Forbes Esqr & Revd Canon Slatter visited in the morning.

---

[113] This figure substituted for '107'.

Readers for combined Stds.[114]

IV	Geography Europe IV–VII
	History Std IV. Nat Soct's III
V	do. Stds V–VII. Moffatt's V Higher Grade
VI	IV Std Literary Reader Technical Std IV
VII	V–VII Swiss Family Robinson —

Appd CDDP
HW

Recitation Pieces for 1886.
Standd

I	Good-Night & Good-morning
II	Complaints of the Poor
III	George Nidiver (Emerson)
IV	Gelert
V–VII	Goldsmith's Deserted Village.

13 The Carpenter put 4 new ventilators in the Senr Department similar to those recently placed in the Infant Room, & recommended by H.M. Inspector. They will prevent the down draught from the upper windows, which has always been uncomfortable, whenever the windows have been opened for ventilation. **15** No school has been held since the Examn as the children were promised their holidays after the Examn instead of at Xmas.

Jan. 18 Re-opened school, and arranged the children in their new standards. **22** Ernest & Wm Simmonds, & Elizth Barrett have been absent with scarlet fever. Mary Lewendon also has been advised to stay away because she lives near the Barretts. Owing to snow the attendance during the week has been very low. Av. 103.

Jan. 25 Heavy fall of snow — only 40 scholars put in an appearance. The Registers were not marked, and the children were sent home for the day. Very poor attendance, owing to the bad condition of the roads. 14 out of 30 Infants were away. **27** Received the Report of H.M. Inspector

Whitchurch (Reading) Parl School.

Mixed School. This continues a very good school. If the quality of the work done in the upper Standards were equal to that of the lower Standard work, the School would be an Excellent one. I think the exceptions numbered 45 and 46 on the Examination Schedule must have been proposed under a misapprehension; they were clearly not cases for withdrawal from examination, but they might have been (apparently) rightly presented for examination in last year's standard.[115]

---

[114] This was written in another hand — probably that of H.M.I. Du Port, or of his assistant. The recommendation of books, in 1886 and subsequent years, was, incidentally, frowned upon by the *Final Report* of the Cross Commission in 1888 (P.P. 1888, xxxv, p. 78), which pointed out that it was 'no part of the duty of the officers of the Department to prescribe or to recommend particular books for use in school'.

[115] This may have meant that in the previous year they had either failed in all three basic subjects, or passed only one; they could then repeat that standard.

Infants' Class. I am much pleased with the new Mistress' work here, and with the general tone of her management of the Infants. The Objects' [sic] Lessons were the only point really below par.

F. A. Tomlin has passed fairly

Herbert W. Winchester   Certd Teacher 2nd Class

Ada Wrightson   Assistant Teacher

Elizabeth Stowe   Assistant Teacher

Fanny A. Tomlin   Pupil Teacher, 3rd Year.

ALEXANDER C. FORBES, Correspondent

27 F. A. Tomlin has been too ill to attend to her duties during the last 3 days. All the Higleys away owing to John having the measles. Commenced using Moffatt's Historical Readers in Standards V–VII instead of Natl Society's. Louisa Shaw, Allen Wells, John Gutteridge, Arthur Hall, & Joseph Hutt have been returned to the Infant's Class for another year, as they are in such a backward state that they cannot possibly do the work of the First Standard by the end of the year. Henry Head, Jas. Wallis, Thos Wallis, Edith Bartlett, Joseph Ridge & Emily Winch have left school & their names have been removed.   **29** Owing to bad weather, and sickness, the attendance during the past week has been very low. Average 94. No. of [sic] Books 120.

Feb. 2 Revd Canon Slatter visited and verified the registers. Bartw Higley & Louisa Gutteridge away with measles; & Sarah Dicker with a cold. Admitted Alfred Morland, who, although 5½ years old, had not attended any school previously.   **3** The attendance officer called respecting the Morlands, some of whom are not attending any school.   **4** Revd Canon Slatter called and reported that The Managers had decided on giving Miss Stowe a month's notice as they were not satisfied with her conduct out of school.[116]   **5** In consequence of Measles, scarlet fever &c. twelve children have been away all the week; and the attendance greatly reduced. Average for the week 101. On Books 121.

Feb. 8 Admitted Annie Morland, who had not attended any school although over 7 years old. Received a Medical certificate for Elizth Goodall, who is suffering from measles. Mary Lewendon returned to school after an absence of a month. Walter Taylor, who was away last week with sore throat, came back in the morning & in the afternoon it was reported that Henry and Elizth Taylor had the Scarlet Fever. All the Painters were advised to stay away too. Sent to ask the Doctor if the Taylors really had the fever, and received answer to the effect that

---

[116] The isolation of women teachers in country districts was summed up by H.M.I. Brodie in 1894: 'Forlorn indeed is the lot of the young mistress in some of these outlying rural nooks. They have perhaps been pupil teachers in towns, and then trained in some college, and accustomed to social intercourse. Suddenly, they are moved off to distant, secluded spots, where there is little or no society . . .' (quoted in Gordon, *The Victorian School Manager*, p. 50). Miss Stowe's post was advertised in *The Schoolmaster* on 13 Feb. 1886, at a salary of £40 per year to teach Infants. An ex-pupil teacher was specified, and as with all assistant mistress's posts at the school in the 1880s, applications and testimonials had to be sent to Winchester himself.

he was convinced the complaint was only German measles. The Painters were, therefore, permitted to come back to school. All they [sic] Higleys are still absent owing to measles. Also Louisa Gutteridge & Elizth Goodall. Satisfactory progress has been made by all those who have attended regularly. Chas Lewendon was put back in Std 3, he was unable to cope with Std 4 work.   12 Received notice from the doctor that the Taylors really only had the German measles, but that the sanitary inspector had given orders that those who resided in the Bridge Cottages were not to attend school at present. I therefore sent to the Sany Inspector to ask if he could permit them to come next Monday. Average for the past week = 97. On books 121.

Feb. 15 Received an answer from the attendance officer, saying the children in the Bridge Cottages could not attend school at present. A. C. Forbes Esq. called in the morning.   **18** Received the books, Swiss Family Robinson, for Standards 5–7 — from Natl Socy.   **19** Eighteen children have been absent all the week — bringing the average for the present year down to 97. The School Managers have appointed Miss S. King to succeed Miss Stowe on March 8th.

Feb. 22 All the Higleys and Painters returned to school. Taylors still absent with measles.   **26** For the future Standard II will reverse the last two lessons on Friday mornings. During the week all the Turners (5) have been away, owing to measles in the family. The attendance has improved slightly, as several children, who have been absent for 5 weeks, have come back to school. Average for the week = 104, on books 120.

Mar. 1 Heavy fall of snow. No school was held.   **2** Many children away owing to bad weather. The Taylors returned to school.   **4** Miss Stowe terminated her duties as Assistant.   **5** Miss S. King entered upon her duties as Infant's Mistress. Revd Canon Slatter visited in the afternoon. Recd Medical certificate for Sarah Dicker, who was suffering from Neuralgia. Albert Hine has been absent for a fortnight with an injured foot. Average for the week only 92 on books 120.

Mar. 8 William Simmonds returned to school after several weeks' serious illness.   **9** Received notice from the Education Dept that Miss Wrightson had gained a Second Class certificate at the recent examination.   **12** Sent a list off [sic] irregular scholars to Bradfield. Took Fredk & Arthur Hall, & Fanny Simmonds off books. There has been a slight improvement in the attendance during the week — especially in the Infants' dept. All the Turners still away with measles. Sent a copy of the Balance Sheet, for last year, to the printers. Good progress has been made by the regular children during the last two months.

Mar. 19 During the week the attendance, owing to sickness, has been only fair. Harry Smith, Hephh Bartlett, James Hearn, in addition to the Turners, have been away all the week. The dinners to the poorer children have been discontinued. Av. for wk 103. On books 119.

Mar. 21 Albert & Louisa Sargent, & Julia Ward absent owing to Scarlet fever. The Turners have not returned to school.   **25** A. C. Forbes Esqr & Mrs Forbes visited in the afternoon.   **26** Owing to sickness, the attendance during the week has again been only fair. Average 104. On books 118.

Mar. 30 All the Turners returned to school after an absence of 5 weeks. Re-admitted Wm Robinson.   **31** Recd Medl certificate for Elizth House. Heavy thunder shower in the afternoon; several Infants away.   **Apr. 2** General progress during the week — good. The children, who have been absent through sickness, are still in a backward state. Average for the week 103. On books 119.

Apr. 5 Admitted Elizth Streak. Emma Wallis also returned to school after an absence of 5 months.   **6** Verified the Register. 77 B & G & 32 Infts. Total 109. JOHN SLATTER   **9** A. C. Forbes Esq. visited in the morning. Punished 6 boys for throwing stones in the playground. The Infants are making very satisfactory progress under the new mistress. Average for the week = 105.3. On books 121.

Apr. 12 Admitted Ernest Davis and Emma Lyford. Recd notice that Arthur Cook had left school.   **14** The Attendance Officer called for a list of irregular scholars. Only one name was given.   **16** Took H. Bartlett & Arthur Cook off books. During the past few days the attendance has very much improved. Average for the week = 110. On books 123. Good progress has been made during the week.

Apr. 19 Admitted two new scholars.   **21** Attendance Officer visited. The Sanitary Inspector called to enquire about the school drains.   **22** Attendance during the week — good. Av. 113. Closed school for Easter Holidays. To re-open on May 3rd.

May 3 Re-opened school. Attendance only fair owing to sickness. All the Bartletts, Greens & Sargents absent through scarlet fever. Louisa Bushnell returned after 5 months' illness. Admitted Edward Pocock.   **5** Sent Ellen Knight & Herbert Ward's names to the attendance officer.   **7** Commenced the use of disinfectants in school, owing to the prevalence of fever. Fourteen children have been away all the week, which has considerably lowered the average. Very satisfactory progress has been made during the week. Average for the week 103. On books 125. Although the average appears very low, the attendance of those who have been able to come, has been very satisfactory.

May 10 Admitted James Goodenough and Harry Adams.   **14** The Pupil Teacher has been absent through illness during the past 3 days. The weather for some days has continued very unsettled, and has greatly interfered with the attendance, especially of the infants. I examined Std 3 in all subjects on the 12th inst. and was much pleased with the progress made during the past few weeks. Herbert Ward was sent home for his school money on the 13th, and has not yet returned. He has brought no fee for several weeks. The Greens, Sargents and Bartletts still absent. Average for the week = 107. On books 127.

May 17 Admitted Thos Smith. Miss Wrightson has sent her resignation to the School Managers. She will leave on the 17th prox.[117]   **21** Attendance during the week has been good.   The three Sargents & Julia Ward returned to school on the17th inst. after an absence of 8 weeks. The Bartletts and Greens still away through fever. Owing to better attendance lately, good progress has been made in all standards. Average for the past week =113. On books 128. Commenced teaching the new recitation pieces, would would [*sic*] have been done earlier had there not been so many scholars continuously absent from school.

May 24 Admitted Harry Hutt. Examined Stds I & II and found good progress had been made during the last month.   **28** Attendance good throughout the week — although the weather has been very unsettled and damp. Bartletts & Greens have not yet returned. Average for the week = 116. On books 127.

May 31 The Bartletts returned to school after an absence of 6 weeks. Admitted 3 new children. Miss Annie Long, late P. T. in Naphill school, Hughenden, Bucks. has been appointed Asst Mistress, in place of Miss Wrightson — to begin duties on the 21st inst.   **June 1** A. C. Forbes Esq. visited in the morning.   **4** Good attendance, except during one day, throughout the week. The Infants' room seems to be filling rapidly — more scholars being on the books than for some time past.

June 7 Admitted Thos Wallis.   **9** Revd Canon Slatter visited in the morning & reproved some boys for doing damage in a meadow. Good attendance. 123 present. Most of the children have returned to school, who have been away with fever &c. Louisa Smith still absent with inflamed eyes.

June 21 Miss A. Long entered upon her duties as Assistant Teacher — Miss Wrightson left on the 17th inst. Admitted Fredk Jeacocke. Many away with whooping cough.   **25** Visited to check the register. Found 73 B & G & 35 I. Total 108. JOHN SLATTER   Rev. Canon Slatter visited and reported a girl who was not attending any school although over 7 years of age. Recd information that Thomas Lewis and Albt Newman had gone to work — having passed the exemption standard. Miss Long appears to be a good teacher & disciplinarian, and one likely to give satisfaction. Only a fair attendance during the past week — Whooping cough appears to be on the increase. Average 113. On books 134.

June 28 More absent with Whooping cough. Received Medl Certificate of Herbert & Joseph Hutt, Elizth Sharp, Harry Bushnell, & Emma Thorpe. **July 2** Transferred Mary Turner from the 4th to the 3rd Standard — as I found she could not cope with the work of the former Standard. She has always been very dull; was two years in doing the work of Std 2, and failed in Reading in Std 3. The attendance during the week has been good in the senior dept — but very low indeed in the Infants' dept, the latter having an average of 34 only out of 50 on books. The last few days have been very warm, & in the afternoons the children

---

[117] The post was advertised in *The Schoolmaster* on 22 May 1886, at a salary of £40 a year to teach 'Standards I and II, and sewing'.

have been tired and not able to do the usual amount of work generally accomplished. Av. for wk 113. On books 133.

July 5 Received notice that Geo. Davis and his brother would not attend school any more as they were leaving the parish. **7** Albert & Wm Newman played truant. **9** Very many Infants have been absent all the week with whooping cough. Took Thos Lewis & Geo. & E. Davis off books. Average for the week = 110. On books 134.

July 12 Admitted Frank Simmonds. **15** Many scholars went to a 'Band of Hope' festival. Half-holiday was given in the afternoon. **16** Several Infants have again been away all the week with whooping cough — but the attendance has slightly increased. Medical certificates have been received for Sarah Wallis, & Amy Terry. Average for the week = 115. On books 132.

July 21 All the Hutts were sent home in the afternoon, as they were in such a dirty state about the head that they were not fit to be with other children. The Hutts returned to school, in, apparently, a much cleaner condition, and so were permitted to stay. **23** Slightly improved attendance during the week, in the Infants' Department; although a great number have again been absent all the time. Average for the week = 117. On books 132.

July 25 Visited to pass Register. In Great Room 79 — Infants 37. 116 Total. [J. SLATTER] Revd Canon Slatter visited, and reproved some boys for running about in an improper manner whilst bathing. **28** The attendance officer called, & reported that Allen Wells was suffering from Scarlet fever, and that, in consequence, Wm & Thos Smith, who reside next door, would be compelled to stay at home, for some weeks. **29** Saw Mrs Newman concerning her boy William playing truant. She was not aware that he had been absent so many times — and promised to see to the matter. The boy promised that he would not stay away again. **30** Revd W. C. Cluff heard the 1st Class read from the bible, and afterwards asked questions upon what had been read. The Flower show was held on the 27th inst — and a half holiday was given in the afternoon. Attendance throughout the week fairly good.

Aug. 2 Bank Holiday. No school was held. **3** Sarah Wallis, Edwd & Julia Simmons, & Thos & Wm Smith away on account of Allen Wells having the fever. **6** Attendance during the week fairly good. Closed School for the usual Summer holidays. To re-open on Septr 13th.

Sept. 13 Re-opened school with a good attendance. Admitted Sydney Turner, and re-admitted Alice Detfield, Alice Weller & Hephh Bartlett. Some of the children appear to have forgotten a good deal during the holidays. **15** Had to punish 4 boys for throwing stones in the playground. **17** Wm Wayman, & Sarah Wallis & Lilian Jeacocke have been absent, through illness, all the week. Medl Certificate received for Wm Smith. Revd W. C. Cluff called on the 13th inst. Average for the week 122. No. on books 137. Received notice that Albert

Newman & Sarah Dicker had left school, having passed the standard for Exemption last January. Took Fredk Jeacocke's name off Infants' Register, as he had been absent for 10 weeks, and was not likely to attend again for some months.

Sept. 21 Received notice that the Pupil Teacher's Annual Examination would be held in the British Schools, Reading on Saturday Octr 30th at 9.50 a.m. Several of the Choir Boys visited the Colonial Exhibition.[118] **24** Lilian Jeacocke has been absent during the last fortnight through illness. The children appear to be getting over their holidays and brightening up again in their lessons. Mrs Young & two Gentlemen visited and heard the Infants sing. The attendance during the week has been good. Average 120.7. On books 136.

Sept. 28 Herbert Ward and Joseph & Harry Hutt were sent home, as they were in such a dirty condition that they were not fit to mix with the other scholars. A message was also sent to the parents, that the children would not be permitted to attend School until the matter had been submitted to the School Managers. **Oct. 1** During the week the attendance has been fairly good. Av. for the week = 124.7. On books 138.

Oct. 7 Sent a list of Irregular scholars to Bradfield, and informed the Attendance Officer that I had sent the Wards & Hutts home for dirtiness. **8** A. C. Forbes Esqre visited in the morning. Owing to two wet days the attendance has fallen slightly during the week. Good progress has been made during the past month, the attendance having been much better. Average for the week = 122. On books 137.

Oct. 13 A. C. Forbes Esqr called, and was informed that the Hutts had been refused admittance for being dirty. He afterwards went to see the attendance officer about the matter, who also visited later in the morning, & then proceeded to see the parents. **15** The weather was very wet and boisterous; still the attendance was very good. Average for the week = 124. On Books 137. Took Albert Newman & Sarah Dicker off books. Both have passed Std 5, and gone to work.

Oct. 19 The School Managers held a meeting to consider the school accounts. Finding they were likely to be about £50 deficient at the end of the year, they decided that next year the staff should be reduced, and a paid monitress should supply the place of an Assistant Mistress. **20** A. C. Forbes Esq. called and informed me of the decision of the Managers. Such a dreadful thunder storm prevailed during the morning, that only 20 children presented themselves. No registers were marked, and no work done. In the afternoon the usual work was done. 82 scholars being present. The Attendance Officer called for the attendances of the Hutts, whose parents were to be summoned. **21** Rev. Canon Slatter

[118] The Indian and Colonial Exhibition, held at South Kensington, had been opened by the Queen on 4 May. It remained open for several months and the South Western Railway advertised special day and half-day excursions from Reading; the third-class adult fare for a half-day excursion was 2s. 6d. (Information kindly provided by Reading Reference Library.)

called and gave notice that probably the Scripture Examn would be held on Nov 11th.   **22** The Managers, at their meeting on the 19th inst also decided that on and after the 25th inst there should be an alteration in the school fees — the first child in each family was to pay 2d. & every other in the same family 1d. The returning of the 1d. would be discontinued. Average for wk 122. On books 135.

Oct. 25 Admitted Rose Knight.   **29** Satisfactory progress has been made during the past week — owing to good attendance. Florence Excell began duties as Monitress on the 25th inst. in view of the contemplated change in the staff next year. She had not previously had any experience as a teacher, and so she was placed in the Infants' Room for a short time, among the smaller children. Sent a list of Irregular scholars to the Bradfield Atte Committee. Average for the week = 125. On books 137.   **30** The Annual Examination for Pupil Teachers was held in the British School, Reading.

Nov. 1 Admitted Edith Morland. Good attendance.   **2** I visited this School & found all going well. S. G. TREMENHEERE, H.M.I.   P.S. I find however that the P.Ts are about to receive their private instruction, as they have received it during the whole of the School year, without the presence of a woman (See Art. 35 small print)[119] S.G.T.   **3** A. C. Forbes Esq. visited the school. Attendance officer visited, and took the names of 5 children who had been rather irregular during the month of October.   **4** Visited to verify the Register. 82 B & G 49 I. Total 131. JS   **5** Very wet indeed in the afternoon; and many children were away. Average for the week = 127. On books 137.

Nov. [9] Report of Visit without Notice, by H.M.I.

Education Department   November 8th 1886
The ordinary work was going on steadily and orderly, but I ascertained that the terms of Article 35 have not been complied with for some considerable time. This regulation must be scrupulously observed in future.
ALEXANDER C. FORBES   (Correspondent) of the Managers

10 The weather was very damp, and consequently many children were absent. Only 25 Infants were present in the morning, & 26 in the afternoon. Gave standard 4–6 girls an extra lesson at their needlework — as some of them, owing to illness, seemed behind.   **11** The school was examined by the Diocesan Inspector. No registers were marked. No school was held in the afternoon. Frank Grist had Prize.   **12** Since the 7th inst. the weather has been very unsettled, and consequently the attendance, especially in the Infants' Deptt has been greatly reduced in numbers. Average for the week = 116. No. on books 137. Diocesan Report

Whitchurch Church of England School
The result of the Diocesan Inspection is again very satisfactory throughout the School. Old Testament — very accurate & good. New Testament — good.

---

[119] Even in the early stages of the Code, the presence of a woman had been insisted upon, where the teacher was male and the pupil teachers female. See, for example, Art. 70(c) of the New Code of 1871.

Church Catechism — intelligently learned. Writing — excellent. Singing — pleasing.

The Infant School shows the result of loving and careful instruction.

Diocesan Prize — Frank Grist Commended — A. Pocock M. Cross M. Grist
C. G. WODEHOUSE Diocesan Inspector

Nov. 17 The attendance Officer called for the attendance of Herbert Ward & Emma Thorpe — whose parents were to be proceeded against. **19** Received notice that Minnie Tomlin, Elizth Goodall & Chas Chapman had left school. The attendance during the week has been very good, in spite of one or two very damp days. Commenced using some of Moffatt's Copy Books in the upper standards — instead of Longmans. Average for the wk = 121. On books 137.

Nov. 26 Owing to fine weather the attendance has been very good, and satisfactory progress has been made during the week. Took Alfred House off books, as he had not attended for several weeks, and his mother said she should not send him again during the winter months. Average 125. On books 135.

Nov. 29 From now till the Govt Examn secular instruction will be given during the time entered on the time-table for religious instruction. Gertrude Ashley returned to school, after an absence of several months. **30** Louisa Bushnell has been ordered, by the doctor, to go away for the benefit of her health. She has gone to the convalescent home at St Leonards for a month. Good attendance. **Dec. 1** Sent the names of Chas Barrett and Wm Wayman to the Bradfield Sch. Att. Committee. Yesterday 6 choir boys attended to sing at the funeral of Mrs Slatter in the afternoon. Recd the Examination Schedules from the Education Dept on the 27th ult. **3** Took Elizth Goodall's name off books — as her mother said she wished her to leave school, to help her grandmother. She was 13 years of age on Novr 2nd — as was proved by an application made to the Registrar, although her age according to the school books was only 12. The wrong date of birth must have been given at her admission. During the week most of the children have attended properly. Average for the wk = 125. On books 135.

Dec. 8 Very stormy weather during the whole day, & consequently many children were away. Only 24 out of 52 Infants were present. **10** Miss King was too ill to attend to her duties and the P.T. was placed in charge of the Infants for the day. A. C. Forbes visited on the 9th inst. Examined standard 3 during the week, and found their work very satisfactory. Std 4 have very much improved in their grammar during the past month. Owing to extremely unsettled weather during the week, the attendance has not been so satisfactory as usual. Average for the week = 116. On books 134.

Dec. 17 There has been a good attendance during the whole week, and good progress has been made. Examined standards I & II on the 14th inst. & the results were very satisfactory. William Wayman has been absent during the last fortnight with a severe cold &c. Louisa Bushnell is still absent, at the St Leonard's Convalescent Home. Sent a message to Mr Excell, that after today Florence's services would not be required, as after 8 weeks, trial, I found she would not be likely to give satisfaction in her teaching. Martha Cross has been appointed monitress in the place of Florence Excell, and her name will therefore be taken off the books, next week.[120] Average for the week = 123. On books 134. Recd notice that Sydney Turner had gone to the Goring Heath School, and his name has therefore been taken off.

Dec. 20 Martha Cross commenced duties as Paid Monitress.   **22** Attendance Officer called in the morning for the attendances of Charles Barrett & Alfred Wayman. A. C. Forbes Esq. visited in the afternoon.   **23** Received Notice that H.M. Inspector purposed examining this school on Jany 12th 1887. Several 1st class children away. Revd Canon Slatter visited in the afternoon.   **24** No school was held in the afternoon. J. Foster Esq. kindly gave the children a treat, and afterwards an entertainment.[121] Closed school at 12 o'clock for Christmas — to re-open on the 28th inst. Average for the week = 119. No. on books 130.

Dec. 27 Heavy fall of snow during the previous night.   **28** Owing to the snow being very deep, only about 70 children attended.   **29** The attendance slightly improved in both rooms, but, owing to the slippery state of the roads only 27 Infants came. The School Managers have arranged to hold a meeting for Auditing accounts &c. on Saturday Jany 8th. Miss Long was absent on the morning of the 28th inst. — through inability to reach here before 12 o'clock, from her home.   **31** Such has been the state of the weather during the whole of the past week that it has been impossible for very many of the children to come to school. Recd Medical certificates for Elizth & Geo. Barrett. Average for the week = 92. On books 130.

1887

Jan. 3 Weather again very wet and frosty, and owing to the slippery state of the roads only a very few children were able to get to school. The attendance slightly improved in the afternoon. Heard that John Lambourne had cut his leg very badly and probably would not be able to attend school for some days. Louisa Bushnell still absent through the effects of her long illness, and her mother thinks that she ought not to attend school again, as she is in such a weak state. **4** Another very heavy fall of snow — and, as only 14 children put in an appearance, they were sent home again and no school was held.   **5** Heavy fall of snow again. Only 6 boys & 4 girls came. No school was opened.   **6** This morning 51 out of 130 attended, owing to the state of the roads. School was, however, carried on as usual.   **7** Only 76 children were present, although the weather had very much improved. Mrs Forbes kindly sent up some soup for the poorer children.

[120] At nearby Mapledurham in 1889 the monitress was paid £7 a year.
[121] John Foster (1832–1910) had purchased Coombe Park from the Gardiner family and was now lord of the manor of Whitchurch. In 1890 he was High Sheriff of Oxfordshire. He was chairman of directors of John Foster & Sons of Queensbury, near Bradford, and also owned property in Yorkshire. (J. Dale (ed.), *Oxfordshire and Berkshire County Biographies* (London, n.d.) p. 80.)

Average for the whole school during the three days it has been opened = 67 only out of 130 on books.   **8** Meeting of the school Managers to audit accounts &c.

Jan. 12 School visited by H.M. Inspector & Assistant.

Songs 1886 [*sic*]   Senr Dept   1 The Daisy, 2 There is a flower, 3 Sing out you Girls, 4 Hark from Woodlands far away, 5 Whatsoe'er you find to do, 6 Spring has come, 7 The flowers are blooming, 8 The Mill
                                     Infants   1 Tommy's toilet, 2 Snowflakes, 3 Buttercups & Daisies, 4 Baby's Welcome

Object Lessons   (Infants)   1 Clock, 2 Chair, 3 Pin, 4 Table, 5 Thimble, 6 Lead pencil, 7 A Letter, 8 Bird's Egg, 9 Window, 10 Wool, 11 Sugar, 12 Coal, 13 Salt, 14 Chalk, 15 Silk, 16 Soap, 17 Cotton, 18 Trees, 19 Grass, 20 Daisy, 21 Dandelion, 22 The Cow, 23 Cat, 24 Mouse, 25 Dog, 26 Horse, 27 Bee, 28 Duck, 29 Owl, 30 Swan, 31 Goat, 32 Robin, 33 Bat, 34 Reindeer, 35 Rat, 36 Codfish, 37 Mackerel, 38 Teeth, 39 Eyes, 40 Hands

Poetry for 1887   St i   Child's First Grief
                              ii }
                              iii } We are Seven
                         iv–vii   Extract from Merchant of Venice
Readers   i   Marshall's & Moffatt's
                             ii   Moffatt's Explanatory & Geog.
                             iii   New London, Gill's Stories fr. Eng. Hist.,
                                   Moffatt's Geog.
                         iv–vii   Merchant of Venice, World at Home (World),
                                   Nat. Soc.'s Hist. Part IV
                                                                    S.G.T.

Revd Canon Slatter & A. C. Forbes Esqr two of the school managers attended during the morning. Several of the Infants were absent owing to the bad state of the roads, but all who were not ill put in an appearance in the senr Department. **13** Re-arranged standards. Drafted all over 7 from the Infants' Dept to Senr Room, and began to work in accordance with the New Time Table. The Pupil Teacher commenced the management of standards II & III with the assistance of the Monitress. The Assistant Mistress was placed in charge of Std I — in order to give them a good drilling in the new work during the remainder of her stay here. The school was closed at 12 o'clock until the following Monday. The Builder came to see to the alterations required with regard to the gallery in Infant Room. Sent to Moffatt's for the new books required in the upper Standards. Average for the 5 times the school has been open = 107.

Jan. 17 Most of the children put in an appearance. A few Infants however were away. The carpenters came on the 14 & 15 inst. and made the required improvements in the Infants gallery.   **18** Recd and commenced using, Nelson's 'World at Home' Geographical Reader for Std 6. They seem rather difficult for the 4th Std.   **21** Took off several names of scholars who had passed Std 5, and had left school. Average for the week = 113. On Books 125.

Jan. 24 The attendance greatly improved, especially in the Infant's Department. Several little ones, who had been away for some weeks, owing to bad weather, returned. The New Time-Table seems to work very satisfactorily. No time being set apart on the same for the Lessons to be given by the Pupil Teacher, she will give one lesson in each week during the time — 9.30–9.50 — allotted to Mental Arithc & Marking Registers. **25** The children appear interested in the new Geographical Readers. Commenced coming to school at 2 p.m. instead of 1.45 p.m. **28** Sent the Names of Chas Barrett & Rosa Lewendon to the School Attendance Committee. Sent Arthur Sargent back in the Infants' Room on the 24th inst. as he was in such a backward state that it would have been impossible for him to have done the 1st Std work in a year. During the week the attendance has been very satisfactory, and great progress has been made in the new work by each standard. Miss A. Long resigned the post of Assistant Mistress. For the future the P.T. will have charge of standards II & III, and the monitress that of Std 1. Mrs Winchester will superintend the Needlework. Average for the week = 117. On books 127.

Jan. 30 Recd the Govt Report

Whitchurch (Reading) Parl School

Mixed School. The children are in very good order, and, with the exception of the Arithmetic of the Upper Standards, the instruction is sound and intelligent throughout. The three lower standards have passed with very high credit. There is some room for improvement in the Needlework of the elder girls.

Infants' Class. The children are kindly managed and acquit themselves well in the Elementary and Object lessons. The Occupations should be so conducted as to give them a more real educational value, and for this end suitable apparatus should be provided. Singing, drill, Needlework and discipline are fair, but some of the children are rather inclined to be inattentive and talkative. The railing in front of the gallery should be removed and another step added.

F. A. Tomlin has passed well.

H. W. Winchester   Certd Teacher 2nd Class

Susan King   Asst Teacher

F. A. Tomlin   P.T. 4th Year

ALEXANDER C. FORBES   Correspondent

31 Mrs Winchester commenced superintending the needlework — assisted by the Pupil Teacher. **Feb. 2** Recd notice from the School Attendance Officer that the Committee would not notice the children who had only passed Std 5 in two subjects. **3** A. C. Forbes Esq. visited in the morning, and looked at the alteration recently made in the Infants' Room. The School Managers presented the Pupil Teacher with a cheque for £5, to assist her in paying her lodgings, as her parents had recently left the neighbourhood. **4** Herbert Ward has been absent through illness all the week. Recd information that Fred Woolford had left the parish; and Julia Ward had gone to the Union,[122] and would not therefore attend school again. Wm Wayman Elizth Barrett & Geo. Barrett still away, owing to illness. Average for the week = 112. On books 126. Satisfactory progress has

---

[122] The poor law union workhouse at Bradfield.

been made during the past three weeks, in the various subjects, as the attendance has been good.

Feb. 7 Harry Adams, & Geo. & Elizth Barrett returned to school after an absence of several weeks.   **11** Herbert Ward has been away through illness for the past fortnight — and Alice Lewendon for the past week. The Attendance during the week has been very good and great progress has been made. A much better start has been obtained than was possible during the early part of 1886. Average for the week = 114. On books 126.

Feb. 14 Herbert Ward returned to school. A. C. Forbes Esqre & another gentleman visited in the morning.   **18** Wet day; only 14 Infants present, and several of the older school were away in consequence. Satisfactory progress has been made during the week. Attendance during the past few days has been very fair. Average for the week = 109. On books 124.

Feb. 21 Admitted Fredk Painter Robt Hearn & Wm Taylor in the Infants' Class.   **23** Sent a message to the Attendance Officer that a boy named Fredk Beeson, living at Hardwick, was not attending any school, although over 5 years of age.   **25** Recd a note to say that Fredk Beeson would come to school on the 28th inst. Recd Blackie's 'Merchant of Venice' for use as a reading book in Std 4–7. Finished going through the Geogl. Reader (World) for the first time in the upper standards. During the week several children have been absent owing to severe colds &c. and consequently the attendance has not been so good as usual. Average for the week = 108.5. On books 127.

Feb. 28 Admitted Fredk Beeson, who was in a backward condition, not having attended any school previously.   **Mar. 1** Recd the Chequered Drawing slates recommended by H.M. Inspector, for the Infants. Also some cards for Pricking & Embroidery work, as a varied occupation. Commenced Reading 'Merchant of Venice' on the 28th ult. Some of the children appeared to like it — but others found some difficulty in understanding it.   **4** Having gone through the prose version of the play, the 1st Class seem to appreciate the blank verse of the Merchant of Venice, and are progressing favo[u]rably with it; especially a few of the more intelligent scholars. Edwin Chambers & Emily Kirk have been absent all the week through illness. Good progress has been made during the week. The names of Wm Wayman & Chas Barrett have been taken off; as their parents sent word that they would not atend school any more. George Detfield has also gone to work as the Bradfield Attendance Committee do not compel the boys to attend School if they have passed Std 5 in two subjects — although according to the Education Code they should pass in all three subjects to be exempt from attending. During the present month the poorer children will have dinners given them twice, instead of three times a week.   **5** Had a man to cut the ivy on the Infants' Room wall, as it had got so thick as to endanger the coping, in a high wind.

Mar. 9 Sent a list of irregular scholars to the Bradfield Sch. Attendance Committee.   **11** I find the arrangement of the New Time Table to have grammar or Geography during the last lesson every day works extremely well. Finished reading through the 'Merchant of Venice' for the first time; some of the children appear to understand and appreciate it; but a few of the dull ones do not take much interest in it. However, that may not be the case after another trial or so — when they get used to the style. The children have attended very well during the week, and good progress has been made in all subjects. Average for the week = 117.1. On books 125. Edwin Chambers has been absent all the week with an injured foot: & Emma Thorpe with a bad cold &c. Recd Med. Certificate for Emma Thorpe.

Mar. 17 Standard I being in rather a backward state, I placed that class with Std 3 under the P.T. and gave Std 2 in charge of the Monitress for a time. During the time the Stds are thus arranged, the Geography Lesson for Std 1 will be given on Friday morning from 10.45–11.30 instead of on Thursday, Reading[123] taking the place of Geog. on Thursday. **18** Owing to inclement weather, the attendance during the past week has been very poor. Average 100. On books 124. Sent Sarah Knight & Louisa Shaw home yesterday as they were in such a very dirty state about their head.

Mar. 23 The Hutts were again in such a dirty state, that I sent them home, until the fact could be laid before the school Managers. Many complaints have been made by the parents of other children, who have been obliged to sit next to the Hutts; and also the other boys have asked that they might not sit close to them. Their bodies & clothes were always in such a condition that it quite made one feel sick when anywhere near them. **25** During the week six Infants and three elders [*sic*] children have been absent through illness, and the attendance has fallen off in consequence. Recd notice that Mary Lewendon had left school, having attained the age of 13 years on the 23rd inst. Average for the week = 104.3. On books 124.

Mar. 28 Admitted Fredk Wallis. **30** Visited for purpose of verifying Registers — present 116.[124] J.S. Mentioned the matter concerning the Hutts, to the Revd Canon Slatter, who considered it best to ask the Educn Department — what ought to be done in such a case. He knew they were always in a filthy state, owing to the condition of their home. **31** Put some curtains up at the back windows, as the chalk reflected such a strong light on bright days that it became almost unbearable to the teacher facing that way. During the week the weather has been nice & bright but it suddenly changed to snow and hail this morning, and consequently many of the children were away — only 22 infants present, in the morning, and 24 in the afternoon. The progress made in the week has been generally very satisfactory. Average for the week = 112.3. No. on books, 125.

Apr. 4 The Attendance officer called respecting the Hutts; the school Managers having decided that they could not admit that family in such a dirty condition. **5** Revd Canon Slatter visited in the morning, and asked the children if they would like to contribute something towards the maintenance of the London

---

[123] This word substituted for 'writing'.
[124] This figure substituted for '117', with note: 'F. Smith counted'.

Hospital for children; in commemoration of Her Majesty's Jubilee.   **6** Emma Thorpe has been transferred from Std 4 to Std 3. She has always suffered very much from nervous headaches, and so many certificates from the Doctor have been recd, that I was afraid to press her on with the work of Std 4, which she seemed unable to cope with.   **7** Thos Painter has been absent all the week with a bad mouth, & Emily Kirk the same owing to her brother having German Measles. Closed school at 12 o'clock for the usual Easter Holidays. Average for the week = 112. On books 125.

Apr. 18 Re-opened school after Easter Holidays. Admitted three new scholars. Good attendance. The School Managers have notified to Mrs Hutt that her children will be permitted to attend school on condition that they are thoroughly clean both with regard to clothes and body.   **22** The attendance during the week has been very good. Average 121. On books 128. Elizth Sharp has been transferred to Std I again as she seems unable to make any progress in the work of Std 2. She is an undergrown girl; very dull; & failed in Arithc in Std I at the last examination. It will [be] much better for her to have a few months longer in the same class, than to be pressed with the work of a higher standard.

Apr. 25 Re-admitted Thomas Wallis in the Infants' Class. The men finished painting the outside of the School, & Teacher's house.   **29** Examined Standard I in all subjects and found the children had made great progress during the past month. The general advance of all the School during the last 3 months has been very good, owing to the very regular atttendance of all the children. Average for the past week = 122. On books 129.

May 2 Admitted Maurice Simmonds, in the Infants' Class. Recd Med. Cert. for Edward Pocock, who had the chicken pox.   **5** Alfred House returned to School after several weeks' absence.   **6** The weather was very damp in the afternoon, and consequently several Infants were away. The general attendance during the week — good. Average for the week = 120. On books 130. Satisfactory progress has been made in all subjects during the week.

May 9 Edwd Pocock returned to School, having recovered from the chicken pox.   **11** The attendance Officer visited — but there were no cases of irregular scholars to report for the past month.   **13** All the children have attended very regularly during the week and the average is, therefore, much higher than it has been for some time past, — viz. 123. On books 130. William Cox has been transferred to Stand III again. He has had a good trial in Std 4 and seems quite unable to make any progress in any of the subjects. He has already been presented twice in the lower Std — but has failed in Arithc each year. Owing to good attendance very satisfactory progress has been made during the week.

May 18 Thoroughly examined Standard I, with a view to ascertaining if there were any who really ought to be transfered to the Infants' class as unable to cope with the work of Std I. Found Ernest Simmonds, Annie Higley, Albert Detfield, Louisa Shaw & Alfd Morland in a backward condition, especially with regard to spelling — but resolved to give them a further trial of a few weeks to see what improvement could be made.   **20** All the Standards have begun to learn their new poetry. Recd notice that Wm & Edith Brewer had left the parish and gone to Reading — and their names were removed from the books. The weather was very stormy, and, in consequence, several Infants were away. Sent a message to the parents of E. Simmonds asking them to be good enough, for the sake of the boy's progress, to send him more regularly to school, in the future. Harry Adams ill all the week. Attendance during the past week lower than usual. Average 117; on books 130.

May 23 Recd notice that Elizabeth Barrett had left the parish and gone to Reading — and therefore would not attend this school again.   **24** Louisa Sargent sent a message that, as her mother wanted her at home, she would not come to school any more. Admitted Sarah Jane Day, and her sister Louisa Day, on the 23rd inst. They had previously been in attendance at Hurst Natl Schools. Sarah Jane, although nearly 7 years of age, was in a very backward condition, and was therefore placed in the Infants' class till the end of the year. Louisa had previously been presented in Std 3, but, as her mother said, had failed in Writing & Arithc; she was placed in Standard III — and a letter sent to the teacher of her late school asking for information.   **27** During the past week the attendance has only been very fair. Average 114. No school was held in the afternoon, and a holiday was also given for Whit Monday & Tuesday, as usual.

June 1 Several children absent. Recd notice that Emma Wallis had removed to Goring Heath and would in future attend the Goring Heath School. Sent the names of Alfred & Edith Morland to the Attendance Officer.   **3** The weather throughout the day was very wet and consequently very many scholars were away. Seven Infants have been absent all the week — also M. Grist, Edith Ashby & Sarah Wallis in the Senr Depart. Average for the 3 days the school has been open = 104, on books 127.

June 6 Recd a reply from Miss Stallard, Hurst Girls' Sch. to the effect that Louisa Day was presented in the 3rd Standd but failed in two Subjects.   **9** Miss Slatter visited, and said that Mrs Foster had expressed a wish that the children should learn a few songs to sing at the Jubilee Festival to be given by John Foster Esqr, one of the School Managers, sometime in July.   **10** Good progress has been made during the week. Thos Goodall away all the week — suffering from general weakness.

June 13 The Attendance Officer called respecting the attendance of the Morlands. Thos Goodall returned to School.   **14** Admitted Ernest Terry & Arthur Lewendon. Recd Med. Cert. for Wm Cox, who was suffering from General debility &c. Med. Cert. recd for Emma Turner.   **15** Attended to check register, found present 35 Infts 76 B & G total 111. J.S. N.B. certain children named Hutt & Ward of the same mother are excluded from attendance on account of their persistent filthy condition, owing to neglect of the mother. J.S.   **17** Several children went to a School Treat at Goring Heath. The attendance of the Infants during the past few days has not been at all good. This morning only 28 out of 44 were present. Fredk Jeacocke had to go home soon after the roll was called — so his mark for atte was cancelled. Thoroughly examined std I, on the 16th inst — & decided to transfer Louisa Shaw, an undergrown & very dull child, to the Infants' Dept, as she seemed totally unable to make any progress in the work of the 1st Standd. Average for the week = 108. On books 126. Jas Goodenough has been absent all the week with the measles.

June 20 Admitted David Thomson, who was staying with his aunt in the village, for a few weeks.   **21** A holiday was given on account of Her Majesty's Jubilee — it being a general holiday.   **22** Several children absent.   **23** A. C. Forbes Esqre called. Recd Medl Certe for Chas Yates who was suffering from measles.   **24** Miss Forbes visited. Several children went home in the afternoon to mind babies whilst their mothers went to a meeting at Hillside. During the week the attendance has again been very low; and not very much progress has been made. Average for the wk = 105. On books 127. Recd information that Wm Turner had the Whooping Cough.

July 1 The weather during the week has been very sultry and depressing in the afternoons, and the children have appeared very tired by closing time. Jas Goodenough and Chas Yates have been absent all the week owing to measles — & Wm Turner with the whooping cough. On the 30th ult. the 1st Standard was again thoroughly examined, and the results were more satisfactory. Edwd Jeacocke has been away in Reading for the past fortnight. Average for the past week = 113. On books 127.

July 4 Sent the names of irregular scholars to Bradfield S.A. Committee. Chas Yates returned to School. Admitted Ruby Cockell, who was staying with her aunt for a few weeks.   **6** Jubilee celebration at Pangbourne, but only two of our boys went.   **8** Good attendance throughout the week in the senr Departt — but only fair in the Infants'. Alfred Hine away with inflamed eyes. A. C. Forbes Esq. called in the morning. Average for the week = 115. On books 128. Satisfactory progress has been made.

July 11 The managers decided that the roof of the Teacher's house should be thoroughly repaired — as it had got into a very unsafe condition.   **13** Recd a message from the Revd Canon Slatter — saying that Mrs Hutt had been to see him, and said that the Attendance Officer had reported her children to be in a fit condition for attendance at School — and that the woman had been told that they would be permitted to come to school so long as they were clean and not a nuisance to other children.   **14** Harry & Willm Hutt returned to School, apparently in a clean condition. Great Temperance Fete was held at Bere Court — many of our children went. A holiday was given in the afternoon.   **15** Good attendance throughout the week — and satisfactory progress made. Average for the week = 117. On books 128.

July 20 Attendance Officer visited — and advised that Louisa Shaw should be sent home on account of the dirty state of her head. Recd a note from the Revd Canon Slatter to the effect that the School Attendance Committee had decided that the Hutts were to be excluded, so long as they were in an unfit condition to mix with the other scholars.   **21** Celebration of Her Majesty's Jubilee. Holiday given.[125] Recd notice that Henry Thompson had gone away again. Verified Register in P.M. 74 B & G & 44 In. Total 118 J.S.   Thos Goodall advised by the Doctor to stay at home as his sister had the measles. Good attendance throughout the School. The men began repairing the roof of the Teacher's House. Thoroughly examined the work of Stds 2 and 3, and with the exception of C. Yates, & Louisa Day in dictation, the results were very good for the time of the year. The work of Std I has also progressed satisfactorily, although some of the children are rather careless over their arithmetic.   **29** The Pupil Teacher was absent on the 25th inst. with a sore throat. The Hutts put in an appearance but there seemed no improvement in their condition, & so they were sent back again. Although their hair had been cut very short, still, what remained was covered with nits. Thos Goodall has been absent all the week, as his sister has the measles. All the standards have finished learning their recitation. Sent a list of 8 irregular scholars to Bradfield. Throughout the week the attendance has been very fair. Average 114. On books 127.

Aug. 1 Although it was a Bank Holiday, no holiday was given as it was thought the better plan to let the children have the day extra at the end of the week when the school would close for Harvest Holidays. The Hutts again came but they were far from being in a satisfactory state and were sent back again. Recd notice that Alfred Hine had left this parish and gone to live at Reading. **3** The Attendance Officer called, and brought Mrs Hutt and her children for me to inspect. The mother had evidently searched the boys' heads well (although vermin was still visible) and then complained that I had previously sent them home without reason — which was not the truth. I told her to take them to the School Managers for inspection.   **4** The attendance during the week has been very low owing to harvest operations. Average for the wk = 96. On books 128. Closed School for 6 weeks' holiday.

Sept. 19 Re-opened school. During the vacation very many scholars have suffered from the measles — and some still have the complaint. Recd information that the Jeacockes were about to leave the parish and probably would not attend this school again.[126] They were nice bright children, and their absence will be felt. Examined all the Standards with the view of ascertaining if they had gone back much during the holidays — and found the 1st Std had forgotten a good deal of their arithmetic. During the holidays notice was recd that the Examn of Pupil Teachers would be held in the Greyfriars school, Reading on Octr 15th at 9.45 a.m.   **21** A. C. Forbes Esq. visited in the morning.

[125] According to the *Reading Mercury* of 23 July 1887, the celebrations included races and sports, plus a fireworks display in the evening: 'at night the village was illuminated from end to end . . . nearly every house being lit up with varicoloured lamps'. However, 'the prettiest sights of all were the "Maypole" dances . . . in which about 25 little children danced round a "crowned" pole to the merry tunes played by Miss Foster on a piano . . . At 5 o'clock several hundred children sat down in a large marquee for tea. Mrs. Foster gave away the prizes in the evening'.
[126] Caleb Jeacocke had kept the Royal Oak public house in Whitchurch.

23 About 20 children have been away all the week, and consequently the average is only 106, out of 128 on Books. Satisfactory progress has been made.

Sept. 26 Admitted John Tyrell, from Goring Heath School; & Edward Simmonds. All the children, who were absent last week with measles &c., returned to School.   **29** The Attendance Officer called for the attendance of the Hutts, whose parents had again been summoned. He also proposed seeing the mother of Mary Turner, about the child's recent irregular attendance. Had an open grate placed in the Infants' Room in the place of the stove.   **30** The 1st Class began drawing their maps from memory, and appeared to do them fairly satisfactorily. Recd a note from A. C. Forbes Esq. to the effect that the Sun Insurance Office had forwarded £5.3.6 for the erection of a shed, copper, &c in the yard behind the Master's house. The attendance in both rooms has been good. Average 115.1. On Books 130.

Oct. 4 Admitted Lily Hutt, who, although over 7 years old had not attended any school before, owing to ill-health, and, therefore, did not know her letters. **5** Punished Thos Goodall for playing truant, on the 4th inst.   **6** Admitted Walter Kirk. Thoroughly examined std 3, and found two children were not quite sure of their long division sums, and also that some were rather careless over their dictation — otherwise the work was very well done for the time of year. **7** A. C. Forbes Esq. called in the morning. Average for the week = 120. On books 133.

Oct. 12 Revd W. C. Cluff, the Curate, visited to wish the Teachers & scholars farewell, as he was leaving the parish, after a stay of 4 years.   **13** The weather suddenly set in cold and damp, and some of the Infants were away.   **14** Recd a note from the attendance Officer asking for the attendance of the Hutts. Weather still cold and dreary. Good progress throughout the week. Average 121. On Books 130. Recd information that the Morlands had left this parish and gone to Goring to reside.

Oct. 17 Visited to verify register found 72 B & G & 46 Infts Total 118 JOHN SLATTER   Recd notice that the Diocesan Inspector would visit these schools on Novr 7th (Monday), and put up the same in school as recommended. Took Annie, Alfred, & Edith Morland off the books as they had removed to Goring Parish.   **19** Examined Stds II & III — Std II did their work very well, but the other class seemed still careless over the spelling of small words. Reading and arithc throughout very satisfactory.   **20** Examined Std I. With the exception of Joseph Hutt, who had been absent so much, the work was done very satisfactorily. The children have attended well since the holidays, and great progress has been made in consequence.   **21** Received notice that Fredk Wm & Winifred Robinson had left the Parish. Average for the week = 117.9. On books 127.

Oct. 24 Admitted Charlotte Streak and Louisa Turner, who had not attended any school previously.   **27** The weather was very wet and dull. Several of the Infants were away.   **28** Satisfactory progress has been made during the week, in all classes; and the attendance has also been good. Average for the week = 116. On books 128.

Oct. 31 Recd information that Alfred Hine had removed to Goring. **Nov. 1** The weather was very boisterous and wet and consequently many Infants, & some of the older scholars were absent. **2** Recd, & began using, in Stds III–VII, the Schedule Arithc Cards. **4** Owing to bad weather, the attendance during the week has been much lower than usual. Average 109. On books 124.

Nov. 7 The Schools were examined by the Diocesan Inspector. Holiday was given in the afternoon. No registers were marked. **11** Revd Canon Slatter visited, and brought the report of the Scripture Examination. Average for the week = 111. On books 124. The weather during the whole of the past week has been very damp, and the attendance somewhat diminished in consequence, especially in the Infants' Department. Satisfactory progress has been made. Standard I children have much improved in carefulness in their Arithc and nearly always produce accurate answers. John Gutteridge has not yet succeeded in understanding the method of doing subtraction.

Report of the Diocesan Inspector

Infants' Departt. The Infants have been carefully taught, and, in many respects, passed a good examination. The children repeated Catechism, Hymns, Texts &c carefully, and answered very fairly. I would however recommend the use of the Diocesan Syllabus.

Mixed Departt. The Religious Instruction has been painstaking and good. The Scripture subjects were very well known in both Divisions. The Catechism was very accurately repeated and written out and its meaning was intelligently[127] known. The written work was, as a rule, excellent. The order and discipline are quite satisfactory.

Dioc. Prize   Albert Pocock   }   1st Div
Commd   Fred Green   Mary Grist   }

Commended Alice Weller, Emma Thorpe, Emma Bartlett, Julia Simmonds, Chas Excell — 2nd Div.

CHARLES E. ADAMS

Nov. 14 Received notice from Mrs Fuller, that Emma Thorpe would not attend school again. **15** The weather set in extremely cold; some of the little ones were away, in consequence. **16** Thoroughly examined Std 3 in all subjects. With the exception of Louisa Day's dictation the work done was very satisfactory. **18** The attendance during the week has been good, considering the state of the weather. Average, 114. No. on books 124.

Nov. 21 Several children away with the Mumps. **25** Owing to the prevalence of Mumps the attendance during the past week has been very low indeed.

---

[127] This word substituted for 'very accurately'.

Average in the Mixed Departt.   =   66. On books,   73.
  do.   in the Infants'   do.   =   32   do.   49.

              Total   98   122

Recd the Examination Schedules from the Educn Depart. Examined Std II and found everything in a very satisfactory state. Revd Canon Slatter visited in the afternoon. Miss C. M. Heasman, late P.T. in St Jude's Sch. Southsea, has been appointed Asst Mistress; to commence duties after the Govt Examination.

Nov. 28 A good many of the children who had been absent with mumps, returned to school. A few fresh cases occurred.   **Dec. 2** Eliza Turner and John Gutteridge have been away with the mumps all the week; in the Senior Department; and about 8 Infants, so that the average for both rooms is only 106, out of 122 on the books. During the week I have thoroughly examined all the Standards. In the 1st class, Herbert Ward, Edward Simmonds and Thomas Goodall seemed backward in their spelling, and in the lower classes, Chas Yate[s], Louisa Day & Ernest Simmonds were weak in Reading & spelling. Thomas Goodall & Herbert Ward showed inability to do grammar well.

Dec. 6 Some of those who had been away with the mumps returned; but others fell with the same complaint.   **9** Miss Forbes visited in the afternoon. In consequence of bad weather and illness, the attendance has been very low, the average being only 103, out of 122. Considering the numbers present, satisfactory work has been done during [the week], and most of the scholars seem to be pretty well up in their subjects.

Dec. 16 Elizth Streak, Alice Bartlett, Edith Ashby, Emily Kirk, Frank Fabry, Rosa Weller & John Tyrell away all the week with the mumps. The Monitress, Martha Cross has also been absent with the same complaint. During the past few days the weather has been very damp and has thinned the attendance of the Infants somewhat. Sent a list of irregular scholars to the Attendance officer on the 14th inst. On the 13 inst. Miss Forbes attended after the morning meeting and distributed the boots to the children who had subscribed to the Boot Club during the year. Owing to the prevalence of the Mumps the average for the week = 100 only, out of 120 on the books. Examined Stds II & III in the 3 Rs on the 14th inst and received satisfactory results, with the exception of the spelling of Louisa Day, and Charles Yates. Edwin Chambers absent with a bad foot. Albert Pocock has had charge of Standard I during the week, in the place of the Monitress.

Dec. 19 Several fresh children away with the Mumps. The Monitress, and some of the others returned to school. Weather still dull and damp. Examined standard I, and found the results satisfactory, with the exception of the spelling of Ernest Simmonds.   **23** Recd notice that H.M. Inspector would visit these schools on Thursday Jany 12th 1888 at 9.15 a.m. Mrs Foster kindly gave all the children some oranges and buns. Average for the week = 109. On books 120 Closed school at 12 o'clock till Tuesday the 27th inst.

Dec. 27 More cases of Mumps. Poor attendance, especially in the Infants' Departt. Recd notice that Louisa Shaw had left the parish, and gone to live with her aunt, as her father had recently died.   **29** Several children went to an entertainment at Mapledurham, in the afternoon.   **30** During the past week 12 scholars have been away all the time, with the Mumps, colds &c. and consequently the average only = 99 out of 120 on the books.

1888

Jan. 2 Admitted Thomas Earwaker. Most of the children returned to school. **4** The attendance Officer called.   **5** A. C. Forbes Esq. visited in the morning. **6** Arthur Smith, Harry Smith, Frank Lewendon, Elizth House and Wm Chambers have been away all the week with the Mumps. Omitting the above children, the attendance has been very good all through the week, and has proved of great benefit, especially to the Infants' Dept. — where there has been a very poor attendance during the past few weeks, in consequence of the Mumps. Average for the week = 110. On books 121.   **7** The Managers met to audit accounts &c.

Jan. 12 School visited by HM Inspector of Schools; Revd Canon Slatter, & A. C. Forbes Esq. attended. Holiday given in the afternoon.   **13** No school was held. Sent for Readers reqd for standard IV–VII. Good attendance during the week. Took Louisa Shaw's name off the books, as she had left the Parish and gone to Goring.

Songs [for 1888] Senr Dept.   1 The Farmer's Boy, 2 I love to wander forth and sing, 3 There are hearts in staunch old England, 4 Up with the dawn ye sons of toil, 5 The lark
              Infants   1 The Sparrow's Nest, 2 The Bees, 3 The Cobbler.

Infants [Object] Lessons   1 Minerals, 2 do., 3 Ice & Snow, 4 Bread, 5 do., 6 Iron, 7 do., 8 Clay, 9 Lead I & II, 10 The hare, 11 Sea Gull, 12 Ostrich, 13 Camel, 14 Squirrel, 15 Mole, 16 Eagle, 17 Spider, 18 do., 19 Frost, 20 Water, 21 Seasons, 22 Rainbow, 23 Thunderstorm, 24 Frog, 25 Wild Flowers, 26 Primrose, 27 Holly Tree, 28 Oats, 29 Barley, 30 The Ears, 31 Breath, 32 Voice, 33 Nose, 34 Face, 35 Money, 36 Railways, 37 Umbrella, 38 Boots & Shoes, 39 Paper, 40 Lead II

Readers for 1889[128]
St. i.   Moffatt's Geog. & Explanatory.
  ii   do.   do.
  iii   New London, Gill's Hist.; Moffatt's Geog.
iv–vii   Glimpses of the Globe (Oceans)
              Short History of Engld Marcus Ward
              King John
    Poetry
St i   Streamlet
  ii & iii Lucy Gray
  iv–vii   Extract from King John.   S.G.T.

[128] The books included William Moffatt's *Readings in Geography* and *Explanatory Readers* both published in 1882, and J. G. Hefford (ed.), *A Short History of England* published by Marcus Ward in *c.* 1883.

Jan. 16 Recd the Duplicate Schedule. Miss C. Heasman began duties. Arranged classes in their new standards, and commenced the fresh work. Received 'Glimpses of the Globe' (Oceans &c) for Stds IV–VII and began reading the books. **18** The attendance Officer called. No cases of irregular scholars to report. **20** Took the names off the books of some who had passed Std 5 and gone to work. Average for the week 106. On Bks 120.

Jan. 23 Admitted Adelaide Barnes, & Frank Cross, and re-admitted Walter Kirk. Charlotte Streak away with the Chicken-pox. **24** Good attendance in both rooms. **27** Good progress has been made during the week and a very satisfactory start has been made in the new work in each standard. Average for the week = 107.

Jan. 30 Several children away with bad colds &c. and consequently a poor attendance. Fall of snow in the afternoon. Commenced reading Moffatt's Explanatory Readers in Standard I. The children appeared interested in the stories. **[31]**

Whitchurch (Reading) Parochial School Jan. 30th
Mixed School. The Arithmetic of the Standards above the third, though improved, is still only very fair, but in all other respects an excellent Examination has been passed in Elementary and Class Subjects. Needlework is pretty good.
Infants' Class. The Elementary Instruction is good, especially in Reading, and the Varied Occupations, with the exception of Recitation, are very satisfactory. Object Lessons are fair, and Needlework pretty good.
F. A. Tomlin has passed fairly. She should be informed that she is now qualified under both Articles 50 and 52.
Herbert W. Winchester　Certd Teacher 2nd Class
Susan King　Assistant Teacher
Caroline M. Heasman　Asst Teacher
ALEXANDER C. FORBES, Correspondent

Feb. 2 A. C. Forbes Esq. visited in the morning. **3** There has been much sickness among the scholars during the past week. No less than 18 have been absent all the time, and several others nearly the whole week. In most cases the cause of absence has been a cold or sore throat. Commenced reading King John in Stds IV–VII. Average for the week = 90.4. On books 117.

Feb. 7 The morning was very wet and kept many away from School. **8** Sent a list of irregular scholars to the Attendance Committee. Recd a med. certificate for Harry Adams. **9** Finished reading Glimpses of the Globe in the upper Standards: and commenced King John. **10** Satisfactory progress has been made during the week. The attendance in the Infants' class has been very low, owing to sickness and inclement weather. Average for the week 100.2. On books 117.

Feb. 17 No school has been held during the week, since the 13th inst. owing to snow.

Feb. 24 The School has only been opened three days during the past week. Average for that time very low indeed.

Feb. 29 Visited in Aftn to verify register. Found 26 I. 74 B & G. Total 100 J.S. The snowy weather has greatly interfered with the attendance and especially of the younger children. J.S.   Mrs Foster kindly gave a treat to the schoolchildren after the afternoon meeting.   **Mar. 2** Took Edwd Simmonds, Wm Cox & Annie Lewendon off the books, as they had left the school. The attendance during the week has again been very low, owing to the bad weather, & sickness. Average = 93.6. On books 117. In spite of the bad attendance, satisfactory progress appears to have been made in all the standard work; but the Infants have been greatly hindered.

Mar. 5 Most of the Infants, who had been away with colds &c. came back to school, and consequently there was an improved attendance, which was more encouraging to the Teachers.   **6** Examined standards 2 & 3 in the afternoon, and found everything, with the exception of the spelling of two or three in Std 2, very satisfactory for the time of year.   **9** Wm Painter absent with an inflamed eye lid, and Edith Terry with a scalp wound. The attendance during the week has been very fair the average being 101 out of 114 on the books. During the past two months the number of children on the books has very much diminished, owing to the elder ones leaving and no fresh scholars being admitted to fill the vacancies.

Mar. 12 Admitted Frank Beeson, who ought to have been attending school over 4 months before.   **16** Several children have again been absent all the week, and consequently the average = 100.6 only out of 115 on books. Satisfactory progress has been made in the lower Standards, but the upper class has been much hindered by irregularity, which has caused so much repetition of work.

Mar. 23 There has been another week of very unsettled weather, and the attendance has again been very low indeed, especially in the Infants' Class. Average for the week = 92. On books 115. Owing to the unpropitious weather during the past 6 weeks, the average since Jan. 1st has been reduced to 100 only.

Mar. 26 The attendance slightly improved.   **29** During the last 2 days the weather has again been such as prevented many children from putting in an appearance. Average for week = 86. On books 115. School closed for Easter Holidays. To re-open on April 9th.

Apr. 9 Re-opened school with a very good attendance. Admitted 5 new scholars. Recd notice that Herbert Ward had left the school.   **11** Examined Std I: and found the results fairly satisfactory. Reading was the strongest subject. The Arithc rather weak.   **13** Received, and commenced using, Marcus Wards Historical Readers, which appeared rather difficult for Standard 4. Average for the past week. 110.8. On books 120.

Apr. 16 Recd notice that Fredk Green & Chas Terry had left school & gone to work.   **17** Several of the choir children went to sing at a funeral in the afternoon. Recd notice that Rosa Lewendon had left the school.   **18** Informed the attendance Officer that there was a child over 5 yrs of age, not attending any school. Wet day. Several children away in consequence.   **19** Examined Standards II & III, and found everything in a satisfactory state, with the exception of the spelling of 3 or 4 children [in] Std 2. Recd a medical Certificate for Alfred House who was suffering from an inflamed foot.   **20** The attendance during the week has been very fair. Average for the week = 104.9. On books 120.

Apr. 27 The attendance during the week has been very fair. Elizth Lewendon has been away for a fortnight with a bad foot. Average for the week = 105. On Books 120.

Apr. 30 Admitted James Streak & Elizth Goodenough. Elizth Lewendon returned to school. Recd notice that Kate Hole had left the parish. Commenced learning the repetition in the upper standards.   **May 2** The Attendance Officer visited. Wet afternoon.   **3** No school was held, owing to the Funeral of the Master's little son, Leonard.   **4** Began the poetry in the Lower Standards. Average for the week = 110. On books 121.

May 7 Admitted Millicent Dean (who ought to have been at school two months earlier), and Edwd Weller. Good attendance in both rooms.   **8** Admitted Thomas Lewendon, aged 3. Received a Medical Certificate for Harry Bushnell, who was suffering from Rheumatism of the thigh.   **11** The children have attended very well during the past week — as the weather has been nice and bright — and great progress has taken place throughout the school. Examined standards I–III, on the 9th inst. and found everything in a satisfactory condition. Average for the week = 112.9. On books 119.

May 15 A Confirmation was held in the Church in the afternoon, and the Choir children attended.   **17** The morning was very wet, and only 19 Infants presented themselves. Nine of the older scholars were also away.   **18** The weather was again very wet in the early part of the day, and prevented some of the children attending school. The Asst Mistress was unavoidably absent. Average for the week = 101.3. On books 119. Closed school until the 23rd inst.

May 23 Re-admitted Arthur Day. Several children away.   **25** There has been a very good attendance in the Senior Department; by [*sic*] only a fair one in the Infants' Class, 8 children having been away all the week. Had a blind fixed to the outside of the west window, and found it a great boon in excluding the sun's rays in the afternoon. Average for the week = 104. On books 120.

June 1 Good progress has been made during the past week. The Lower Standards have commenced their Repetition. Four scholars have been away, through sickness all the week. Received a medical Certificate for Millicent Deane. Examined Std I on the 29th ult. and the results were generally satisfactory. Average for the week = 109. On Books 119.

June 3 Sent the names of Sarah and Frank Wallis to the Attendance Officer. Examined standard 3 and found some of the children rather weak in spelling, and others careless over their Arithmetic. Reading was good in most cases. Most of the scholars were present.   **8** Although the weather was rather damp, most of the children were present. In the afternoon 3 boys went on the river instead of coming to school. Harry and Arthur Smith also went home to dinner and did not return. Satisfactory progress has been made during the week, and most of the children appear in a good state for the time of year. Average for the week = 108.5. On Books 119.

June 11 Admitted Edwd Higley and Fredk Allwright. Good attendance in both rooms.   **12** Admitted Emily Detfield.   **15** Wet day. Several scholars absent. The Attendance throughout the week has been good, on the whole. Average 114.7. On Books 122.

June 18 The Infants' Assistant was unavoidably absent, & her place was taken by Mrs Winchester.   **19** Charlotte Turner, Alice Weller, & Alice Bartlett away, suffering from bad colds.   **22** Louisa Gutteridge and Julia Ridge absent with severe colds. Satisfactory progress has been made during the week. Examined Std I on the 21st inst. and found the children had greatly improved in their Arithmetic and writing. Average for the week 111.7; on books 122.

June 25 The Attendance Officer called and took the name of 3 or 4 children who had been rather irregular during the past few weeks. No school was held in the afternoon, as there was a treat on the Hill for most of the children residing in that district. Several Infants were away in the morning.   **26** Most of the children were present.   **29** During the week the attendance has been very fair. Thoroughly examined Stds I–III on the 27th inst. and the results were generally satisfactory. All the Taylors have left the parish and gone to reside in Reading. They were all well up in their work, and will be missed. Average for the week = 108. On Books 122.

July 2 Admitted Alice Clark. The weather was very wet, and a great number of children were unable to attend school. A. C. Forbes Esqre visited on the 29th ult, and heard the singing.   **3** Admitted Mary Ann Weller, Edith Hedges and Sarah Smith — all Infants. Edith Hedges ought to have attended school in February as she was 5 years old on the 13th of that month.   **6** Received a Medical certificate for Julia Ridge, who was suffering from an inflamed gland. During the week the children have attended very well, and very satisfactory progress has been made. For the time of year, most of the scholars are well up in the Standard work. Average for the week = 108.8. On books 121.

July 9 Admitted Selina & Thomas Wallis.   **11** Wet day; many scholars absent in consequence.   **12** Several children went to a Temperance Fête at Bere Court. Fair attendance.   **13** Average for the week = 105.8. On books 124. Louisa Smith, Ethel Lewendon, & Julia Ridge have been away all the week, owing to sickness &c.

July 18 Received Medical Certificates for Harry Painter (bad eyes) Elizth Streak (enlarged glands), George Gutteridge (severe cold) & Emily Terry (severe cold & enlarged gland). Julia Ridge still absent.   **19** Thoroughly examined Stds 2 and 3, in all subjects, and found the results satisfactory with the exception of the work of two boys in dictation, and of one girl in arithmetic. In Std I John Gutteridge & Wm Smith still fail to make any progress in Arithc. Most of the children in all standards have learned all their repetition.   **20** The morning was very wet indeed and many scholars were absent throughout the day. Average for the week = 104. On books 123.

July 25 Louisa Fabry away with a sore throat and head-ache. Sarah Wallis also absent with a bad cold. The weather still very damp, but the attendance was good, considering the great number absent through sickness. Sent a message to Mrs Newman on the 24th inst. informing her that Wm Newman had been absent from school several times during the last few days, and asking for an explanation as, some time since, he played the truant once or twice.   **27** Louisa Fabry returned to school. There was a Sunday School Treat at Goring Heath and several children went to it, as they attended that Sunday School. There has been only a fair attendance during the past week, no less than eight children having been away during the whole time. Average 105.7. On books 123. Sent a list of defaulters to Bradfield.

July 30 Admitted Percy Bartlett aged 4 years.   **Aug. 1** The weather was extremely wet, and there were present only 64   Senr Dept 45 Infants 19. A holiday was given in the afternoon as there was a Flower Show at Coombe Park, Whitchurch.   **2** Improved attendance. Fine weather having set in.   **3** Average for the week 103. On books 124. Closed school for Harvest Holidays. 5 weeks.

Sept. 10 Reopened school. Owing to extremely unsettled weather, the harvest operations have progressed very slowly and a great number of children failed to present themselves. Admitted four new scholars.   **11** The Attendance improved slightly.   **14** Many children have been absent all the week and the Average = 76 only. On books 129.

Sept. 17 Admitted Henry F. Smith. Many scholars, who had been gleaning, came back to school. A few, however, were again absent. Received notice that George Kelly, and Thomas Earwaker had left the parish, and also that Ada Lewendon & Elizth Higley had left school.   **21** Harry Bushnell has been ill with a bad leg &c all the week, and it has been decided by the doctor that he ought to be removed to the Reading Hospital. Charlotte Turner has also been away all the week with a bad cold. Very fair progress has been made during the week. Average 108. On books 130. Recd Notice that the Annual Examination of Pupil Teachers would take place on October 20th at Greyfriars Sch. Reading.

Sept. 24 In the morning the weather was very wet, & consequently many children were absent.   **25** The attendance much improved.   **28** Harry Bushnell still too ill to attend school. Emma & Thos Wallas have been absent during the whole week. Satisfactory work has been done this week.

Oct. 1 Admitted Fredk Luker. George Gutteridge returned to school. **5** There has been a full school throughout the week; and very satisfactory work done. Harry Bushnell still too ill to attend. Average for the week 112. On books 124.

Oct. 8 Admitted Annie and May Pocock. Received a Medl Certificate for George Gutteridge, who was suffering from a severe cough. **12** Several Infants absent, only 39 present in the morning. The standard work has greatly improved during the past three weeks, owing to good attendance, and most of the children appear to be in a satisfactory state for the time of year. Commenced using the Sovereign Arithc Cards on the 8th inst. Average for the week = 110. On books 123.

Oct. 15 Harry Bushnell, George Gutteridge, Alice Detfield and Emily Detfield still absent. **18** Thoroughly examined Standards II & III in all subjects and the results were very satisfactory especially in reading and arithmetic. **19** Four Infants have been absent with bad colds &c. during the whole of the past week; and several others have been very irregular. So that the usual progress has not been made. Average for the week = 108. On books 122.

Oct. 24 Verified the Register — B & G 67 I. 42 — 109 present. [J. SLATTER] **26** The children have attended school very well during the week and a good amount of work has been done. The Assistant Mistress was absent this morning owing to indisposition, but attended as usual this afternoon. On the 29th inst the afternoon meetings will begin at 1.45 instead of 2 o'clock. Harry Bushnell, Alice & Emily Detfield, and George Gutteridge still absent through illness. Average for the week = 110. On books 122. Recd notice that the Scripture Examination would be held on November 20th at 10 a.m.

Oct. 29 The weather set in very wet which prevented many children attending school. **Nov. 2** Owing to the very unsettled damp state of the weather during the whole week, the attendance has been very low. Average 101. Received information that Henry Higley would not attend school again until the spring, and his name was, therefore, removed from the register.

Nov. 5 Revd Canon Slatter, and the Revd — Cudmore, the recently appointed Curate, visited in the morning.[129] **9** During the past week, the Curate has attended and examined the 1st Class on the Acts of the Apostles, each morning, from 9 till 9.30. The weather was very damp and only 29 Infants presented themselves in the morning and 31 in the afternoon. The Attendance Officer visited on the 7th inst. Average for the week = 104.8. On books 120.

[129] The Rev. Richard Paul Cudmore (a non-Collegiate Oxford graduate from Cork) remained at Whitchurch for a few months only; in Crockford's *Clerical Directory* his stay at Whitchurch is not even mentioned, and from 1888 to 1890 he is shown as curate of Greenham in Berkshire. His immediate predecessor at Whitchurch, the Rev. Samuel Thorn Gwillam (licensed 1 Dec. 1887) is not mentioned in the log book; and neither Cudmore nor Hemsworth (see p. 149, n. 133) is listed among the Curates of Whitchurch in W. J. Oldfield's MS Parochial Index in Bodl.

Nov. 16 The Revd — Cudmore has visited each morning during the week and examined the upper standards in Scripture. The attendance of the Infants has been much hindered by bad weather. On the 12th inst Standards III–VI began using Matthew's Unexcelled Arithc Test cards, and seemed to work most of the sums correctly. Average for the week = 105. On books 121. Attended to examine Register. Present 42 I. 68 B & G. J.S.

Nov. 20 The School was examined by the Revd C. G. Wodehouse, the Diocesan Inspector. Half holiday in the afternoon.   **22** The Revd Canon, & Miss Slatter visited in the afternoon, and brought the Report of the Diocesan Inspector:—

Diocesan Report
Whitchurch C.E. Schools — examined Nov 20th 1888

The children have a very accurate knowledge of Holy Scripture and of the Church Catechism, and answer very readily and intelligently. The Paper-work is creditable, Writing and spelling very fair. The Repetition of Hymns and Texts was correct. The Tone is very satisfactory. The Infants have been very well taught and answer with intelligence. It would be well if more children in the Vth Standard were instructed in writing brief biographies of some of the leading characters of the Bible.

Dioc. Prize   Fredk Ashby   Highly commended   Louisa Fabry
C. G. WODEHOUSE   Diocesan Inspector of Schools

23 The scholars have attended well during the week, and satisfactory work has been done. Some of the Infants have been absent for several weeks. On the 16th inst the Revd Canon Slatter called and examined the upper Standards in the 7th Std Geography. Average for the week = 107. On books 121.

Nov. 26 Attended to examine & count. I 43 B & G 67. J.S. Admitted Caroline Hunt, who was 8 years of age, and in a very backward state, so that it was necessary to place her in the second class in the Infants' room. Received information that John, Edwd & George Gutteridge had left the parish and would not attend these schools again.   **27** Revd — Cudmore visited.   **29** The Misses Forbes called in the afternoon and asked for a list of all the children as it was proposed to provide a christmas tree.   **30** The weather was extremely wet throughout the day, and reduced the attendance to an average of 104 for the week. On books 122. Recd the Examination Forms from the Educn Departt.

Dec. 5 Sent a list of Irregular scholars to the Attendance Officer.   **7** During the past week the attendance, owing to improved weather, has been much better and good progress has been made. Alice & Emily Detfield have not attended at all since Octr 8th in consequence of eruptions on their heads. Louisa Gutteridge has not been able to attend for over a week, from want of boots. Average for the week = 112.5. On books 122.

Dec. 14 The Attendance officer called on the 12th inst. Several children have been absent all the week, and consequently the average is only 107.6 out of 122 on the books. Thoroughly examined all the standard work during the week and found everything satisfactory.

Dec. 21 Wm Hedges has been away for a fortnight with bad eyes. The weather set in very wet at noon, and several children were absent in the afternoon. Julia Simmonds has not been able to attend since the 18th inst. owing to sickness. Average for the past week = 108 out of 122 on books. Sarah Knight was admitted on the 17th inst. Miss Forbes visited on the 20th inst and distributed the boots to the children who had paid subscriptions to the Boot Club during the year, after the afternoon meeting. During the week all the standards have again undergone a thorough examination and, in most instances, satisfactory results have been obtained.

Dec. 24 The morning was very wet and only 98 scholars presented themselves. 62 Senrs & 36 Infants. Closed school until the 27th inst.

Dec. 27 The attendance improved slightly. **28** Received notice that these schools would be visited on Tuesday, Jany 15th 1889 at 9.15 a.m. by H.M. Inspector of Schools. Another wet day, and bad attendance. Average for the week = 94. On books = 121.

Dec. 31 Alice Detfield returned to school after an absence of 12 weeks. Emily Detfield still too ill to attend. The attendance throughout the School greatly improved. **Jan. 4** Harry Adams, Harry Painter, Millie Dean, Frank Beeson & Emily Hedges absent all the week. Average for the week = 110. On books 122. **5** Managers met at the Schools to Audit the Accounts &c. and found a deficiency of £45.

1889

Jan. 11 There has been a good attendance during the whole of the week although the weather has not been in a settled state. Average for the week = 113.3. on books 122.

Jan. 15 The Schools were examined by H.M. Inspector & his Assistant. All the Std children were present. Revd Canon Slatter visited. Holiday was given in the afternoon. **16** Arranged the children in their new Standards. Drafted 18 infants into the 1st Standard. Commenced the new work for 1889. **18** Made some slight alterations in the Time-Table (sanctioned by H.M. Inspector) which were necessary on account of Stds I & II being grouped for Geography.

Songs [for 1889] Mixed Dept 1 The Coach, 2 In Summertime, 3 The River, 4 Boys wanted, 5 Where is the land

Infants 1 The Threshers, 2 The Thrashing Machine, 3 The Robin

Object Lessons 1 Silver, 2 Fur, 3 Wool, 4 Cotton I, 5 do. II, 6 Silk, 7 do. II, 8 Tea I, 9 do. II, 10 Metals I, 11 do. II, 12 Lion, 13 Fly I, 14 do. II, 15 Bat, 16 Horse, 17 Cow, 18 Cat, 19 Pig, 20 Salmon, 21 Parrot, 22 The Snake I, 23 do. II, 24 Birds of prey, 25 Beasts do., 26 Stork. 27 A Tree, 28 Fir Tree, 29 Grass, 30 Leaves, 31 Corn, 32 Oranges, 33 Sky, 34 Sea, 35 Vapour, 36 Rain, 37 Sun, 38 Matches, 39 A Straw hat, 40 A Slate

Readers for 1890
Sts. i & ii   see p. 388 [i.e. 13 Jan. 1888]
  iii   Moffatt's Explanatory, Gill's Hist: & Moffatt's Geog.
  iv–vii   Gill's Brit. Isles & Colonies
    do. Annals of England
    Henry V   S.G.T.
[Poetry]
  i   The Pert Chicken
  ii & iii   George Nidiver
  iv–vii   Extract from Henry V.   S.G.T.
In Geogy Sts. i & ii are grouped & take in 1890 the work of St. ii. S.G.T.

18   During the past week the attendance has been very good indeed, which has enable[d] the teachers to make a satisfactory start in the new work. Average for the week = 112. On books 122.

Jan. 20 Received the Duplicate Examination schedules, and found that the only failures throughout the schools were Julia Ridge, and Wm Newman, who both failed in Arithc.

Jan. 28 No school was held last week, owing to the rooms being required for a Dramatic Entertainment.   **30** Mary Grist has been appointed to succeed Martha Cross as Monitress, to commence duties on Feb. 1st.   **Feb. 1** Florence Smith and John Terry were admitted on the 28th ult. During the week the attendance in the Senr Dept has been remarkably good and much work has been done in all subjects. Average for the week = 109. The School Managers have offered the appointment of Asst Mistress in the schools, to Miss E. Agnes Green of Witham, Essex, who will begin duties on March 1st in the Senr Department — Miss King leaving and Miss Heasman taking the Infants on the same date.

  Feby 2nd Whitchurch (Reading) Parochial School (Oxford)
  Mixed School. The children are in very good order and have again passed an excellent examination. The only points requiring attention are the needlework of the second standard and the style of setting out the Arithmetic on paper.
  Infants' Class. Considering the amount of absence, through sickness during the year, the elementary attainments are satisfactory and the occupations good. The Object Lessons, however, fail to interest the children, and during them very lax discipline is allowed to prevail. Improvement must be shown in these subjects, as a condition of the renewed recommendation of the present scale of merit grant.
  Herbert W. Winchester   Certd Teacher 1st Class[130]
  Susan King   Asst Teacher
  Caroline M. Heasman   Asst teacher.
        ALEXANDER C. FORBES   (Correspondent)

---

[130] Under the Code, teachers' certificates of the second class could be raised to a first by 'good service'.

Feb. 8 The School Managers have appointed Miss Janet Blacklaws (not Miss Green, as entered on page 414 [*i.e. 1 Feb. 1889*]) of Locherbie [*sic*], Scotland, as Assistant in the place of Miss King; to commence duties on March 1st. Most of the children have attended regularly during the week, and very satisfactory progress has been made in all the classes. Mary Grist began her duties as Monitress, in the place of M. Cross, on the 1st inst. Harry Bushnell has been absent during the past fortnight with rheumatism, and George Barrett for a week with a cold on the liver. Average for the week = 109. On books 116.

Feb. 11 There was such a deep snow that not a single child came, so that the Schools were not opened.   **12** Only 45 children attended but the registers were marked, and the usual work done.   **13** A thaw set in the previous night and several additional scholars put in an appearance in the morning. A. C. Forbes Esq. called in the afternoon & suggested that an Extract from the Report of H.M. Inspector should be inserted in the Annual Balance Sheets.   **15** Although the weather has been nice and bright, during the last two days, a great number of the children have not come to school. Average for the week = 81. On books 117. Received notice from the Education Department that Miss S. King & Miss C. Heasman would be permitted to sit at the Certificate Examination in Decr 1889 providing they received a report on their Recitation from H.M. inspector.

Feb. 18 Re-admitted Edward Higley.   **20** Arthur Chambers; Emily Kirk, Millie Dean, George Barrett, & Sarah Smith absent through illness. Harry Bushnell has not been able to attend school for several weeks owing to a severe attack of rheumatism. Wm & Walter Willis have left the parish & gone to Caversham to live. Their names have therefore been removed from the books. **22** Average for the week = 105. On books 118.

Feb. 25 The weather was very cold, and snowy, and very many children were away. Only 17 out of 34 Infants were present.   **Mar. 1** During the past week there has been a great deal of irregularity, owing to bad weather and sickness, consequently the usual amount of progress has not been made. Miss King left on the 28th ult; and today Miss Heasman has commenced working with the Infants' Class. The Girls did not have any sewing in the afternoon, owing to the absence of an assistant — it having been arranged that Miss J. Blacklaws should commence duties on the 4th inst. Average for the week = 91.5. On books 118.

Mar. 4 Miss Janet Blacklaws began duties as Assistant Mistress.   **6** A. C. Forbes Esq. called.   **8** During the week a great number of children have been absent: and the average attendance only reached 88 out of 117 on the registers. Progress has been greatly retarded in consequence.

Mar. 15 During the week several scholars have been away with chicken pox. Good work has been done in the senr department, and everything seems in a satisfactory state for the time of year. Average for the week = 97. On books 117.

Mar. 18 Admitted three new scholars — Infants.   **20** Visited to verify Registers. I 27. B & G 75. Total 102. J.S.   **21** Owing to rain and snow, very many scholars did not attend. Only about 50 were present in the morning; and a few additional ones in the afternoon.   **22** A. C. Forbes Esq. attended at 12 o'clock and distributed prizes to all children who passed in the three R's at the Govt Examination in January. There was a good attendance. Average for the week = 89.9. On Books 116.

Mar. 29 Several children have been away all the week with colds or chicken-pox. A. C. Forbes Esq. called on the 25th and again on the 28th inst and complained of boys breaking an iron fencing, and destroying some young trees, and threatened proceedings. The Upper Standards began reading Cassell's Shakespeare's Henry V on the 25th inst, and seemed greatly interested in the subject matter. Average for the week = 101.9. On books 118. Two new scholars were admitted on the 25th inst.

Apr. 1 Sarah & William Day returned to school after being away with Chicken Pox.   **5** For the past few days the attendance has been very good, and satisfactory progress has been made. on the 1st inst. Elizth Streak & Thomas Smith were transferred to the Infants' Class as they were in such a backward state, owing to deficiency in intelligence, that it would have been an impossibility for them to have accomplished the work of Standard I by the end of the year. Average for the week = 107. On books 119.

Apr. 12 Satisfactory work has been done during the past week, in both rooms. Annie Painter, aged 3 years, was admitted on the 8th inst. *Also Frank Wallis & Walter Kirk. Elizth Streak has been away all the week with sickness*. Average for the week = 104. On books 120.

Apr. [14] Began using Evan's [sic] Midland Arithmetical Examinations in the upper standards on the 14th inst. and found them very good. The children appreciated them because they contained no catchy questions.   **17** Charlotte Turner absent with a bad cold. Closed school until the 29th inst. During the holidays it has been arranged for the rooms to be thoroughly cleaned, white-washed, painted &c. During the three days the Schools have been opened the attendance has been very fair. On the 15th inst. Miss Heasman went to Reading in the afternoon to say her recitation to H.M. Inspector. Miss Blacklaws took the Infants so that the senior girls did not have any needlework.

Apr. 29 Re-opened school with a very good number. Admitted Florence Grist and Edith Pocock.   **May 1** A. C. Forbes Esq. called in the morning.   **2** The Rev. R. P. Cudmore, the Curate, visited in the afternoon.   **3** During the week the attendances have been very good and very satisfactory work done. Average 110. On books 121.

May 6 Admitted Albert Kent. Attendance very good.   **8** The Attendance Officer visited to see if there were any defaulters for April.   **10** Charlotte Turner has been absent all the week with a severe cold & cough. The morning was wet —

and many little ones absent. Satisfactory work has been done during the week. Average 112. On books 122.

May 17 Chas[131] Lewendon, Elizth Wallis & Ellen Hearn were admitted on the 13th inst. Frank & Sarah Wallis, and Charlotte Turner have been away, with severe colds, all the week. All the Standards began learning their repetition pieces early in the week, and seemed interested in them. During the week all the standards have been thoroughly examined in every subject and, with the exception of the spelling of some of the standard I boys, very satisfactory results have been obtained. Average for the week = 115.5. No. on books 126.

May 23 Visited to verify the numbers. 74 B & G. 45 I. Total 119. [J. SLATTER] **24** Charlotte Turner, Sarah & Frank Wallis, and George Gutteridge still absent. Alfred Shaw, aged 3, was admitted on the 20th inst. Good progress in all classes, has been made during the week, owing to regular attendance. Average 119. On books 127. During the past 3 months the Infants have made good progress in every respect under Miss Heasman, and the discipline has been much improved.

May 27 Only 60 children attended as the day was very stormy. **28** Sarah Wallis & Char. Turner returned after a month's absence through sickness. George Barrett, who had been in the Reading Hospital since February 4th, came back to school, of course knowing nothing of the work of standard 4. **31** Since the 27th inst. satisfactory work has been accomplished. Average for the week = 106.3. On Books 127.

June 7 There was a thunderstorm in the early morning and many Infants stayed away from School. Closed school at 12 o'clk until the 12th inst.

June 14 The children have attended very fairly during the last three days. Average 114. On books 127. Miss Heasman has sent in her resignation to the School Managers, having been offered a more lucrative appointment near her home at Southsea.[132] George Barrett has made very good progress in the work of Std 4 since the 28th ult.

June 19 The Attendance Officer visited, and promised to see the parents of three children who were over 5 years of age and not attending any school. **21** Great progress has been made during the past week owing to good attendance. Average for the week = 118. On books 127. The Lower Standards have finished learning the repetition pieces, and Std IV–VII have nearly done so. The Upper classes began using Gill's Annals of History, on the 20th inst. having thoroughly mastered the contents of the Geogy & Shakespeare Readers.

---

[131] This name substituted for Thos.'.
[132] The Whitchurch vacancy was advertised in *The Schoolmaster* of 22 June 1889, as for an Assistant to teach infants in an 'Excellent' school. 'Salary £35 (monthly payments), plus £1 for "Excellent".' The term 'Excellent' referred to the school's classification under the Merit Grant system then in operation.

June 24 Admitted Mary Ann Hutt who was over 6 years old (Date of birth Jan. 14, 1883) and had not attended school previously, although she had always resided in the parish.   **28** The attendance has been very good during the week. Av. 118. On books 128. Satisfactory work in all standards has been done.

July 5 Miss Heasman was unavoidably absent in the morning. There was a half-holiday in the afternoon. The children have attended well during the week — average 121, on books 126. Satisfactory progress has been made.

July 8 Admitted a new scholar.   **10** The weather was very unsettled throughout the day, consequently many infants did not attend school. Miss J. B. Forder of Wolverton has been appointed Assistant for the Infants in the place of Miss Heasman who will leave on September 1st.   **12** Good work has been done during the week. Most scholars now know their repetition. A few standard I children are still in a backward state as regards spelling. Average for the week 117. On books 126.

July 16 Good attendance.   **17** There was a Temperance Fête at Purley, and a good number of our scholars went to it, as they were members of the Band of Hope.   **19** On the whole the attendance has been good during the week and good progress has been made. Average 114. On books 127.

July 24 The Attendance Officer visited. Admitted Fredk Spokes on the 22nd inst.   **26** Five Infants and one sen scholar have been prevented attending school during the week, by illness. Satisfactory work has been done. Average for the week = 112. On books 127.

Aug. 1 The Attendance Officer called on the 31st ult. to see if there were any defaulters for July. A. C. Forbes Esq. visited in the morning — and proposed the school should be closed this week for the Harvest holidays. The children have attended very well during the past week. Average 115. On books 127. The schools were closed after the afternoon meeting — to reopen on Sept. 16th.

Sept. 16 Attended on some business — took occasion to count. 71 B & G, 45 I = 116. J.S.   Re-opened school. Some of the Infants away with whooping-cough. Canon Slatter visited in the morning, and brought notice from the Diocesan Inspector that he wished to examine the schools on the 8th of October instead of in November.   **17** Revd W. B. Hemsworth, the recently appointed Curate, called in the morning to make arrangements for giving some lessons in Scripture.[133] **20** Allowing for absence through sickness, the attendance has been good during the whole week. Average 115. On books 126. Mervin Marlor and Millie Dean have left the parish and their names have been removed from the books. Miss

---

[133] The Rev. William Barker Hemsworth, Jesus College, Cambridge (1855–1930), remained at Whitchurch (his third curacy) for a short time only, and moved in 1890 to become curate of Gimingham, Norfolk.

Jane Bound Forder began duties as Assistant Teacher for Infants (in the place of Miss Heasman) on the 16th inst.

Sept. 24 Stormy weather prevailed throughout the whole day and consequently many children were away.   **25** The Attendance Officer called in the morning to enquire about the attendance of Sarah & Frank Wallis.   **27** Several Infants have been absent during the past fortnight with whooping cough. In the afternoon three little children presented themselves after the registers had been marked. Good progress has been made. Average 108. On books 126. Miss Forder appears to manage the Infants well.

Oct. 1 A. C. Forbes Esq. visited in the afternoon.   **4** The morning was very wet and many scholars were absent, only about 80 were present. A few more attended in the afternoon. Commenced using the Minerva series of Arithmetic Test Cards. Six Infants have been ill all the week. Edith Ashby still away with a severe cold &c. Average for the week = 106.4. On books 126.

Oct. 8 The school was Examined by the Revd C. G. Wodehouse, Diocesan Inspector of Schools. Half holiday was given in the afternoon.   **9** Punished Joseph and Harry Hutt for absenting themselves when sent to school. **11** Edmund & Lily Pocock still away with whooping cough, & Elizth Goodenough with German Measles. Examined all standards during the week and found everything in a satisfactory state. Average for the week = 113. On books 128.

Oct. 14 Admitted four scholars from Goring Heath schools.   **18** Elizth Goodenough still away with German Measles & Edd & Lily Pocock with Whooping Cough. The children have attended extremely well during the past week and much good work has been done. Average 124. On books 131.

Oct. 23 Revd W. B. Hemsworth visited in the afternoon.   **25** Sarah Wallis has been absent for over a fortnight with a pain in her side. Elizth Goodenough has not yet returned to school. During the past week there has been a good attendance each day. Average for the week = 120. On books 132.

Oct. 28 All the Hedges have left the parish.   **30** Sent the names of three defaulters to Bradfield S.A. Committee.   **Nov. 1** A. C. Forbes Esq. called during the morning. Many children absent owing to bad weather. Average for the week 115. On books 130.

Nov. 4 Harry Bushnell returned to school, having been absent, in the Hospital since January 18th. He was, therefore, placed in standard II, as it would have been useless to have put him in standard III.   **7** Ten boys were taken to sing songs at a Mothers' Meeting on the Hill, in the afternoon.   **8** Two pipes have been added to the stoves which give much greater heat than formerly. Satisfactory work has been accomplished during the week owing to good attendance. Average = 124. On books 132.

Nov. 15 The children have again attended well during the week, and good progress has been made. Average for the week = 125.4. On books 132.

Nov. 22 Miss Forbes & Miss Grey visited in the morning and heard the children sing. Joseph Hutt has played truant all the week. All the Hurfords have left the parish. Satisfactory work has been done during the week. Average attendance 120.3. On books 132.

Nov. 25 Miss E. Forbes attended at 12 o'clock to distribute the boots.   **29** Sent a list of 4 scholars to the Bradfield S.A. Committee. Joseph Hutt has again played truant all the week. Received the Examination Schedules from the Educn Dept. Average for the week = 118.

Dec. 2 A. C. Forbes Esq. called in the morning.   **4** Joseph Hutt returned to school after playing truant for 3 weeks. Chas Detfield has scalded his leg, and is unable to attend school.   **6** Satisfactory work has been done during the week, owing to good attendance Average = 119.5. On registers 127.

Dec. 13 Sarah Wallis and Charlotte Turner have been unable to attend school during the last two days, owing to bad colds. During the week all standards have had a thorough examination. The results, with the exception of the arithmetic of John Gutteridge and William Newman, were satisfactory. Average for the week = 117. On books 127. Joseph Hutt stole another boy's food yesterday and has not attended school since.

Dec. 16 Admitted William Sharp, who, although over 6 years of age, did not know his letters. Joseph Hutt played truant, met with an accident, and was conveyed to the Reading Hospital.   **19** Verified the Register. 70+42. Total 112. J.S.   Revd Canon Slatter visited, and brought the Report of the Diocesan Inspector.

Scripture Report

The children acquitted themselves very creditably; their knowledge of the facts of Holy Scripture and of the Church Catechism is accurate.

The Paper-work shewed good writing & spelling — the children evidently took great pains with their work.

The Infants promise well.

Diocesan Prize — Julia Simmonds   Std 5.

Commended	Edwin Chambers	
	Florence Smith	} Std iii
	Elizth House	
	Lilian Winchester	Std ii

C. G. WODEHOUSE   Diocesan Inspector of Schools

Wet day, many scholars absent. The usual work has been done during the past week. Average attendance 113.5. On books 127.

Dec. 25 Received notice that the Annual Inspection would be held on January 24th 1890.   **27** — Wilson Esq. Chairman of the Reading School Board, & Miss

A. Forbes called in the morning and heard the children sing their school songs. Several scholars absent. Average for the week = 115. On books 127.

1890

Jan. 3 Miss Blacklaws was absent through illness, so the girls did not have any sewing lesson in the afternoon. Sent a list of defaulters to the S.A. Committee. Joseph Hutt still playing truant. Satisfactory work has been done during the past week. Average attendance 115. On books 127.

Jan. 9 A. C. Forbes Esq. & J. Foster Esq. visited in the afternoon and proposed holding the Annual Meeting of Managers, on Saturday the 18th inst. to examine accounts &c. **10** Joseph Hutt has again played truant all the week. There has been a very good attendance during each day for the past week — and good work has been done. Average = 120. On books 127.

Jan. 13 Several children away with colds &c. **15** The attendance officer called respecting Joseph Hutt's non-attendance at school. **17** A. C. Forbes Esqre visited in the morning. Nine scholars absent in the Senr Dept. Average for the week = 117.3. On books 127. **18** The School Managers met at the Rectory to Audit accounts &c.

Jan. 24 The schools were visited by H.M. Inspector and his Assistant. Only Charlotte Turner was absent in the Standards. A. C. Forbes Esq. was present during the Examination H.M. Inspector recommended the use of desks in the Infants' Department. Average for the week = 117.

Jan. 27 Took Fred Ashby's name off the books.
Songs [for 1890]   Mixed Department   1 The River, 2 The Lark, 3 The Ship, 4 Lullaby, 5 Father Christmas
Infants' Department   1 The Robins, 2 The Showman, 3 The Daisy
Object Lessons   1 Clock, 2 Chair, 3 Pin, 4 Table, 5 Thimble, 6 Sugar, 7 Lead-pencil, 8 A Letter, 9 Window, 10 Coal, 11 Salt, 12 Chalk, 13 Cotton, 14 Daisy, 15 Dandelion, 16 Dog, 17 Goat, 18 Teeth, 19 Eyes, 20 Hands, 21 Potatoes, 22 Sheep, 23 Baker, 24 Carpenter, 25 Schoolroom, 26 River (I), 27 River (II), 28 Iron, 29 Frog, 30 Donkey, 31 Tiger, 32 Elephant, 33 Camel, 34 Hen's egg, 35 A Book, 36 Rat
Readers for 1891[134]
St   i & ii   see p. 388
     iii   ,, ,, 413
     iv–vii   Royal Geogy. (Europe)
          Easy Hist: for Upper Std:
          Richard iii

[134] H.M.I. Tremenheere continued to recommend books even though the Minutes and Instructions to Inspectors for 1890 clearly stated: 'The officers of this Department are not at liberty to prescribe or to recommend particular books, apparatus or school requisites for use in schools' (para. 21).

Poetry
    i   Past & Present (T. Hood)
  ii & iii   We are Seven
  iv–vii Richard iii

                                                  S.G.T.
Sts i & ii grouped take St. i Geog.   S.G.T.

28 Received the Duplicate Schedule and found only 5 failures: viz. 4 in Arithc & 1 in composition. **31** Several Children who passed Std V at the Examn left School. The Attendance Officer called on the 29th inst. Average for the week was only 107, out of 129, owing [to] the prevalence of Influenza. On the 27th inst. May Elliott was admitted.

Feb. 3 Several additional children away with Influenza. Took the names of scholars who had left, off the books. Admitted Kate Weller. **5** More children absent with Influenza, & the attendance was very low. **8** Satisfactory work has been done, during the week by those who have attended. Joseph Hutt again played truant. Average for the week = 104. On books 124. Received the Report of H.M. Inspector.

Mixed School. Reading, though quite good, is not up to last year's level, and written Arithmetic is only fair in the standards above the fourth, but the Writing, Spelling and Arithmetic of the four lower standards deserve the highest praise. The Class Subjects and Needlework are very satisfactory on the whole, but the first class should answer more readily in Grammar, and Map-drawing requires attention. The discipline is very good. The boys' offices should be provided with doors.

Infants' Class. The Reading of the first class and the Writing of the third should be better, but otherwise the Elementary Instruction is very satisfactory. The rest of the routine is fairly well carried out, but the younger children should be encouraged to take a more active part in the Object Lessons, and more use should be made of smart bright drill. The discipline is good, except in regard to the personal cleanliness of the boys. Some desks are required.

  Herbert W. Winchester Certd. Teacher 1st Class
  Janet Blacklaws   Asst   do.
  Jane Bound Forder   do.   do.
                    ALEXANDER C. FORBES   Correspondent

Feb. 11 A. C. Forbes Esq. visited in the Afternoon. Several additional children away with Influenza &c. The Hutts were sent home, for they were in such a filthy condition that they were totally unfit to sit near other children. **14** Received 60 new slates and ruled them to a pattern suggested by H.M. Inspector. Also ruled the blackboards to match. New desks for Infants were ordered on the 8th inst. Irregularity has much impeded the progress of the children in their new work. Average for the week = 104. On books 124. Miss Blacklaws terminated her duties. The appointed [sic] of Miss L. Burch was notified to the Educn Departt on the 9th inst.

Feb. 17 Miss Burch began work. Recd a letter from the Educn Department saying that Miss Burch was not qualified under Article 50 but that she might serve under Article 84 — subject to the approval of H.M. Inspector at next year's inspection.[135] Some of the children returned — others were away. **20** A. C. Forbes Esq. called in the afternoon. **21** The attendance has slightly improved during the week. Average 110.2; on books 124. Miss Burch has been suffering from Influenza, since the 18th inst., so the girls have not had any needlework during the last 4 days.

Feb. 24 Miss Burch returned to her duties. Several other scholars absent with Influenza. Attendance only fair; about 20 away. **26** Miss Forder has been absent during the last two days with neuralgia &c. Received 3 desks for the Infants' Room. **28** During the week 20 per cent of the children have been absent with Influenza &c. Sent a list of irregular Scholars to Bradfield. Took Thos Whiting's name off books as he had passed the sixth standard & gone to work. Average for the week = 104.

Mar. 6 Still several children away with Influenza. Considering the absence through sickness, satisfactory progress has been made during the week. Mr Sellwood called on the 5th inst. and complained of children damaging a shed.

Mar. 10 The morning was very wet and many children were away. **11** Nearly all children presented themselves. **14** Good progress has been made during the week. Amy & Ernest Terry absent with severe colds; & Albert Turner with a bad leg. Average for the week = 110. On books 123.

Mar. 17 Admitted Alice House. **19** Several children away with bad coughs. **20** Wet day. Many scholars absent. **21** William Newman went home at 10.30 a.m. because he was punished for idleness. Average for the week = 105. On books 124. Willm Newman returned in the afternoon, with an apology from his mother.

Mar. 24 About 30 absent with bad coughs. **25** Sent word to the Attendance Officer that Joseph Hutt had played truant for over 6 weeks. No notice was taken of his absence last month, by the Attendance Committee, although the matter was reported on the usual monthly return form — on the 1st instant. **28** The progress has been greatly retarded this week by irregular attendance, owing to severe colds. No less than 19 children have been absent all the week. Average 92. No on books 124.

Apr. 1 Most of the elder scholars returned to school, several Infants still away. A. C. Forbes Esq. visited in the afternoon. Called to verify registers.

---

[135] Article 84 of the Code stated: 'In mixed, girls', and infant schools, a woman over 18 years of age, and approved by the Inspector, who is employed during the whole of the school hours in the general instruction of the scholars and in teaching needlework, is accepted as equivalent to a pupil teacher'. An Article 84 teacher was thus without any formal training or qualification whatever. Miss Burch had been appointed as a result of an advertisement of the vacancy appearing in *The Schoolmaster* on 4 Jan. 1890 for an Assistant to teach Standards II and III, plus Needlework at a salary of £35 a year with '£1 bonus if Schools classed "Excellent"'.

Present 80 B & G, 33 Infts, total 113. I have been prevented by illness from calling earlier. [J. SLATTER] **3** Closed school for Easter Holiday — one week. The Attendance Officer called on the 2nd inst.

Apr. 14 Re-opened school. Several children still absent with bad colds &c. Received notice that Albert Kent had the Diphtheria. In the afternoon the Sanitary Inspector called to see what other children were away from school, and the reasons for their absence.   **15** Albert Kent died.   **18** The average for the week was only 106 out of 124 on the books. The New Curate called on the 14th & 15th inst.

Apr. 21 All the Terrys were ordered by the Doctor to stay at home owing to illness of their brother.   **22** The Curate gave a Scripture Lesson to Std IV–VII.[136] Joseph Hutt returned to school on the 21st inst after playing truant for 10 weeks. He was absent again in the afternoon — without leave.   **25** The attendance during the whole week has been very low, owing to sickness. Ruby Cockell has left the parish — and her name has been taken off the books. The weather this morning was very damp, and only about 70 children attended; in the afternoon there was some improvement both in the weather and in the attendance.

Apr. 29 The Curate gave a scripture lesson to Stds IV–VI.   **30** Fred. Smith took Mary Grist's place as teacher of Std I for a short time. The Curate visited in the morning.   **May 2** During the week the numbers have slightly improved; still the average has only reached 106.9 out of 122 on the books. Arthur Chambers, May Elliott, & Harry Bushnell still away from Whitchurch owing to fear of Diphtheria, although no other cases have been reported.

May 5 Harry Bushnell returned to school.   **6** The Curate took Stds IV–VI in scripture.   **9** Elizth Streak, Rosa Weller, Robt Hearn & Fred. Luker have been absent, through sickness, all the week. A good many of the children are behind in the work, especially in spelling, for the time of year, owing to irregularity of attendance, caused by influenza, sore-throats &c. since January. Average for the week 104. On books 122.

May 16 The Revd Rowley gave a scripture lesson to the 1st class, on Thursday, 9–9.30 a.m. During the week great progress has been made, owing to good attendance. Emily Kirk & Eliz Streak absent all the week with bad colds. Joseph Hutt has only attended half-a-day and has played truant the rest of the time. Average for the week = 108. On books 120.

May 19 Admitted two new scholars in the Infant Room.   **23** Good progress has been made during the week. Joseph Hutt has only been present twice during

---

[136] In March 1890, Canon Slatter reported to Bishop Stubbs that religious instruction was being given in the day schools by 'the Curate who lives close by the school' (1890 Clergy Visitation Returns, Bodl. MS. Oxf. Dioc. Pp. c. 356). This (new) Curate was James Farmer Rowley, who remained at Whitchurch from 1890 to 1894, before moving to Stourpaine in Dorset.

the week. Examined Std I and found Thos & Sarah Smith very backward in their spelling, otherwise·the· work was done very satisfactorily for the time of year. Average for the week = 110.1. On books 122. Closed school till Wednesday the 28th inst.

May 28 Re-opened school. Several children away.   **29** The Curate gave a scripture lesson to Std iv–vi.   **30** The morning was very wet & many scholars were· absent. A few additional ones came in the afternoon as it cleared off. Average for last 3 days = 103. On books 124. Two new children were admitted on the 28th inst. Sent five names of defaulters to the Bradfield S.A. Committee.

June 2 Elizth Streak returned to school after an illness of 5 weeks.   **6** Examined Standard II in Arithmetic and found Jas Goodenough, Fred Beeson, Arthur Chambers & Elizth Weller shaky over short division. Satisfactory work has been done during the week. Attendance good. Average for the week = 116. On books 127.   **7** The Attendance Officer called respecting the defaulters in May.

June 12 A. C. Forbes Esqre called to enquire about Joseph Hutt, who had been prosecuted for taking a nest of partridge's eggs.   **13** Damp morning; several away. The attendance improved in the afternoon. Good work has been done during the week. Average for the week = 117. No. on books 127.

June 16 Admitted Harry Goodenough. Good attendance.   **17** A. C. Forbes Esq. visited, and said the magistrates had decided on sending Joseph Hutt to an Industrial School until he was 16 years old.[137]   **19** The Curate gave a Scripture lesson to Stds iv–vi.   **20** Miss Forder was too ill to attend school on the 18th inst. Monitors supplied her place. During the week very satisfactory progress has been made. Average for the week = 119. On books 128. Nelson's Queen Royal Reader was introduced in the Infant's Room last week. Christopher Turner has been away ill, for a fortnight.

June 25 Received notice that Sydney, Christ., Alb. & Fred Turner had left the parish.   **26** P.M. called to verify registers. 103 present (B G & I) J.S.   The morning was very wet and only 94 children attended. Improvement in the afternoon.   **27** Owing to two wet days, the average for the week was only 113.3. On books 129. The four Turners have been taken off the books. Examined Stds II & III and found the spelling of Std II rather weak.

July 1 Thoroughly examined Std I and found everything in a very satisfactory state, with the exception of the reading of Thos Smith and Louisa Turner and the writing of Sarah Knight.   **3** Miss Forder was away in the afternoon, and the

---

[137] Industrial Schools were designed to give training and education to youngsters who had 'not yet fallen into actual crime but who are almost certain from their ignorance, destitution and the circumstances in which they are growing up, to do so if a helping hand be not extended to them'. Horn, *Victorian Country Child*, p. 188.

Infants were taught by monitresses.   **4** Minnie Luker has been absent, through illness for 4 days. Average for the week = 116. On books 123.

July 11 The usual progress has been done during the past week. Attendance very fair, on books 123. Average 112.

July 14 Admitted John Knight.   **16** A Band of Hope Festival was held at Purley & several boys and girls went in the afternoon. Good progress has been made during the week. Attendance very good. Av. 117. On books 124.

July 25 The usual work has been done during the past week. Miss Burch was absent on the 24th inst. Average for the week = 114. On books 124.

Aug. 1 Walter Kirk & John Terry absent with colds all the week. Sent a list of irregular scholars to Bradfield S.A. committee. The usual progress has been made during the week. Average 110. On books 124. Closed school for harvest holidays; 6 weeks.

Sept. 15 Re-opened school. Attendance very good. Harvest quite finished. Miss Harriett Berrington commenced teaching in the Infants' Room in the place of Miss Forder. Admitted 3 new scholars.   **19** Good work has been done during the week owing to bright weather & good attendance. Average 116. On books 125.

Sept. 22 Admitted Philip Rosier. Walter Smith away with inflamed eyes. Thoroughly examined Standards ii & iii during the afternoon — the results were satisfactory on the whole; found Fred. Beeson, Edith Weller & Emma Turner very backward in reading & spelling, and Ruby Cockell in Arithc in Std ii, also Harry Painter & Charles Whiting in Arithc in Std iii. Commenced Arithc in Stds iii–vi on foolscap.   **26** The usual work has been done during the week. The weather has been nice and open and the attendance very good. Average for the week = 120. On books 126. Revd Canon Slatter visited and brought notice that the Diocesan Inspector intended examining the Schools on Tuesday, Octr 14th at 9.30 a.m.   **27** Recd another notice that the visit of the Diocesan Inspector had been postponed till November.

Sept. 29 I visited the School officially to verify the Registers & found present 76 B & G & 40 I. J.S.   **30** Miss L. Burch sent in her resignation, as she had been offered an appointment near her home.   **Oct. 3** Florence Lewendon & Chas Lewendon have been away with sore throats all the past week. The attendance has been good: and satisfactory work done.

Oct. 10 Revd Canon Slatter visited during the morning, and stayed some time to hear the singing lesson. Three boys were absent, blackberrying, in the afternoon. Attendance during the week, very fair.   **11** Miss L. Cooper, Assistant in Catsfield Natl Schools has been appointed Asst Teacher in the place of Miss Burch. To commence duties on Monday Nov. 3rd.

Oct. 17 Revd Canon Slatter & A. C. Forbes Esqre visited on the 16th inst. and gave the children a lecture about throwing stones at the walnuts. The attendance during the week has been very good in the Infants' class and very fair in the Senr Department. The managers have cautioned Fanny Lewendon, about being absent from school. Elizth Wallis has left the parish. Began fires in school on the 12th inst., as the weather set in very cold. Miss Slatter called in the afternoon.

Oct. 22 The Attendance Officer visited. **23** Revd Canon Slatter called in the morning & mentioned that Mrs Foster proposed giving an entertainment to the school children on Monday Novr 3rd in the afternoon at Coombe Park. The work done during the week has been very satisfactory, on the whole. recd a 'Memorandum of suggested arrangements for Examination under the New Code' & filed the same in the Log Book.[138] The attendance during the week was very good. Average 114. On books 124.

Oct. 31 Miss L. Burch terminated her duties as Asst Teacher. Frank & Sarah Wallis were away with bad colds all the week. During the week I examined all the Stands and found they were in a satisfactory state for the time of year. Harry Hutt played truant in the afternoon. The average for the week was 114. On the 29th inst the choir boys were entertained at tea &c in the afternoon at Mrs Williams-Freeman's — about 20 children were absent.[139] Sent a list of defaulters to Bradfield S.A. Com.

Nov. 3 Miss L. Cooper began duties as Assistant Mistress in the Mixed Department. Miss Burch terminated her engagement on the 31st ult. In the afternoon all the scholars were entertained at a treat by Mrs Foster at Coombe Park. **7** Several children were absent without leave, and went out in the woods getting acorns.[140] Sarah Knight was ill all the week. With the exception of Friday afternoon the attendance was very good. Examined Std II on the 6th and found one or two very weak in reading and spelling, but the arithc was very good throughout. Average for the week was 116. On books 124.

---

[138] This brought to an end the 'payment by results' system for the three R's. Although variable grants were retained for class and specific subjects, needlework and singing, the attendance and standard subjects grants were to be replaced by a larger 'principal grant' per child in average attendance of either 12s. 6d. or 14s. — the higher grant to be paid if the scholars 'throughout the school are satisfactorily taught Recitation'. (Art. 101(a)(iii)). To the 'principal grant' a 'discipline and organization' grant of 1s. or 1s. 6d. per child could be added. This was not a 'revamped merit grant but a grant for moral tone and atmosphere, and a happy cheerful school'. For a discussion of these and other aspects of the New Code, see Sutherland, *Policy-Making in Elementary Education*, pp. 279–82; for the Code itself see P.P. 1890, xxviii. Grants under the new Code became operative from 31 August 1890.

[139] Mrs Williams-Freeman lived at Walliscote House, Whitchurch.

[140] The estate records of the Blount family at Mapledurham show that payments of 1s. a bushel were made for collecting acorns — see, for example, July–December 1900 at Whittle's Farm (Bodl. MS. D.D. Blount c. 192). The acorns were fed to the pigs.

Nov. 10 Miss Cooper sent in her resignation to the School Managers, with an intimation that she would be willing to leave as soon as another teacher could be secured, as she did not like her work. The Managers decided that she might go at once and her place supplied by temporary monitors, Mrs Winchester looking after the needlework till an Assistant should be obtained.[141]

Report of the Diocesan Inspector of schools   Novr 8th 1890
The School has passed an Excellent Examination in a somewhat too limited range of subjects.
The Answering in each class was very good especially in Holy Scripture.
The Catechism was most accurately repeated, and portions of it were faultlessly written out, but its meaning and teaching were not sufficiently understood.
The written work of the Upper Standards was, in itself, excellent, but they should be practised in answering questions on paper.
I venture to hope that the New Diocesan Syllabus may now be followed.
Diocesan prize   Adelaide Barnes
Commended   Frank Cross, Chas Excell, Geo. Barrett, Wm Smith, Edw. Chambers, Flo. Smith, Eliz. Sharp, Emma Wallis, Minnie Luker, Emma Lyford, Thos Wallis, Rob. Hearn, Chas Whiting, Hy Bushnell, Flor. Grist, Jno. Holmes, Ellen Hearn, Edwd Simmonds.

CHAS E. ADAMS   D.I.S.

12 The morning was very wet and many were away, but several attended in the afternoon as the weather became finer.   **14** Minnie Luker, Chas Lewendon & Wm Newman were ill all the week. Caroline Hunt was admitted on the 10th inst. Mary Grist took charge of Standard I & Fred Smith assisted with Stds ii & iii. Very satisfactory work was done. The average for the week was only 109, out of 123 on the Books. During the month Stds v & vi practised drawing the lines of Latitude & Longitude (required by the New Code) and made very good progress, although some were rather slow in calculating the measurements with the ruler.

Nov. 21 Revd Canon Slatter visited in the afternoon. Chas & Thos Lewendon, Allen Wells, Arthur Day & Charlotte Turner were away through illness during the whole week. The Attendance Officer called to enquire about the Hutts and Wallises whose names were returned last month. The working of the school deviated slightly from the Timetable so as to allow the sewing lessons to be held on Tuesday and Thursday all the afternoon, as Mrs Winchester was not able to teach every afternoon. The attendance was only very fair.

Nov. 28 The School was conducted as in the previous week, as no assistant had been secured. A. C. Forbes Esqre visited & brought the Forms from the Education Department. The attendance throughout the week was very low indeed, owing to the prevalence of severe colds, caused by a sudden change in the weather. The average for the week was only 102, out of 123 on the books. Took Adelaide Barnes off the books, as she had been appointed monitress for Std I.

---

[141] The vacancy was advertised in *The Schoolmaster* on 15 Nov. 1890 for an Assistant '(Ex-P.T.) for Standards II and III. Needlework. £35 paid monthly'.

Dec. 4 Visited to verify & inspect Registers   found present 76 B & G & 36 I = 112 Total. J.S.   **5** Miss Margaret Roberts, Pupil Teacher, Katesgrove Board School, Reading, began duties as Assistant Teacher for Stds ii & iii, on the 1st inst. The Curate called in the morning. The Misses Forbes visited on the 3rd inst. In consequence of the prevalence of bad coughs & colds the attendance was only very fair, although an improvement on that of the previous week. Good work was done in the Senior department. Average for the week was 112; on books 123.

Dec. 8 There was a heavy fall of snow in the morning and a great number of children were absent.   **12** The Revd Canon Slatter called in the Afternoon. A great number of children were away all the week with bad colds, headaches &c. and the average was only 104 out of 123 on books.

Dec. 15 The morning was very damp, and a great many scholars were away. A few additional ones came in the afternoon.   **19** Three children in the senior department, and six Infants were ill all the week; and the average only reached 102 out of 121 on the books.

Dec. 24 Owing to a heavy fall of snow, and sharp frosts, the attendance, during the 3 days the schools were opened, was very low indeed. The average was only 72 out of 121 on the books. The Curate called in the morning. Received notice that the schools would be examined on Wednesday Jany 14th 1891. The schools were closed at 12 o'clock till the 29th inst.

Dec. 29 The snow was still thick upon the ground and nearly half the Infants were again away but most of the Senior scholars presented themselves. **Jan. 1** A. C. Forbes Esqre called in the afternoon, and proposed a meeting on the 10th inst for auditing the accounts &c.   **2** Eleven Infants were absent all the week, owing to the severity of the weather, and the average for the whole school was only 99 out of 121 on the books.

1891

Jan. 5 Admitted two new scholars.   **6** A. C. Forbes Esqre visited in the afternoon.   **9** The attendance of the Infants has been very low indeed for several weeks, owing to the severe weather. Received information that Edith Ashby had scalded both feet and probably would not be able to attend school for some days.

Songs [for 1891]   Senr Department   1 The Blacksmith, 2 The Daisy, 3 The Laughing Rill, 4 Down by the greenwood, 5 The sun is in the golden west

Infants' Class   1 The Bees, 2 The Fox, 3 The Robin, 4 The sailor Boy

Object Lessons   1 Bat, 2 Lion, 3 Cow, 4 Wolf, 5 Snake, 6 Swan, 7 Mouse, 8 Monkey, 9 Birds, 10 Fish, 11 Bread, 12 Candles, 13 Soap, 14 Stone, 15 A straw Hat, 16 An Umbrella, 17 Ships, 18 Coins, 19 Butcher, 20 Fisherman, 21 Sailor, 22 Postman, 23 Railway, 24 Oak, 25 Beech, 26 Walnut, 27 Strawberry, 28 Currant, 29 An Orange, 30 Silver

Readers for 1892
Sts. i & ii   see p. 388 [*i.e. 13 Feb. 1888*]
    iii   do.   413 [*i.e. 18 Jan. 1889*]
  iv – vii   Chambers' Geogy (for St. vi)
        Natl Soc.'s Hist. (Part iv)
        Merchant of Venice
Recitation
      i   Traveller's Return (Southey)[142]
  ii & iii   Lucy Gray
  iv & vii   Extract from Merchant of Venice

                                                 S.G.T.

Jan. 14 The schools were visited by H.M. Inspector & his Assistant. A. C. Forbes Esqre attended. Half-holiday was given in the afternoon. **15** Re-arranged the children in their new standards. The schools were closed at 12 o'clock till the following Monday.

Jan. 21 Received the Duplicate Schedule of the children who had been examined for Labour certificates, and found Edwd Gutteridge had failed in Arithc and Composition & William Newman and Alice Bartlett in Arithmetic. **23** Miss Slatter called in the afternoon. Owing to the slippery state of the roads, and sickness, the attendance during the week was very low. The average of the Infants was 17 out of 26, & of the older scholars, 82 out of 94 — total 99 out of 119.

Jan. 28 The attendance Officer called, and was informed of the fact that Joseph Hutt was illegally employed on the examination day. He promised to submit the matter to the S.A. Committee at the next meeting at Bradfield. **30** The attendance of the Infants somewhat improved during the week, but several of the elder children were absent through illness so that the average only reached 104 out of 119. Received Moffatt's Test Maps of England and British Colonies &c. Good progress was made by the scholars present.

Feb. 2 A. C. Forbes Esq. called in the morning. Elizth Wallis returned to school after an absence of many weeks. **4** The attendance Officer called and took a list of children, in Whitchurch Parish, who attended the Goring Heath Schools. He promised to make enquiries as to their attendances. **6** Several children were absent during some part of the week with sore throats, colds &c. and consequently the attendance was not very satisfactory; except in the Infants' Room where it was very good. The Balance Sheet was affixed to the School Door in accordance with Article 89.

Feby 2nd   Copy of Report

Mixed School   The children are in very good discipline, and have passed an excellent examination. They have been most carefully and intelligently taught.

---

[142] This title substituted for The Pert Chicken.

The Managers should verify the Registration at least once in each quarter, at irregular intervals.

Infants' Class The infants are pleasantly managed, and have made most gratifying progress. With the exception of the Needlework of the second class, their work has been very well done.

Herbert Walter Winchester Certd Teacher 1st Class
Margaret Roberts Asst Teacher
Harriett Matilda Berrington Asst Teacher

ALEXANDER C. FORBES Correspondent

Feb. 13 The Infants attended very well during the week; but in the Senr Department the average was very low owing [to] several scholars being absent with sore throat & toothache. Took Rosa Weller's name off the books as she had passed Std V & left school.[143] Admitted three new scholars on the 9th inst. — Martha Whiting, and two Elliotts, the later two were in a very backward state considering their ages; one was placed in the Infants' Class and the other in Std I. The average for both rooms was 105. On books 119.

Feb. 20 Prizes were distributed to the 23 children who had made the most attendances during the year 1890. Three children were absent, through sickness during the whole week. The attendance in the Senior department was again low. On books 87: av. 78. Good progress was made in most of the subjects. The Infants attended very well.

Feb. 23 Admitted Thos & Wm Fry. **27** Luke Lambourne, Chas Yates & John Knight were ill all the week. Sent a list of irregular scholars to the Bradfield S.A. Committee. No notice of the list for January was taken, although some of the defaulters had attended very irregularly. Satisfactory work was done, considering the average was only 106 out of 120 on books.

Mar. 2 Admitted Lily Wackford, who had come to reside temporarily with her aunt, at Bridge House. **3** Made a slight alteration in the Time-Table so that the Boys might have their drawing lesson from 3.30–4.15 instead of 2–2.45 on Tuesday & Thursday. Commenced teaching Drawing on slates. **4** Visited to test the Register. 114 in 84 in B G Sch. 30 Infts found 1 more present but not marked by good time. J.S. **6** There was considerable improvement in the attendance during the week and very satisfactory progress was made in every subject. Samuel Smith & Minnie Luker were ill all the week. Took Susan & Jas Rawle off the books — left parish.

Mar. 9 Several Infants were absent with bad colds &c. **10** A fearful snow-storm occurred during the previous night, which rendered the roads quite impassable. Not a single child put in an appearance. **13** The Schools were not

---

[143] Even when the formal '3 R' examination was ended for younger pupils, those who wished to leave school — to gain their 'Labour Certificate' — took the relevant leaving examination. In the case of Whitchurch this was for Standard V, under the Bradfield Committee bye-laws. See Minutes and Instructions to Her Majesty's Inspectors on the Code of 1890, para. 15.

opened for four days owing to the continuation of snow. Although a thaw set in during the daytime, the nights were frosty and the depth of snow on the hill made it impossible for the children to attend. Average for 9th inst. 107. On Books 119.

Mar. 17 Admitted Alice Weller, who was five years old in October 1890, but had not been to any school previously, and consequently did not know her letters. **18** A. C. Forbes Esqre called and signed the title pages of the Registers in accordance with the latest instructions on keeping school records. Commenced marking absentees with 'O' instead of 'a', in attendance registers. Satisfactory progress was made during the week; and the attendance was very good.

Mar. 24 Closed school for the Easter Holidays.

Apr. 6 Admitted Jessie Smith, who ought to have come to school last November. **8** Admitted Edith Messenger. No notice whatever was taken, by the Bradfield Attendance Committee, of the Returns for February. Consequence — greater irregularity during March. **10** Emma Wallis & Fred Spokes were absent all the week. They were running about the whole time, although the reason given for non-attendance was "want of shoes". Satisfactory progress was made. Average for the week 112. On books 123. Began using Cassells Library Edition of Merchant of Venice in Stds iv–vii.

Apr. 14 Received notice from the Department of Science and Art that the Schools would be examined in the month of December — together with the Illustrated Syllabus of Drawing. **17** Joseph Hutt played truant for two days. His absence on the occasion of the visit of H.M. Inspector, was notified, in February, to the Bradfield S.A. Committee, but nothing was done. During the week the attendance was very good. Average 116. On books 121. The names of Edwin Chambers & Chas Excell were removed from the books, the former having left the parish, & the latter appointed monitor for Std i.

Apr. 20 Jos. & Harry Hutt played truant again. Admitted a new scholar in the Infants' class. **21** Admitted Albert Higley. **23** Joseph Hutt was away again. **24** Satisfactory work was done during the week, as the attendance was good. Received notice that John Knight would not attend school again. Sent a list of defaulters to Bradfield S.A. Committee.

Apr. 28 Admitted Emma Turner. **29** The attendance Officer called during the morning. **May 1** A. C. Forbes Esq. called in the morning. Good average attendance for the week, satisfactory work was done.

May 4 Received a medical certificate stating Cecil Holmes was suffering from Chicken pox — so John Holmes also was advised to stay away. The Terrys removed from the village to Pangbourne. Harry & Joseph Hutt played truant again. **6** Wrote a note to the Attendance Officer, intimating that, if no proceedings were taken against the Hutts, other similar cases would soon occur. **8** The attendance during the week was only very fair. Average 109. On books 122.

May 11 Admitted Edgar Goodall in the Infants' class.   **12** Half holiday was given in the afternoon, as the Head Teacher was away on business, connected with the teaching [of] drawing.   **15** The attendance during the week was fairly good, average 109, on books 119. Examined all the Standards in their work & found very good progress had been made during the past 4 months.

May 18 & 19 Whitsuntide Holidays.   **20** Re-opened school. Very poor attendance.   **22** Joseph Hutt played truant since 14th inst. No notice whatever was taken of the irregular scholars during April by the Bradfield S.A. Committee. The average for the 3 days the schools were opened was only 101 out of 120 on books.

May 25 Admitted 3 new scholars named Wigmore who were, considering their ages, in rather a backward condition. The attendance somewhat improved.   **28** Admitted Mary Wallis, an Infant.   **29** John & Cecil Holmes were away with Chicken pox for a fortnight. The attendance during the week was only very fair. Sent a list of irregular scholars (Joseph & Harry Hutt & Frank Wallis) to the Bradfield School atte Committee. Joseph Hutt had only made 18 out of 35, & Frank Wallis only 19.

June 4 The morning was very wet, and a great many children were away. There was a slight improvement in the afternoon.   **5** Punished Frank Cross for dis-obedience in not holding out his hand when requested. Notified to the Attendance officer that Mary Lewendon, Path Hill, was not attending school, although over 5 years of age. The Hutts did not attend school all the week.

June 8 Admitted a new scholar in the Infants' Department.   **10** No school was held, as the Head Teacher was out for the day.   **12** Joseph & Harry Hutt did not come all the week. No notice was taken by the S.A. Come of the last return. The average for the week was only 112 out of 127.

June 17 The Attendance Officer called, and intimated that he had received instructions to summon the parents of the Hutts. The girl Lewendon (see above) attended Goring Heath School on the 15th inst. Received notice that the Wigmores had left the parish. The Upper Stds began learning their recitation. (Extract from Merchant of Venice).   **18** Thos & Frank Wallis played truant, all day. Average for the week 114.5. On books 127.

June 24 Attended to verify Register in the P.M. I found 78 B & G & 39 I — Total 117 — J.S.   Examined Standards I and II in Arithmetic and found Thos Lewendon & Lily Pocock, in Std I, weak in subtraction; and Charlotte Streak in Std II, weak in multiplication. A. C. Forbes Esqre visited and proposed holding a meeting at 7.30 on the 25th inst., to consider what should be done by the County Council in the Matter of Technical Education.   **26** The Hutts (Jos. & Harry) absent all the week. A. C. Forbes Esq. & two other gentlemen visited on the 25th inst. Average for the week was 115, on Books 128.

July 1 Reported the fact that Joseph & Harry Hutt had not attended school during June.   **3** May Goddard and Wm Simmonds were away all the week owing to illness. The attendance for the week was good. Average 115. On Books 125. Took Wm Newman's name off, as he had gone to work, legally. Received notice from the County Council for Oxfordshire that a scheme had been set on foot for the purpose of sending certain certificated Teachers to Oxford, during August, to receive Lectures on Botany & Geology.

July 10 Very satisfactory progress was made during the week as the attendance was very good. Joseph Hutt did not attend all the week. The average for the week was 115. On books 124.

July 13 Received notice that Thomas Painter had gone to work, & that Chas Yates was leaving the parish.   **15** A Band of Hope Fête was held at Purley, and nearly half the scholars were absent in the afternoon — some of them played truant. Mr Ashby sent word that, as his son Fred had the scarlet fever, Edith Ashby would be away for some time.   **17** Thos Wallis & Harry Hutt played truant 2½ days. The average for the week was only 110, on books 123.

July 24 Joseph Hutt was playing truant all the week, & Harry Hutt for 3 days. No notice was taken of their absence, during June, by the S.A. Committee. The average for the week was only 109 out of 123 on the books.

July 27 Very stormy day. Only 81 children present.   **29** A. C. Forbes Esqre visited. Sent a list of irregular children to the attendance officer.   **31** Closed School for harvest holidays: 6 weeks. The average for the week was only 103, out of 123 on the books. Miss Berrington and Miss Roberts sent in their resignations, both having been appointed to more lucrative situations.

Sept. 14 School opened with a very good attendance although, owing to wet weather, the harvest was not finished. Fourteen new scholars were enrolled. Miss Grove & Miss How began duties as Assistant Teachers; the former for Infants & the latter for Stds II & III and needlework. The School Managers, having accepted the 'Fee Grant', the schools were declared 'Free', from the 1st inst.[144]   **18** Revd — Rowley, the curate, called in the morning. The attendance during the week was very good — average 126, on books 136.   **19** Received a form from the Educ. Dept asking for a list of children

    (a) Between 13 and 14 not attending school although they had neither passed Std 4 in all 3 elementary subjects, nor made 250 attendances for 5 years.

    (b) Between 10 and 13 not attending School though they had not passed Std 5 in all three subjects.

[144] Under Section I of the Elementary Education Act 1891, 54 & 55 Vict., Chap. 56, a fee grant was to be made 'in aid of the cost of elementary education in England and Wales at the rate of ten shillings a year for each child of the number of children over three and under fifteen years of age in average attendance at any public elementary school in England and Wales'. Schools whose annual fee per pupil had been 10s. or less thus became free.

(c) Between 5 and 13 attending irregularly without reasonable excuse. Also:—
1. *On the whole* does the Local Authority secure the enrolment of children at 5 years of age?
2. How often has the Attendance Officer visited the school within the last 12 months?

Sept. 21 Admitted two new children. Notified to the Educ. Departt the appointments of the new assistants.   **23** The Attendance Officer called in the morning and said he had instructions to get a summons for the Hutts.   **25** The Curate visited in the morning. During the week the children attended very well. Average 129. On books 139. Harry Hutt & Wm Fry played truant in the afternoon.

Sept. 30 Visited to verify & examine the Registers for the Quarter. Found B & G 84 — Infts 50. Total 134. [J. SLATTER]   **Oct. 2** Sent Joseph Hutt's name to the S.A. Committee. He had not attended for 3 weeks. The attendance during the week was very good; average 131.1 on books 140. Admitted Lilian Chidsey on the 28th ult. Although she was 5 years 5 mths old, she had not been to school previously, i.e. since she attained school age.

Oct. 6 A. C. Forbes Esqre visited. Miss Grove was absent with a sore throat. It was a very wet day, and about 50 scholars were away.   **9** Joseph & Harry Hutt played truant all the week.

Oct. 12 A. C. Forbes Esqre visited in the morning.   **16** Several Infants were away during the week with bad colds &c. Examined Std II in Dictation and found 3 or 4 rather weak in spelling small words. The attendance during the week was very fair. Jos. Hutt played truant all the week, and Harry Hutt 3 days. Average 126. On books 141.

Oct. 23 The weather throughout the whole week was very stormy, and, consequently, the attendance was very low; especially in the Infants' Dept. Received notice from the Secretary of the Technical Education Committee that the County Council had decided on offering open Scholarships of the value of £20 to children who had passed the 5th Std; also that the Examn for same would take place in November.[145] Average for the week = 110.2. On books 141. Harry & Joseph Hutt played truant all the week.

Oct. 26 Admitted two new scholars.   **28** The Attendance Officer called, and took the attendances of Joseph Hutt for 6 months. Several children were away with bad colds &c. Examined Std I, and found their work was satisfactorily done.   **29** A. C. Forbes Esqre visited and cautioned Harry & M. A. Hutt against coming

---

[145] Under the Technical Instruction Act of 1889, County and County Borough Councils (themselves only established in 1888) were empowered to levy a penny rate in order to 'supply or aid in supplying technical or manual instruction'. The Councils were to appoint Technical Instruction Committees which would be represented on the governing body of any school, college, or institution which gave the instruction. See, for example, Barnard, *English Education from 1760*, p. 179. State grants for technical education were offered from 1890.

to school in a dirty condition. Sent a list of defaulters to Bradfield S.A. Committee. The average for the week was 125.4 out of 144 on the books.

Nov. 2 Received notice that Caroline Hunt had left the parish, and also Wm Fry. **6** A. C. Forbes Esqre called in the afternoon, and brought the Drawing Schedules. The attendance for the week was fairly good. Average 126; on books 140.

Nov. 9 Many children were away, owing to very stormy weather. **11** There was a tremendous storm in the early morning, and not a single child put in an appearance, so no school was held. **13** Received a note from the Attendance Officer, asking for the attendances of the Hutt[s] for the past 14 days. Examined Std ii & iii and found Sarah Knight, Fredk Beeson & Charlotte Streak rather backward in spelling; otherwise the work was well done. Average attendance for the week was 123, on books 140.

Nov. 16 Received notice that Edith Short & Robt Wallis (both under 5) would not attend school again till the spring. Frank Wallis played truant all day. **18** Mr Windle, the Sanitary Inspector, reported that the house of the Hutts was in such a filthy condition, that he had threatened the parents with prosecution unless they rendered the home fit for the children to live in.[146] Joseph, Harry & Mary Ann Hutt were therefore sent home till such a time that the Sanitary Inspector should report the residence to be in a satisfactory state. Numerous complaints had previously been made by parents whose children had been sitting near the Hutts in school. **20** Average for the week 118. On books 139.

Nov. 25 Received a note from the Sanitary Inspector saying that, although a material improvement was noticed in the home of the Hutts, the place was still far from satisfactory with regard to its cleanliness. **26** Miss B. Forbes and Mrs Forbes Junr visited in the afternoon, and heard the children sing their school songs. Received Medical Certificates for Thos Lewendon Susan Rawles & Chas Watts, who were suffering from severe colds. &c. A Penny Bank was started on the 23rd inst. and the parents seemed to appreciate it for no less than 17s. 5d. was paid. **27** Recd from the Controller of the Savings Bank Department, various forms &c giving all information for establishing a Penny Bank. The average for the week was 120. On books 135. Received the Government Forms from the Educn Departt.

Dec. 1 Received notice of the Drawing Examn for the 15th inst at 1.30 p.m. **2** A. C. Forbes Esqre visited, and was informed that some of the boys had wilfully broken about 20 rails off the school fence. **3** The Policeman called and took the names of the boys who did the damage to the fence. The attendance officer called on the 2nd inst. **4** Visited in aftn to verify Register — I 41 B & G

---

[146] Thomas Windle of Theale was the Sanitary Inspector and Surveyor for the Bradfield area. The humiliations which the Hutt children had to face over their home conditions and appearance at school perhaps explain the two boys' persistent truancy.

80, 121 present but 120 only to count as one entered after Registers were closed J.S. During the week the attendance was good, and satisfactory progress was made. Average for the week 124. On books 136.

Dec. 7 The weather was very wet, and many scholars were away. **11** Several Infants were absent all the week & the attendance throughout the school was very low. Average 113. On books 136. A Penny Bank was established on the 7th inst. There were 40 Depositors. George & John Tyrell were prosecuted by the School Managers, for doing damage to the fence round the Boys' playground — to the amounts of 7s. 6d. The Managers promised to let them off on condition that they were punished by their father, who refused.

Dec. 15 The Schools were examined in Drawing at 1.30 p.m. — by the Science & Art Inspector. A. C. Forbes Esqre & Canon Slatter were present. The girls did not attend in the afternoon. The boys went home at 2.45. No registers were marked. Joseph Hutt was taken to Bradfield Union, preparatory to his removal to an Industrial School — by order of the Caversham magistrates. **18** Miss How was absent all the week, attending the Certificate Examn — consequently some slight deviations from the time-table were made. Harry & Mary Ann Hutt were permitted to return to school on the 14th inst., as it had been certified that their home had been thoroughly cleansed. The attendance was good in the Senr Dept & very fair in the Infants' Class.

Dec. 24 The weather was very cold during the week, and consequently many children were absent. Twelve did not attend all the week. The average was only 109 out of 135 on books. Closed school at 12 o'clock till the 28th inst.

Dec. 28 Many children were absent with colds &c. **29** Recd notice that H.M. Inspector intended visiting the schools on Wed. Jany 13th 1892. **Jan. 1** Many scholars were absent with Influenza, & owing to the illness of the Head Teacher and the Infants' Assistant, the schools were closed at noon.

1892
Jan. 4 The Influenza continued to spread rapidly, and, acting on the advice of the Doctor, the Managers decided on temporarily closing the schools. **7** A. C. Forbes Esqre called to say that he had received a letter from H.M. Inspector, who recommended an application for Grant under article 85.[147] **8** Received Notice from the Science & Art Departt, that the Schools had received the mark 'Good' for Drawing.

---

[147] Article 84 was probably intended, since this laid down that if 'a continued epidemic or other cause accepted as satisfactory by the Department', prevented a visit by the H.M.I. the grant was 'as a rule, paid at the same rate as that last previously paid'. Article 85, on the other hand, merely dealt with the general conditions as regards premises, staff, furniture, apparatus, etc. needed for a grant to be paid. See the New Code for 1891, P.P. 1890–91, xxvii.

Jan. 23 Information was received that Frank Cross & Albert Sargent had gained Scholarships offered by the Oxfordshire County Council, which would enable them to attend the Kendrick Schools, Reading for two years.[148]

Feb. 1 Re-opened school, after having been closed a month.   **2** Received notice from the Education Department, that no Inspection would take place. Arranged the children in their new Standards, and began the fresh work. **4** Visited & verified the Register. 31 I. 89 B & G. J.S.   **5** During the week the children attended very well, and satisfactory progress was made.   **6** Received Approved Selections of Readers & Recitations for 1892 from H.M. Inspector and filed the same in Log Book.

Feb. 8 Admitted two new Infants.   **12** There was good attendance throughout the week, and much work was done. A. C. Forbes Esqre visited on the 8th inst. & Miss Slatter called on the 9th. Edith Ashby was appointed a Paid Monitress in the place of C. Excell.

Feb. 17 The attendance Officer called.   **18** Many Infants were absent owing to a fall of snow, on the previous evening. Received some pictures, from Messrs Peek Frean & Co. for decorating the school walls.   **20** Received the Govt Report from the Educn Departt.[149]

Feb. 24 Many Infants were away owing to wet weather in the morning. **25** Began teaching 'Drawing to scale' to Std VI.   **26** The average for the week was 115: on books 130. Sent a list of nine irregular scholars to the Bradfield Attendance Committee.

Mar. 4 The weather was very cold all the week, and consequently the average of the Infants was only fair. Minnie Luker was absent with ringworm & May Pocock with a bad leg. Satisfactory progress was made.

Mar. 10 The 'Drawing' Grant, £3 0 0, was received from the Science & Art Dept.   **11** Ruby Cockell & Lily Wackford left the parish. The weather was very cold and wet all the week, and many children were away in consequence. The average was only 115 out of 130 on the books.

Mar. 14 Admitted Ernest Daw.   **18** Frank Wallis was away all the week with the itch & Minnie, Fred. & Elizth Luker with ringworm. Received a note from A. C. Forbes Esqre stating the [sic] Mr Holmes had complained that his son, John, had been 'thrashed' 3 times on the 15th & 4 times on the 16th inst. The boy was, therefore, sent down to the Doctor for examination, and not a single mark could be found on any part of his body.

---

[148] Kendrick Schools were endowed schools which, academically, took 'an intermediate position between the National & Grammar schools' (*Kelly's Dir. Berks.* (1895), pp. 142–3; *V.C.H. Berks.*, iii (1923), 381). The endowment dated back to 1624.
[149] The failure to copy out the Report suggests that with the weakening of the system of 'payment by results' the Report itself had lost some of its terror.

Mar. 25 Sent a list of 4 irregular children to the Bradfield S.A. Committee. Took Ruby Cockell and Lily Wackford off the books, as they had left the parish. The attendance was only very fair during the week, owing to sickness. Average 116, on books 132. Satisfactory progress was made in all subjects.

Mar. 30 The Attendance Officer called, and said the Bradfield S.A. Committee did not take any notice of the return for February, although some of the children had been very irregular. **31** Began using King John in Stds iv–vi. **Apr. 1** The average for the week was only 113 out of 129 on books.

Apr. 4 Admitted Annie & Arthur Aldridge. Minnie, Elizth & Fred Luker, and Frank Wallis returned, after several weeks' absence. The attendance was very good. **7** Admitted Albert Ward in the Infants' Class. **8** Satisfactory progress was made during the week, as the attendance was very good. Began using Poynters Drawing Test cards, on the 7th inst.

Apr. 12 Visited and verified attendance list. Present 86 B & G 41 I — Total 127. J.S. **13** Admitted Percy Simmonds in the Infant Room. **14** There was a good attendance during the week. Closed school for Easter holidays — 1 week.

Apr. 25 Admitted several Infants. **28** No school was held in the afternoon, as the Head Teacher had to go to Reading. **29** Sent a list of 4 scholars to Bradfield.

May 2 Lily Chidsey came back to school after an absence of 4 months. **3** Began using Moffatt's Drawing Test cards Std 4. **4** A. C. Forbes Esqre called in the morning. **6** The attendance was good throughout the week.

May 10 Received medical certificates for Eliz. & Charlotte Street, who were suffering from sore throat. The curate called in the morning. **13** Satisfactory progress was made during the week. Average attendance 131. On books 141.

May 16 Admitted Martha Allwright in the Infants' Class. Decided on giving extra time to Drawing for a few weeks. **18** The Attendance Officer called respecting Daisy Rogers. **19** Received a medical certificate for Annie Painter who was suffering from chicken pox. **20** Several scholars were away with bad colds & sore throats, all the week, and the average was consequently low.

May 27 No school was held, as the Head Teacher was too ill to attend to duties. Average for the week = 125. On books 142.

June 1 Allowed Mr Winchester to make a permanent alteration in the Time Table. ALEXANDER C. FORBES **3** Owing to the inclement weather the average of the week was lower than usual, viz. 118. The schools were closed till the 8th inst.

June 9 Visited the School to inspect registers. Present 42 I 85 B & G. and found the books made up to date. J.S. **10** Several children were away all the week with chicken-pox. Examined Stds ii, iii, and found the girls of St. iii weak in spelling; otherwise the work was very satisfactorily done for the time of year.

June 13 Admitted 3 new scholars. **15** The Attendance Officer called. **17** Most of the children attended very well during the week. Average 127. On books 144.

June 22 A. C. Forbes Esqre called. **23** Wet day; nearly half the scholars were absent. **24** Average 124, on books 145.

July 1 Sent a list of defaulters to Bradfield S.A. Committee. Examined Std 5 in Mapdrawing — results very satisfactory. The average for the week was 131.3

July 6 A holiday was given, owing to a Temperance Fete at Purley. **7** Moffatt's Std III New Schedule Drawing cards were introduced, and found very useful. **8** The attendance during the week was only very fair. Average 127. On books 143.

July 12 The schools were required, in the afternoon for the Girls' Friendly Society & no meeting was held.[150] **13** Drawing & Needlework were taken in the afternoon, as they were omitted on the 12th inst. The Attendance Officer visited. **15** Emma Lyford & Minnie Luker were away, ill, all the week. Average 128. On books 143.

July 21 Called to verify registers. B & G = 85, I = 44 — 129 present. J.S. **22** Satisfactory progress was made during the week in the senior department. The Infants attended badly: their average being only 41 out of 52. Mr Sellwood complained about some of the boys pulling up his carrots in the allotments.

July 25 The Schools were closed in the afternoon on account of a School treat. **29** During the week the attendance was very fair. Closed schools for harvest holidays — six weeks. A. C. Forbes Esqre visited in the morning.

Sept. 12 Re-opened school with a good attendance. Admitted four infants. The Attendance Officer called on Aug 3rd and reported that the S.A. Committee had decided to deal more stringently with defaulters in the future. **14** Examined Std I and found the children had forgotten a good deal during the vacation. **16** Average for the week = 132. On books 145. The Curate visited in the morning, and asked the first class a few questions in scripture.

---

[150] The Girls' Friendly Society was a Church of England organization, established in 1874, 'to meet needs of *body*, *soul* and *mind*' of young working girls — including the organization of suitable social activities. Within ten years of its formation the Society had a membership of over 100,000. See Pamela Horn, *The Rise and Fall of the Victorian Servant* (Dublin, 1975), pp. 106–7.

Sept. 19 Admitted a new scholar in Infants' class. Thoroughly examined Std II, and found the results satisfactory on the whole.   **23** There was a good attendance during the week, except on the 21st inst. when it was very stormy. Average 130. On Books 147.

Sept. 26 Admitted a new Infant.   **30** Sent a list of defaulters to the Attendance officer.   **30** Satisfactory work was done during the week as there was a good attendance. All the Stds finished learning their recitation. Average for the week = 137. On Books 149.

Oct. 7 The usual work was done during the week. The attendance was very good. Average 135. Chas Wm & Albert Watts were away during the whole week.

Oct. 10 Received information that the Watts had left the parish & gone to Maidenhead.   **14** The morning was very stormy and many were away. A few additional children came in the afternoon. Average for the week = 129. On books 145.

Oct. 19 Mrs Thomas (Thames Bank) and another lady visited in the afternoon. 'Form E and Drawing Regulations' from H. Harcourt Smith Esqr, Local Inspector of Drawing.   **21** Good attendance, & good work done, during the week. Average attendance 136. On books 143.

Oct. 28 Visited to verify Registers. B & G — 79, I 45 — Total 124 J.S. I consider the attendance is creditable on such a wet day. J.S. Received notice that the Scripture Examination would be held on Tuesday Novr 15 at 10.30 a.m. Average for the week 122. On books 144. Sent a list of defaulters to the Bradfield S.A. Committee. No notice was taken of the last list.

Nov. 4 Three children were ill all the week. The newly appointed attendance officer called on the 2nd inst. and afterwards went to see the parents of Frank Wallis & Daisy Rogers. Satisfactory work was done during the week. Average 132. On books 145.

Nov. 7 The Kemps removed to London. Had notice that the Drawing Examination would be held on Friday Novr 18th at 2.15 p.m. A. C. Forbes Esqre called. The Boots & Stockings were distributed by Miss B. Forbes.   **11** Good attendance. Average 132. On books 145.

Nov. 15 The schools were examined by the Diocesan Inspector at 10.30 a.m. Miss Slatter & Miss Williams-Freeman visited.   **18** The school was examined in Drawing [by] H. Harcourt-Smith Esqre, in the afternoon.[151] The Girls & Infants had half holiday. A. C. Forbes Esqre was present. Average for the week = 133.

---

[151] Under the Regulations on Drawing in Elementary Schools, issued on 27 January 1891, the work for Standard I comprised: 'Drawing freehand, and with the ruler, of lines, angles, parallels, and the simplest right-lined forms, such as some of those given in Dyce's Drawing Book (To be drawn on slates). Standard II. The same on paper. Standard III. (a) freehand

Nov. 25 The children attended very well during the week. Average 134. On books 145. Received the Forms from the Education Departt. Put the Boys in their new drawing standards, on the 22nd inst.

Dec. 1 A. C. Forbes Esqre visited during the morning. The weather was very wet in the afternoon and many were absent. Sent a list of defaulters to Bradfield S.A. Committee. Average for the week = 130. On books 140.

Dec. 4 Received the result of the Drawing Examn — 'Good'.   **7** The Attendance Officer called in the morning. Several boys away through illness.   **9** The Attendance Officer sent letters of warning to 6 parents.

Dec. 16 The Attendance much improved during the week and the average was 132, out of 140 on the books. Examined Std 1, and found one or two careless over their arithmetic.

Dec. 19 Lily & Edmund Pocock left the parish.   **21** Received notice that the Inspection would take place on Wednesday, Jany 18th at 9.15 a.m.   **23** Several children were absent, without excuse, in the afternoon. The average for the week was 131.

Dec. 26 Bank Holiday. No school was held.   **27** Owing to a severe frost, many children were away during the morning, but the numbers improved in the afternoon.   **30** Verified the Register excep[t] in first many ill — B & G 75 — I. 41 — 116. [J. SLATTER]

1893

Jan. 4 The Attendance Officer called. A. C. Forbes Esqre visited in the morning.   **6** Nearly 20 per cent of the children were ill with sore throats, colds &c all the week.

Jan. 10 Owing to the fact that the two assistant Teachers were laid by [*sic*] with Pleurisy, & that bronchitis, German Measles, & sore throats were increasing very rapidly, the School Managers, acting under Medical Authority considered it advisable to close the Schools for a time.

Feb. 1 Re-opened school after closing 3 weeks. Miss Grove was absent owing to the illness of her mother. Mary Grist rendered assistance with the Infants. A. C. Forbes Esqre & Mrs Forbes visited. Many children were still absent. Recd notice from H.M. Inspector, on the 13th ult., that the examination would be postponed for a time.   **3** About 20 per cent of the scholars were away during the 3 days the schools were open.

---

drawings of regular forms and curved figures from the flat, (b) simple geometrical figures with rulers, etc.' Awards were 1*s*. per pupil for 'fair', 1*s*. 6*d*. for 'good' and 2*s* for 'excellent', and higher standards would, of course, be attempted by the older scholars.

Feb. 6 Admitted John Brown.   **10** Satisfactory progress was made in the Senior Department, but the Infants were still very irregular. Average for the week = 126. On books 141.

Feb. 13 Admitted Horace Munday in the Infants' Class.   **17** The Attendance improved during the week. Average 129. On books 142.

Songs [for 1893]   Senior Department   1 Whatsoe'er you have to do, 2 Boys wanted, 3 The spider, 4 When things don't go to suit us, 5 The River.
                        Infants' Class   1 The naughty little Sparrow, 2 Sing we all merrily, 3 Dollie Deene's Wedding
Object Lessons   Monkey, Camel, Wolf, Goat, Hen, Cow, Dog, Butterfly, Robin, Swan, Tea, Sugar, Coffee, Oranges, Potato, Clock, Pictures, Farm yard, Windows, A Street, Umbrella, Post Office, A Butcher's Shop, Coal, A Country Walk, Sun, Light, Sea, Seasons, Minding Baby
                Copy of Diocesan Report Decr 17th 1892
The general result of the Inspection was 'good'.
Repetition throughout the school was very satisfactory.
The children in the Higher Standard appeared to have a thorough knowledge of the subjects taken.
The second and third standards were rather weak in the Old Testament Subjects.
The Bishop's Prize was awarded to Minnie Luker.
Sarah Day, Ernest Daw, Frank Simmonds and Lilian Winchester also answered excellently.   WM EDWIN BEAUMONT Diocesan Inspector of Schools

Feb. 21 Received notice that the Schools would be examined by H.M. Inspector on Wedy March 1st at 9.10 a.m.   **22** Wet day. Many children, mostly Infants, were absent.   **24** Satisfactory work was done during the week.

[The first entry in the second Whitchurch School log book (O.R.O. T/SL 58 (ii)) duly records the visit on 1 March 1893 of H.M.I. Tremenheere, who was accompanied by an Assistant Inspector, Mr Spikes. Their Report noted of the Mixed School: 'The discipline is good on the whole, although scarcely so steady as has been usual here. The elementary instruction deserves high praise for accuracy, and general intelligence is well developed, but the higher scale of Principal Grant cannot, in future, be recommended, unless Recitation be better said. The Class subjects, as well as Needlework and Drill are good. Altogether the condition of the School is very creditable in spite of some recent sickness'. Of the Infants' School they stated: 'The Kindergarten exercises should be considerably increased in number and treated in a more educative manner, but otherwise the work of the Infants' Room has been well carried out, particularly in the elementary instruction, which is very good. Some better pictures should be provided. Proper provision should be made for hats and cloaks. Unless the infants have room for marching and are provided with adequate accommodation for hats and cloaks, My Lords may be unable to pay the higher Grant under Article 98 (a) of the Code next year'.

In the second Whitchurch log book are recorded the Reports made by H.M.Is. in 1894, 1896–1905, 1907, 1910 and 1912. Until the year of Winchester's illness (1914) both Government and Diocesan Inspectors found much to praise in the school; however, there was another isolated reference in the Government Report of 1896 to 'some laxity in the discipline' (caused by the absence of an Assistant Teacher); and in and after 1902 most such Reports notice some failure in discipline, especially among the older children. From about 1904 Winchester made noticeably fewer entries in the log-book, and at the end of 1914 he fell ill, and never resumed work. On 19 December 1947 his successor Miss F. G. Gwinnell recorded:

'This school closes this afternoon, the Children being transferred to Goring Heath and Woodcote. Miss Ashby retires after over 50 years service in the school. I retire after 32½ years as Head Teacher'. (O.R.O. T/SL 58 (iii), p. 18).]

VII

EXTRACTS FROM WHITCHURCH SCHOOL ACCOUNTS

[There are two volumes of School Accounts for Whitchurch, the first running from 1829 un
1840, and the second from 1840 to 1875. Both are slender volumes, bound in cream colour
imitation leather, and now (1977) preserved with other parish records at Whitchurch rector
School accounts were required to be kept by the school managers; at Whitchurch the incumbe
in practice kept them, though occasionally the schoolmaster himself did so, presumably und
the rector's supervision.]

(a)

1829

Annual Subscribers

	£	s	d
Revd W. A. Hammond	5	5	0
Mrs W. A. Hammond	5	5	0
Mr Gardiner	1	1	0
Mrs Gardiner	1	1	0
Mr Rawson Gardiner	1	1	0
Mrs Pigou	2	2	0
Mr Robt Pigou	1	1	0
Mr Powys	2	2	0
Mrs Powys	1	1	0
Miss Powys	1	1	0
Mr Simeon	2	2	0
Mrs Simeon	1	1	0
Mr Buttin	1	1	0
	£25	4	0

Received	£	s	d
Subscriptions	25	4	0
n. Children's Pence	0	18	0
eb. Do	0	17	0
ar. Do	1	0	1
pr. Do	0	16	6
ay Do	0	12	5
ne Do	0	14	11
ly Do	0	12	2
ug. Do	0	10	9
pt. Do	0	12	4
ct. Do	1	3	0
ov. Do	1	1	9
ec. Do	1	3	5
for Work done at the School	0	13	11¼
for Work bought	1	9	8
	£37	9	11¼

Paid		£	s	d
Jan. 20	Magg's Bill	7	6	6
	29 Bonnets	1	9	0
	Making up 22 Hats, at 4d. each	0	7	4
	4 oz. of white Worsted	0	1	0
	8 Cwt & ½ of Coals	0	15	0
Mar. 25	Mrs Davis Salary for a quarter	5	0	0
	Betsy Davis for do.	0	10	0
	Teacher's pay for do.	0	8	8
	Clock	0	2	0
	Soap bill	0	2	2
June 25	Mrs Davis Salary for a quarter	5	0	0
	Betsey Davis for do.	0	10	0
	Teacher's pay for do.	0	8	0
	Soap bill	0	2	2
	Thread, needles, tape, &c	0	3	0
July 8	Worsted for knitting	0	9	7
Oct. 2	Mrs Davis Salary for a quarter	5	0	0
	Betsy Davis for do.	0	10	0
	Teacher's pay for do.	0	6	4
	Soap bill	0	2	2
	Clock mending	0	1	1
28	2 pieces of green ferret for the girls' bonnets	0	3	0
Dec. 25	Mrs Davis Salary for a quarter	5	0	0
	Betsey Davis Salary for a quarter	0	10	0
	Teacher's pay for do.	0	6	8
	Soap bill	0	2	2
		£34	15	10

(b)   **1838**

Subscribers to Clothing

	£	s	d
Revd W. A. Hammond	2	7	1½
Mr Powys	2	7	1½
Mr Robt Pigou	2	7	1½
Mr Gardiner	2	7	1½
	£9	8	6

Annual Subscribers

	£	s	d
Revd W. A. Hammond	2	2	0
Mrs W. A. Hammond	1	1	0
Mr Powys	2	2	0
Mrs Powys	2	2	0
Mr Robt Pigou	2	2	0
Mr Gardiner	1	1	0
	£9	9	0

Received

		£	s	d
	In hand	2	16	9¾
	Subrs	9	9	0
	Do. for Clothing	9	8	6
	Do. Sunday School	6	10	0
	Children's Pence			
Jan.	Do.	0	11	11
Feb.	Do	0	11	4
Mar.	Do	0	9	1
Apr.	Do	0	15	4
May	Do	0	10	1
June	Do	0	2	6
July	Do	0	8	8
Aug.	Do	0	3	11
Sept.	Do	0	11	6
Oct.	Do	0	10	0
Nov.	Do	0	4	10
Dec.	Do	0	13	6
		£33	16	11¾

Paid

		£	s	d
Jan.	Letchworth, for 12 yds ¼ of Druggett	1	18	9½
	Mrs Clark, for making 10 Cloaks at 9d. & thread	0	7	9
	2 pieces of binding	0	2	8
	Mrs Brown, for cutting out Children's clothes	0	6	0
	Wid. Weller, for making 24 Smock frocks 6d.	0	12	0
	Palmer, for 65 yds Olive Linen [at] 9d.	2	8	9
	57 yds ¼ blue print — wide — 8d.½	2	0	7½
	thread & Cotton	0	7	0½
	Gutteridge, for 23 Bonnets 1/1	1	4	11
	Gutteridge, for 24 Boys' hats 1/1	1	6	0
Mar.	Brooms, & Soap	0	3	5
Apr.	1 piece of green binding	0	2	3
May	print, calico, &c. for work	0	11	0
June	Soap, & brooms	0	4	4
Sept.	Soap, & clock	0	3	10
Dec.	Jas Weller, for a year, Sunday School	5	0	0
	Mrs Davis' yearly Salary	21	16	0
	Brooms, & tape	0	5	8
		£39	1	0

(c)   **1853**

Received							Paid			
	£	s	d	£	s	d		£	s	d
Revd E. Moore	10	0	0				Balance brought			
Saml W. Gardiner Esq.	10	0	0				forward	3	14	2½
Mrs Pigou	10	0	0				Master & Mistress	54	12	0
Admiral Fowler R.N.	10	0	0				Rent of School			
Captain Bacon	5	0	0				Cottage Michs			
Amount of Subscriptions				45	0	0	1853	4	4	0
Children's pence				20	1	9	Fuel	2	3	0
Children's Work				2	3	3½	Messrs Shoolbred			
							& Co. Clothing	2	19	2
				£67	5	0½	Mrs Palmer 13/6			
							makg Smocks 7/6	1	1	0
							Incidental Expenses	1	18	9
							Total Expenditure	70	12	1½
							Total Receipts	67	5	0½
							Balance Carried			
							Ford	3	7	1

B. An examination of the Accounts indicates that in most years during the 1850s a deficit was carried forward to the next year.

(d) **1868**

Received	£	s	d	£	s	d
Revd E. Moore	10	0	0			
Trustees of the late						
S. W. Gardiner Esqr	10	0	0			
Philip Lybbe						
P. Lybbe Esqr	10	0	0			
W. Fanning Esqr	10	0	0			
W. C. Wentworth Esqr	10	0	0			
Captn Fowler R.N.	5	0	0			
A. C. Forbes Esqr	5	0	0			
W. B. Wood Esqr	5	0	0			
John Willan Esqr	5	0	0			
Amount of Subscriptions				70	0	0
Balance brought forward				3	3	0
Aug.9 Collection at Sermon by						
Bishop of Oxford				19	15	6
School pence				14	17	7
Work done for Mrs Forbes					9	0
Mr Rich Briant 1£						
Mr Robt Briant 1£				2	0	0
E Blyth Esq. 2£						
Mr Rowden 1£				3	0	0
Mr Sellwood 10/–						
Mr Whitfield 10/–				1	0	0
Mr Horwood 10/–						
Mrs Troy 5/–					15	0
				£115	0	1

Paid	£	s	d
Miss Cooke's salary			
9 months 1 week	39	12	5
Mr Eastman's			
salary 3 months	17	10	0
Mr Rich. Briant			
cupboard porch			
&c	7	14	9
Mr Robt Briant			
repairs &c	5	7	4
Mr Holmes repairs		19	0
Bill at National			
Society &c.	7	15	4
Rent of Cottage	4	4	0
Material & making			
frocks cloaks &c.	13	5	4
Cleaning school 5/6			
Sundries 11/1		16	7
Mrs Ashley Coals			
2/6/0			
Rch Briant wood			
1/5/0	3	11	0
Gratuity to			
Miss Cooke	1	0	0
Balance in hand	13	4	3
	115	0	1

1873

Dr

	£	s	d
●vernment Grant	36	18	–
v. E. Moore £10 0 0	10	0	0
, Lybbe Powys Lybbe Esqr	10	0	0
W. Gardiner Esqr	10	0	0
●tn R. D. Fowler R.N.	5	0	0
C. Forbes Esqr	5	0	0
Willan Esqr	5	0	0
Fanning Esqr	10	0	0
J. Blyth Esqr	2	0	0
B. Wood Esqr	5	0	0
s Baker	5	0	0
Blyth Esqr	5	5	0
●ool pence as per a/c	22	8	6
s Giles	1	0	0
Sheldon	1	0	0
Cameroux	3	0	0
Sellwood	–	10	–
● Holmes 5/– Mr Tayler 5/–	–	10	–
●s Sykes 9/8			
●iss Fanning 2/8			
●rs Willan 11/5	1	3	9
	138	15	3
To Balance	20	5	5
	159	0	8

Cr

	£	s	d
Mr Litchfield's			
portion of Grant	12	6	–
National Society a/c	1	19	8
Do. Do. a/c	5	6	11
Mr Briant a/c		12	3
Mr Sellwood a/c		8	11
Fuel	8	9	1½
Do. of last years a/c	1	9	–
Sundries for School			
as per School a/c	10	5	9½
Teachers Salaries			
Mar.	25	–	–
June	25	–	–
Sept.	25	–	–
Dec.	25	–	–
Insurance	–	17	–
a/c Paid by the Revd E. Moore for the year 1870 to Mr Withers	5	9	6
Do. Do. for Coals to Mr Withers	1	4	–
Deficit in last years a/c repaid to the Revd E. Moore	8	17	7½
Sundries as per School a/c	1	14	10½
	159	0	8

APPENDIX

LIST OF OXFORDSHIRE SCHOOL LOG BOOKS

In view of the complicated history of many schools, this list (corrected to 1 January 1978) seeks to give only the essential minimum of information. Log books for nearly all schools in that part of Berkshire added to Oxfordshire in 1974 remain in their former county.

* indicates closure of the school
† indicates the presence of Inspectors' Reports at the rear of a book.

Log Books in Oxfordshire County Record Office

CAT. NO. (T/SL)	YEARS	NUMBER OF BOOKS	SCHOOL
103	1909–1949	1	Abingdon
67	1874–1965*	3	Albury and Tiddington
1	1906–1934	1	Ambrosden
2	1863–1913*	3	Ardley
3	1940–1942*	1	Arncott
4	1884–1924	2	Asthall
63			Balscote *See* Wroxton
68	1873–1965	4	Bampton
	1863–1889	2	Banbury (British School)[1]
102	1863–1928	2	Banbury (National School)
6	1881–1934	1	Banbury (Grimsbury Council School)
7	1909–1955	2†	Banbury (Grimsbury, St Leonard's C. of E. School)
89	1887–1943	1	Banbury (Grimsbury Wesleyan; later County Infants', East Street, Banbury)
9	1863–1888	1†	Beckley
10	1863–1888	1†	Benson
11	1941–1946	1	Bignell Park, Chesterton[2]
82	1878–1966*	3	Bix
83	1900–1967*	1	Blackthorn
69	1879–1961*	3	Brightwell Baldwin
12	1873–1910	1	Broadwell

[1] See O.R.O. Catalogue B.B. XI/vii/1 (Girls), 2 (Boys).
[2] Originally evacuated from West Ham to Bicester.

Cat. No. (T/SL)	Years	Number of Books	School
13	1895–1948*	2	Bucknell
14	1871–1908	1	Burcot
93	1863–1920	8	Burford
70	1950–1958*	1	Chalgrove
99	1868–1904	2	Chesterton
			Chesterton, Bignell Park *See* Bignell Park
15	1912–1948*	1	Chilson
27	1924–1959*	2	Church Hanborough
16	1878–1948	2	Claydon
17	1865–1889	1	Clifton Hampden
87	1924–1968*	1	Cottisford
96	1910–1972*	3	Cuddesdon
18	1900–1948	3	Culham[3]
101	1863–1956	2	Cumnor
19	1895–1922*	1	Cuxham
20	1890–1948*	3	Drayton near Banbury
21	1863–1947*	3	Drayton St Leonard
95	1969–1973*	3	Dunsden[4]
88	1917–1969*	2	Duns Tew
22	1881–1955	3	Elsfield
23	1900–1922	1	Epwell
84	1890–1958*	3	Eynsham (Infants')
26			Fawler *See* Finstock and Fawler
73			Fifield *See* Idbury
25	1874–1948	2	Finmere
26	1886–1906	2†	Finstock and Fawler
97	1929–1973*	1	Fulbrook
64	1900–1932	1	Glympton
6, 7, 89			Grimsbury *See* Banbury
79			Guys Green *See* Rotherfield Greys
71	1914–1961	1	Hanwell
28	1910–1929	1	Henley-on-Thames (British School)
29	1899–1973*	2	Hethe
72	1902–1964*	2	Heythrop
80			Highmore *See* Rotherfield Greys
66	1892–1915*	1	Holton
30	1896–1958*	3	Holwell
90	1895–1923	1	Horley
73	1933–1966*	1	Idbury and Fifield
74	1883–1962*	3	Kelmscott
31	1905–1928	1	Kingsey [now Bucks.]

[3] Culham log book for 1868–1900 at the school.
[4] Written in exercise books: the official log book was lost.

Cat. No. (T/SL)	Years	Number of Books	School
32	1865–1879	1	Launton
33	1876–1927	2	Lew
24	1879–1946*	3	Little Faringdon
34	1908–1927	1	Lyneham
94	1885–1973*	3	Mapledurham
8	1873–1908	1	Middle Barton
75	1877–1924	3	Middleton Stoney (Boys')
76	1877–1962*	4	Middleton Stoney (Girls' and Infants')
35	1870–1955*	4	Mixbury
91	1881–1971*	3	Mongewell (Mongewell and North Stoke 1902–57)
57			Morland House Reception Home *See* Wheatley
36	1874–1959*	4	Newton Purcell
37	1864–1946*	3	Noke
65	1924–1955	1	North Aston
38	1873–1931	2	Northmoor
91			North Stoke *See* Mongewell
77	1937–1960*	1	Nuneham Courtenay
39	1900–1933*	1	Over Norton
100	1863–1909	2	Oxford (St Peter's National School)[5]
85	1899–1967*	2	Piddington
40	1904–1932*	1	Pyrton
79	1873–1966*	3	Rotherfield Greys (Greys Green)
80	1901–1954	1	Rotherfield Greys (Highmore)
41	1894–1916*	2	Rotherfield Peppard
81	1927–1966*	1	Sandford-on-Thames
42	1899–1947*	2	Sandford St Martin
27			Sarsden *See* Churchill
43	1870–1970*	4†	Shilton
44	1905–1926	1	Shipton-on-Cherwell
45	1869–1963*	2	Shutford (West Shutford)
46	1869–1907	2	Souldern[6]
47	1911–1946	2	South Leigh
78	1887–1965*	3	South Newington
48	1884–1958*	2	Spelsbury
98	1898–1934	1	Standlake
49	1874–1923	1	Stanton St John
5	1863–1892	1†	Steeple Aston
50	1943–1953*	1	Stoke Talmage
51	1887–1948*	2	Swalcliffe
52	1883–1946	2	Swinbrook and Widford

[5] For other Oxford log books, see below.
[6] Souldern Log Book for 1893–1907 in O.R.O. Misc. Dew. V/I.

Cat. No. (T/SL)	Years	Number of Books	School
53	1878–1948	3	Sydenham
92	1893–1971*	3	Tadmarton
54	1876–1959*	3	Taynton
67			Tiddington *See* Albury and Tiddington
86	1910–1958*	2	Towersey
55	1884–1938*	2	Waterperry
56	1882–1959*	3	Wendlebury
57	1951–1956*	1	Wheatley (Morland House Reception Home)
58	1868–1947*	3	Whitchurch
52			Widford *See* Swinbrook and Widford
59	1923–1958*	1	Wigginton
60	1882–1929*	2	Witney (West End)
61	1891–1927	1	Woodcote
62	1871–1932*	2†	Woodstock (Old Woodstock)
63	1910–1931*	1	Wroxton (Balscote)

Books in Oxford City Archives

Cat. No. (T/SL)	Years	Number of Books	School
1	1942–1958*	1	Church Cowley Infants'
2–4	1873–1949	3	Cowley St John Infants'
5	1930–1943*	1	Cowley Poplars Elementary
6	1881–1898*	1	Cowley St John Intermediate
7	1939–1944	1	Dingle Lane Infants'
8	1930–1948[7]	1	East Oxford Council
9	1944–1950*	1	Emergency School, Cowley Road
10	1872–1910*	1	Holy Trinity Boys'
11, 12	1872–1938*	2	Holywell Mixed
13, 14	1871–1945	2	New Hinksey Boys'
15, 16	1889–1934	2	New Hinksey Girls'
17–19	1881–1952*	3	New Hinksey Infants'
66, 67	1874–1921	2	Oxford Girls' British
20, 21	1876–1914	2	Practising School
22	1924–1946*	1	St Aldate's C. of E.
23	1863–1900	1	St Clement's Boys'
24	1900–1947	1	St Clement's Boys' and Mixed
25, 26	1863–1929*	2	St Clement's Girls

[7] Visitors' Minute Book.

Cat. No. (T/SL)	Years	Number of Books	School
27	1908–1956*	1	St Clement's Infants'
28	1947–1958*	1	St Clement's Mixed and Junior Infants'
29	1940–1963*	1	St Dennis
30	1875–1910	1	St Ebbe's National Girls'
31–34	1872–1956*	4	St Frideswide's Boys'
35, 36	1871–1936	2	St Frideswide's Girls'
37	1863–1884	1	St Giles' Boys'
38, 39	1863–1926*	2	St Giles' Girls'
40–42	1869–1923*	3	St Giles' Infants'
43–45	1873–1904	3	St Mary Magdalen Girls'
46, 47	1904–1926	2	St Mary Magdalen Girls' & Infants'
48, 49	1873–1901*	2	St Mary Magdalen Infants'
50, 51	1864–1927	2	St Thomas' Boys
52, 53	1871–1923	2	St Thomas' Girls'
54, 55	1898–1971*	2	St Thomas' Infants'
56–60	1863–1963*	5	Summertown C. of E. Mixed
61	1903–1935	1	Temple Cowley Church Infants'
62, 63	1863–1928*	2	Wesleyan Boys'
64	1957–1963*	1	West Oxford County Secondary
65	1936–1956*	1	West Oxford Girls' Council

INDEX OF PERSONS

Single references on consecutive pages have been run together in the interests of economy in all indexes.

The following abbreviations are used: A.T. (Assistant Teacher), D.I. (Diocesan Inspector of Schools), H.M.I. (Her Majesty's Inspector of Schools), H.T. (Head Teacher), M.P. (Member of Parliament), and P.T. (Pupil Teacher).

Adults are indicated by status (Rev., Mr, etc.) or occupation; all others indexed are children, nearly all of Whitchurch.

The dates following the descriptions Curate, A.T., or P.T. refer to tenure at Whitchurch.

INDEX OF PLACES

(All in Oxon. before 1974, unless otherwise stated)

INDEX OF SUBJECTS

Accommodation in Oxfordshire schools, xxx–xxxi; in Whitchurch School, liv, 16, 26, 31, 38, 47, 49, 54, 83, 125, 147, 174

Agricultural Children Act (1873), xxxiii

Assistant Teachers, lvii–lviii, 11, 50–51, 53, 58–9, 61–3, 67, 69, 73, 75, 81–2, 85–6, 88–9, 94–9, 101, 107, 109, 114, 116, 119, 121, 123, 125, 139–40, 142, 145–8, 153–4, 157–60, 162; 166. *See also* Index of Persons, *under* Attwood, A.; Berrington, H. M.; Blacklaws, J.; Brown, S. J.; Burch, L.; Clark, E. A.; Cooper, L.; Elliott, R.; Forder, J. B.; Grove, S.; Heasman, C. M.; Higgs, E.; Hills, E.; How, A.; King, S.; Long, A.; McLennan, M. J.; Prestoe, A.; Roberts, M.; Stowe, E.; Watkins, E.; Wrightson, A. For members of Head Teachers' families, see pp. lvi–ii.

Attendance, xxviii, xxxiii–viii, 25, 29–30, 35–7, 41, 46, 50–2, 54–5, 57, 59–62, 64–5, 67, 69–70, 72, 74, 76, 83, 86, 90, 92–3, 97–9, 104, 113–4, 117, 120, 124, 127, 133, 138, 144, 151–2, 157, 163, 165–6, 170

Band of Hope, xl, 19 n., 30, 32, 82, 104, 111, 120, 131, 140, 149, 157, 165, 171

Board of Education, xlv

Boot Club, 100, 135, 144, 151

British and Foreign School Society, xvi–ii, xx, xxii–iii, xxxi

Charitable gifts, xl–xli, 7, 14, 39, 49, 78, 100, 107–8, 114, 117, 124, 127, 135, 176, 178–80

Certification of teachers and certified teachers, xlvi, lvii, 11, 22, 27, 68, 87, 108, 114, 146

Child labour, xii, xxiii, xxviii, xxxvi–xxxviii, 36, 46–7, 50–2, 54–5, 59–60, 63–4, 68–70, 76, 80, 88–9, 95–6, 141, 157–8

Child's school book, 62–3, 76

Closure of school (during epidemics), 168, 173

Code (Revised, 1862), xxiv–v, xlix–l, 11, 27; (1867), 20; (1868), 23; (1871), 1, 54, 79; (1876), 58; (1877), 62; (1882), 86, 93; (1883), li–lii; (1885), 108; (1890), 158–9, 162; (1891), 168

Committee of the Privy Council on Education, xi, xviii, xxiv, xxix–xxx, xlv, 11

Cottage and rural industries, xxviii, liii, 46, 50, 54–5, 59–60, 63–4, 68, 88

Curriculum, xiv, xvi–ii, xxiv–v, xxxix, xl, xlix, lii, 13, 15, 20, 35, 39, 55, 59, 63, 65, 86, 92–3, 102, 107, 115, 125, 136, 144–5, 147, 152–3, 160, 162, 168–70, 172–4

Dame schools, xiii, xvii

Deaths of children, xxxv, 31, 95, 112, 139, 155

Department of Science and Art, xxxix, 163, 168–9

Diocesan Inspectors, xx, 29, 42–3, 52, 57, 65, 71–2, 77, 82, 91, 99–100, 105, 113, 122, 133–4, 143, 151, 159, 174. *See also* Index of Persons *under* Adams, C. E.; Barber, E.; Beaumont, W. E.; Bligh, H.; Williams, T.; Wodehouse, C. G.

Diocesan Visitation Articles, xii, 8–10

Discipline & punishments, xli, lviii, 19, 26–31, 45, 50–1, 69–70, 73, 82, 85, 88–90, 93, 96, 102–4, 106, 109, 111, 118, 120, 133, 145, 150, 154, 164, 168–9, 175

Disinfectants (in fever epidemics), 118

Education Act (1870), xxviii–xxx, xxxix, liii, 8–10, 42, 62; (1876), xxviii, xxxiii, 59, 62–3; (1880), xxviii; (1891), xxxv, 165; (1902), xlv